Chancellorsville and the Germans

Chancellorsville and the Germans

Nativism, Ethnicity, and Civil War Memory

Christian B. Keller

FORDHAM UNIVERSITY PRESS
NEW YORK   2007

Library of Congress Cataloging-in-Publication Data

Keller, Christian B.
  Chancellorsville and the Germans : nativism, ethnicity, and Civil War memory /
Christian B. Keller.—1st ed.
    p.   cm.—(The North's Civil War)
  Includes bibliographical references and index.
  ISBN-13: 978-0-8232-2650-4 (cloth : alk. paper)
  ISBN-10: 0-8232-2650-6 (cloth : alk. paper)
  1. Chancellorsville, Battle of, Chancellorsville, Va., 1863.   2. United States—
History—Civil War, 1861–1865—Participation, German American.   3. United States.
Army of the Potomac. Corps, 11th.   4. German American soldiers—History—19th
century.   5. German Americans—History—19th century.   6. German Americans—
Social conditions—19th century.   7. Nativistic movements—United States—
History—19th century.   I. Title.
  E475.35.K45   2007
  973.7'33—dc22

                                                                            2007017279

Printed in the United States of America
09 08 07   5 4 3 2 1
First edition

For my parents,
who taught me to love history.

Contents

Maps

Acknowledgments

In a project of this size, spanning several years, it is difficult to recognize all the people who helped make it possible. The generous advice, support, professional courtesy, and prompt service that so many individuals provided during the course of researching and writing this book is staggering. If I have inadvertently forgotten someone, the negligence is a result of the passage of time, not the unimportance of the contribution.

Holt Merchant, my undergraduate advisor at Washington and Lee, endured with grace and, dare I say, enthusiasm, an honors thesis on the Germans in the Civil War that sparked my professional interest in the subject. My dissertation committee members at Penn State were the next suffering souls who read more than they probably wanted to about German-American identity, the ethnic regiments, and what it all meant for American history. Mark Neely, Gary Gallagher, Carol Reardon, and Bill Pencak waded through monstrous chapters and heavy-handed historiography that became crisper and more analytical under their tutelage. I owe them each a great deal of thanks.

During my Fulbright year in Germany, I had the pleasure of meeting and befriending several excellent German scholars who share my interest in this subject and helped me conceptualize the book in many discussions over beer, schnapps, or wine: Jörg Nagler, Andrea Mehrländer, Martin Oefele, Wolfgang Hochbruck, and Christoph Hänel all deserve a hearty "Vielen Dank." Andrea and Christoph also assisted with some translations of handwritten German script that I could not personally decipher.

Three American colleagues were kind enough to read portions of the manuscript at different points in its creation and provided insightful and critical suggestions for its improvement: Gary Gallagher, Donald Pfanz, and David Valuska. The book is much better thanks to their input. For that matter, my editors at Fordham University Press, Mary Christian and Nicholas Frankovich, transformed often obtuse prose into flowing narrative, and their endless patience with my e-mails and phone calls helped make the publication experience seamless. Joseph Reinhart came to the rescue more than once with copies of esoteric German-American newspapers that I could not have possibly located in time, and Julie Krick drew up excellent maps for me, displaying incredible fortitude as we exchanged thoughts on how best to portray the Eleventh Corps's fight at Chancellorsville.

Numerous archivists and librarians were indispensable over the many years during which I conducted research. As all historians know, without their friendly assistance our books would never see the light of day. I would especially like to thank Richard Sommers of the United States Military History Institute (now AHEC), Carlisle Barracks; Michael Musick (now retired) of the Military Division of the National Archives; Jonathan Stayer and the staff of the Pennsylvania State Archives; James Green and Charlene Peacock of the Library Company of Philadelphia; Lee Arnold and Max Moeller of the Historical Society of Pennsylvania; and the staffs of the German Society of Pennsylvania, Schwenkfelder Historical Library, and the Manuscripts Division of the Library of Congress.

I am privileged to have received numerous grants over the years that partly or fully funded portions of my research. All of them were gratefully received, but in particular the dissertation scholarship provided by the Friends of the National Parks at Gettysburg and postdoctoral grants from the German Historical Institute, Washington, D.C., and the Historical Society of Pennsylvania, Philadelphia, were integral to the successful completion of this project. Dirk Schumann at the GHI deserves special mention for his receptiveness and interest in my topic. I would also like to thank William Keel, editor of the *Yearbook of German-American Studies*, for his kind permission to reproduce a sizable chunk of chapter five, much of which first appeared in the 2006 edition of the *Yearbook*.

Last, but certainly not least, I owe an enormous debt of gratitude to friends and family who never gave up on me or the book. Some of them fed, housed, and yes, even clothed me during my period of research, whereas others cheered me on later in the game. All of them individually and aggregately contributed the emotional and logistical support that permitted me to finally finish the project. My thanks—and my heart—go out to the following wonderful people: first and foremost, my mother, Patricia F. Keller; Ted and Daphne Sahlin; Norman and Kay Rodriguez; Joseph Walker; Tom and Bev Phillips; Peter and Sandy Clark; Ryan McCann; Andrew Ulsamer; the Rev. Charles Brophy; Warren Mitchell; Jilletta Davis; D.E.B.K.; and my colleagues at the Command and General Staff College, Ft. Belvoir, especially Harry Dinella, Andrew Kirkner, Peter Campbell, Thomas Wingfield, Bill Bryan, Sandy Cochran, and Ed Coss.

Thanks again to all of you, and "Alles Gute!"

Chancellorsville and the Germans

ir sacrifices. Instead of becoming more American throughout the months—
, arguably, years—following Chancellorsville, the North's Germans became
re German. Their reactions to the battle's nativist aftermath brought them
ser together as an ethnic group and heightened their ethnic consciousness at
 expense of Americanization.

ch has been written about the battle of Chancellorsville, Robert E. Lee's
atest victory. But within the volumes of books on the subject comparatively
e has come to light about the actual fighting of the Eleventh Corps on 2
y, and even less regarding the effect of the Federal defeat on both the Ger-
n American troops and their families at home. Horace Greeley's 1867 history
he Civil War, which met with much acclaim among Anglo American read-
 left out the role of the corps' German regiments in the battle. William
nton, in his early chronicle of the Army of the Potomac, devoted half a page
he Eleventh Corps' struggle, indicating, "the dispositions to meet [an]
ck were utterly inadequate," and arguing "in so far as the rout was owing
his circumstance, the author of this disposition must assume responsibil-
' He somewhat exonerated the Germans, correctly stating that only a per-
tage of the Eleventh Corps was actually German, and declared that the corps
 received "exaggerated coloring" by newspaper accounts. But Swinton left
issue at that. So did Abner Doubleday, who in his 1882 reflections on Chan-
orsville and Gettysburg similarly skipped over the actual fighting of the
os and German reactions to the bad press. He summarized the entire affair
laiming, "the Germans were bitterly denounced for this catastrophe, I think
 unjustly." Alfred Pleasonton's 1888 collection of "self-serving and fantastic
ies" remarked very unfavorably on the Germans, and had almost no foun-
on in fact, but quickly became a major source for subsequent veterans' rem-
cences. Theodore Dodge and Samuel Bates, two other early historians of
 battle, sympathized with the Germans to a degree and tried to counteract
sonton, but neither provided a concrete analysis of what actually happened
ag the Orange Plank Road between the Wilderness Church and the Chancel-
House. Bates went so far as to suggest that accusations of cowardice were
id of just discrimination, and conve[y] an impression utterly at variance
 the facts," but said nothing about how those accusations resonated with
Germans.[4]
The two most respected and consulted early histories, those of Augustus C.
nlin and John Bigelow, although more comprehensive than their predeces-
, nonetheless leave much open to question. Hamlin, who served in the Elev-
 Corps, naturally took a very pro-German position and strongly defended
German regiments in his 1896 book. "Upon close investigation," he sarcas-

Introduction

General after Union general appeared before the stern-faced and forthright politicians comprising the powerful Joint Committee on the Conduct of the War
and nervously took their seat, not knowing if they would suddenly find their
careers at an end. These were some of the most important men in the Federal
army: Sickles, Pleasonton, Birney, Warren, Hancock, Butterfield, Devens—even
Joseph Hooker himself. Led by Republican Senators Benjamin F. Wade of Ohio
and Zachariah Chandler of Michigan, the Committee was bent on finding a
scapegoat for the miscarried Chancellorsville campaign of the past spring.
Someone had to officially take the fall for the disaster that befell the Union Army
of the Potomac, then led by Major General Joseph Hooker. There were a plethora of candidates to choose from: Brigadier General Charles Devens, former
commander of the Eleventh Corps' First Division; Major General Carl Schurz,
then in charge of the Third Division; Major General Oliver O. Howard, commander of the Eleventh Corps; and even Hooker himself. But no single man
would end up being blamed for the defeat in the Virginia wilderness. Instead,
an entire corps would be, and by proxy, an entire ethnic group.

The questions from the committee members came fast and furious, and in-
between self-glorifying or exculpating rhetoric uttered by the various generals,
a common theme quickly developed. Major General Dan Sickles thought the
Eleventh Corps "might have fought very well; yet very few in the army believed
it would." Major General Winfield Scott Hancock claimed that the Confederate
attack "overthrew the 11th Corps almost immediately. I have no doubt that
proper precautions had not been taken." Major General Daniel Butterfield testified, "several officers of rank in the army" urged Hooker to break up the Eleventh Corps after the battle.

Benjamin Wade asked Major General Alfred Pleasonton, "Can you tell what
produced the panic in the 11th Corps?"

Response: "The combined effect upon their imagination of the sound of the
musketry and the increasing yells of the rebels, and their increasing artillery
fire. . . . I would have preferred to have sent the 11th Corps to Spotsylvania
Court House. That was an open country there, and Europeans are accustomed
to an open country; they will fight better in an open country than in the
woods."

Question: "This 11th corps being principally foreigners?"

Answer: "Yes, sir; they were in circumstances disadvantageous to themselves."

To Major General David B. Birney: "Do you know the cause of the giving way of the 11th corps, and whether it made any reasonable resistance?"

Response: "I think the 11th corps, through disregard of rules of warfare, had its pickets too close to the main body, and was surprised by the sudden massed attack of the enemy on its right flank and rear, and fled in instant confusion. Portions of it may have fought, but the flight, stampede of artillery, transportation, officers and men, has been described to me, by officers who saw it, as disgraceful in the extreme."

In reply to a later question: "The 11th corps suffered no loss as it fled, except in prisoners."

To Major General Gouvernor K. Warren: "The fact was that [the Eleventh Corps] made no resistance to speak of?"

Response: "Not where I was, they did not. It began, probably, on the right of the line, but there was no resistance made to speak of by their infantry at all."

Hooker then testified, "The 11th corps had been completely surprised and disgracefully routed. . . . No disposition had been made to receive an attack, and there were no pickets on the alert to advise of the approach of an enemy. I only know that my instructions were utterly and criminally disregarded."

The questions and answers recorded during the Joint Committee's investigation reflected the many errors in fact, misconceptions and prejudices that arose in the aftermath of the Chancellorsville campaign. They also indicated that a scapegoat had already been found. Those questioned could rest easy, especially Joseph Hooker. The Eleventh Corps, believed to contain a majority of German-born troops, remained the fall guy. It had been presumed the guilty party from the beginning. Carl Schurz had applied to testify before the Committee, but his request was turned down. He feared "that there was in all the official circles concerned, a powerful influence systematically seeking to prevent the disclosure of the truth." Indeed, someone had to be blamed, and "the 'Dutch corps', which had few friends and that might be abused and slandered and kicked with impunity," was it.[1]

Chancellorsville has always been considered a watershed for German Americans. The attack and rout of the Eleventh Corps by Confederate General "Stonewall" Jackson's flanking columns late in the afternoon and evening of 2 May 1863 set the stage for the strongest nativist and anti-German backlash since the rise of the Know Nothing Party in the previous decade. The uproar over the performance of the German soldiers and regiments spread like wildfire

through the camps of the Army of the Potomac and succe overall morale at the expense of its ethnically German elem filled both English- and German-language newspapers for and created serious antagonism between northern Anglo cans that long outlived the war. It is not an exaggeration to German-born population never got over what happened in in May 1863. Its repercussions shook them throughout the and well into the postwar period.[2]

Historians Gerald Linderman and James McPherson hav the ethic of courage held by most Civil War soldiers. Cour regarded as an essential "manly virtue" that defined the t worth. Especially important in the first years of the war, th courage—which encompassed other Victorian notions of ness, and chivalry—left little room for an acceptable explan worse yet, "skedaddling" in the face of the enemy. Malign ately by their fellow Union soldiers and later by the Ang German soldiers in the Eleventh Corps, forced to retreat and cellorsville, found themselves in a psychological dilemma: fought as well as they could, but had to retreat against over In so doing, they were perceived as "cowards" by other sold ethic of courage. That the German soldiers also believed in courage is unquestionable, but their testimony after the batt they were outraged at being so harshly judged, especially t ethnic prejudice.[3]

Naturally, nearly all German-speaking troops present believed they fought as well as they possibly could. In their their duty, just as they had at the earlier battles of Cross Key assas. Certainly the casualty reports of certain regiments atte Yet much of the blame for the Union defeat was foisted o by Anglo Americans. Shock, indignance, a feeling of betray of the need to unify swept over the German troops of the E the immigrant German press in May and June 1863. The pat siasm with which these soldiers had enlisted, and that sust the bloody and exhausting campaigns of 1862, vanished. Of regiments would fight on, and most Germans would rema was unthinkable to men who had fought alongside the same years.

Nonetheless, most of the North's German-born popula their ardor for the war and began to look within their ow support rather than toward a Union that seemed to despise tically wrote, "it appears that the offense of the Eleventh Corps was chiefly that it did not, singlehanded, pulverize Jackson and his greatly superior army for their presumption in attacking the Eleventh in the rear and far away from any support; that it did not change front and fortify without permission from its superior officers; that it did have in its ranks many volunteers of German birth or of other nationalities who had offered their services in defense of the government," and that those officers were well educated and invited jealousy from others. Hamlin took his time in research, carefully gathering primary sources from surviving veterans, corresponding with them, and walking the ground where the Eleventh Corps fought. Yet he was too quick to absolve the Germans from any blame whatsoever and positively excoriated army commander Joseph Hooker, Eleventh Corps commander Oliver O. Howard, and First Division commander Charles Devens for the disaster. He also did not consult any period German-language newspapers and thus was unable to truly examine German American home front opinion.[5]

Hamlin's work preceded Bigelow's 1910 campaign study, which seemed to return to the old line that the Germans had shamefully run during the battle without putting up much of a fight. While admitting, "such a disaster would have happened to any body of troops situated as the XI Corps was when Jackson struck it," Bigelow added, "other men might have comported themselves with more dignity, or less ignominy, even while running for their lives." The last statement was "supported" with descriptions of how "American" soldiers typically deserted the field of battle: "coolly and collectedly," in comparison with foreign-born soldiers, who usually abandoned themselves to wild panic. Bigelow unsuccessfully tried to ameliorate the castigation of the Eleventh Corps Germans by stating "their courage can hardly be impugned without reflecting to some extent upon the people among whom they had lived as citizens," meaning their fellow Americans. He offered an equally unconvincing argument about why German soldiers often made poor fighters: "An appreciable proportion of our German population comes to our country to escape from military service, and for this reason is not representative of the military population of Germany," which he lauded as among the best in the world. Obviously, Bigelow failed to consider the strong military backgrounds of many northern Germans who had fought in the Civil War.[6]

Bigelow's work has unfortunately superseded Hamlin's in historical memory if the accounts of more recent historians of Chancellorsville are to be believed. Edward Stackpole, for instance, in *Chancellorsville: Lee's Greatest Battle* (1958), focused on the Confederate side of the campaign and described the stand of the Eleventh Corps thus: "Wild with enthusiasm, the irresistible Confederates rolled over brigade after brigade of the successive lines of Howard's corps, as the retrograde movement of the overwhelmed regiments quickly turned into a confused rout." Why did the corps perform poorly? "Its low morale . . . and the lack of confidence that the higher commanders displayed in so many of its regiments, were enough to make the corps a sitting duck for the Confederate hunters almost without the assistance gratuitously made by the generals of the corps." Such generalized and biased statements are absent from the latest chronicles of the battle, but even with the vast advantages available to the modern researcher, both Ernest B. Furgurson and Stephen W. Sears fail to adequately analyze the various components of the Eleventh Corps' stand on 2 May as well as the German American reaction to the battle. That may be due to their neglect of German-language sources. They are, however, more astute than Stackpole in placing the blame for the debacle where it belongs and much more detailed in their descriptions of the corps' retreat and Anglo American criticisms of the Germans. Both authors show some professional sympathy for the beleaguered German soldiers of the Eleventh Corps, but neither adequately documents their reactions to becoming the scapegoats for the entire Union army.[7]

This book is first and foremost a history of northern German Americans during and after the battle of Chancellorsville. Thus, it is a work of both ethnic and Civil War history, but it is more firmly rooted in the latter. My goal is to create a greater understanding of the United States' largest ethnic group during the Civil War by carefully examining the event that proved most pivotal to it. I want to analyze how well the German regiments in the battle actually performed by reconstructing their actions through the eyes of those who fought. I want to determine the extent of the Anglo American criticism that followed the battle, and ascertain if it was justified. Most importantly, I want to document the German American reactions to that criticism and how it affected the Germans' thinking and behavior later in the war, and even in the postwar period. Embedded in that analysis is the larger question of whether or not the Civil War helped to assimilate the German-born immigrants who lived and fought through it. I take issue with the claims of previous historians, especially Ella Lonn, John Higham, and William Burton, who claim that it did. The primary source material, especially that written in the German language, points strongly in the other direction.[8]

    The chapters follow a rough chronology but engage only those issues and events relevant to the German Americans, their ethnic identity, and nativism. Ethnic identity, a term that I conflate with "ethnicity" throughout the book, is "an attitude toward oneself and one's cultural world which is shaped in individuals and eventually in groups through contact with other self-conscious groups of human beings." Don Yoder, the author of this definition, argues (and I agree) that a "sense of group identification exists" in most ethnic groups, and the German immigrants of the nineteenth century were no exception. Differences between individuals and communities in how they perceived their ethnicity, or how strongly they defended it, were often linked to the strength of the nativistic impulse in their given locales. Nativism, simply stated, is an anti-immigrant attitude espoused by long-time residents of a certain geographic area, strongly influenced by xenophobic and nationalistic sentiments. Less pronounced in modern American society, nativism was a real presence in the lives of antebellum Americans, and, as this study will show, only intensified during the Civil War, creating immense problems for German and other foreign-born citizens.[9]

A few other preliminary notes are worth mentioning. I cheerfully admit to an Eastern bias in my research and conclusions because the German regiments in the Eleventh Corps primarily hailed from New York and Pennsylvania. The majority of German Americans living in the United States at the time also resided in the East. I have therefore received much direction in the narrative from my source material. Nonetheless, I endeavored to include as much commentary as possible about those from Ohio, Illinois, Wisconsin, and other western states, because no general observations can be made about *all* northern Germans without considering the large ethnic populations living west of the Appalachians. Finally, my emphasis on the importance of ethnicity and nativism to German Americans certainly should not be understood to mean that these issues were the only ones facing them during the war. Indeed, partisan politics, economic hardship, and personal and individual tragedies affected them, just as they did Anglo Americans. Yet both ethnicity and nativism became extremely important, both to the average German infantry private and his forty-eighter colonel, and, as we shall see, had longer staying power in German American memory than most other Civil War issues.

The idea for this book emerged precisely because no one had yet tried to analyze, in any systematic or comprehensive fashion, how the German American soldiers of the Eleventh Corps and their communities at home felt about being stigmatized as "cowards" and blamed for the defeat. This appeared to be a glaring omission in Civil War historiography by itself, but after delving a bit into the neglected German-language sources about the battle, it became obvious that Chancellorsville meant much more than simply a lost battle to the North's German immigrants. They took the accusations emanating from the Anglo American soldiers and English-language press to heart, characterizing them as a rebirth of the old nativism of the 1850s. They grew indignant and felt betrayed by their comrades and adopted homeland. Ultimately, they grew

closer together as a national ethnic group in unified response to the post-Chancellorsville prejudice and seriously questioned the wisdom of quickly assimilat-
ing with the very people who only recently had so maligned them. As the first
chapter demonstrates, nativistic tendencies among Anglo Americans appeared
well before the war, and German Americans had already begun to show a
strengthening of ethnic consciousness before 1861. Once the war began, this
new ethnic consensus only grew stronger in response to anti-German reports
and jibes in both the army and the northern press. The second chapter traces
some of these incidents in the context of the first battles of the East and daily
life in the German regiments, explaining how the stage was set for the explosion
of nativism—and the German reactions to it—that occurred after Chancellorsville. In many ways Chancellorsville accelerated processes already in motion.[10]

But the climactic battle in the thick underbrush of the Virginia wilderness
that shattered Joseph Hooker's grand plan to subdue Lee also undoubtedly
became the major event of the war for the North's German-born population
and the most written-about Civil War battle in German American editorials
and private letters. Chapter three examines what happened on 2 May 1863, and
assesses how well the German American soldiers in the Eleventh Corps fought.
Did they deserve the criticism that was heaped upon them? Naturally, the Germans thought they fought well and most Anglo Americans argued they did not,
although elements of each group broke ranks with their respective choruses and
offered contrary opinions. Chapters four and five analyze these issues and suggest that the German regiments, caught in their poor positions by a numerically
superior enemy, did resist as long and as well as could be expected. The German
American editors and disgruntled officers of the Eleventh Corps had a right,
then, to feel aggrieved, and they took those grievances with them into the last
years of the war, especially into the political arena, as chapter six points out.
Although some scholars may disagree, I believe the editorials of the major
newspapers represented the public consensus of the papers' readerships. Ethnic
editors were powerful people in their respective communities and played a
major role in how members of those communities interpreted the world
around them. What they wrote clearly mattered, and strongly influenced public
opinion to the point that the editorials provide excellent windows into the
thought processes of the North's German-born population. Chapters five and
six trace those thoughts as they related to the nativism born of Chancellorsville.

No sooner had the smoke drifted off the bloody fields around Dowdall's
Tavern than the battle for historical memory began. Before Lee even surrend-
ered in 1865 and throughout the postwar decades, German veterans and historians would constantly hearken back to the dismal spring of 1863 as a
Wendepunkt, a point of reference, a time of reckoning. Chancellorsville took

center stage in their memories. It was burned into them. An event of such significance for the antebellum North's largest ethnic minority—a component of
the citizenry not dissimilar in size, political and economic power, and potential
from today's Latino Americans—cried out for further examination. Chapter
seven analyzes how the memory of the battle and the war in general affected
German Americans and their attempts to assimilate into the greater American
population. German-language sources such as period newspapers, regimental
books, soldiers' letters, and postwar histories and journals, although scarce,
explain that German immigrants decided to Americanize slowly and carefully—on their own terms, in other words—partially as a result of their experiences with nativism during the war. A plethora of mainly untapped English-
language sources dealing with Germans in the conflict also beckoned, likewise
concentrated in newspapers, soldiers' letters, and postwar veterans' serials.
Using such German- and English-language materials, it was possible to recon-
struct how and why Chancellorsville became the key event of the nineteenth
century for the nation's largest ethnicity.

1 German Americans, Know Nothings, and the Outbreak of the War

The most significant reason Chancellorsville later became so important for German Americans had to do with a pre–Civil War sociopolitical movement called the "Know Nothing" or "American" Party. This nativistic, anti-immigrant group of Anglo Americans strove to curtail immigrant voting rights, attacked immigrant religion and culture—especially German and Irish beer, whiskey, and Catholicism—blamed those groups for fomenting crime, and urged quick assimilation of immigrant communities into the mainstream of American life. Although the Know Nothings were themselves a party created mainly out of irrational xenophobia, they represented a powerful and deep-set impulse within American society that inherently distrusted the foreigner and associated with him much that was perceived as negative in nineteenth-century American life: unemployment, lethargy, immorality, and Romanism.

German-born immigrants (who numbered almost a third of the foreign-born population in 1860, 1,301,136 souls) not only were forced to confront this threat against their collective rights in the 1850s, but also were struggling to define themselves within American society as an ethnic group and sort out internal differences that kept them strongly divided. Many of these differences stemmed from the old country, where Prussians and Badeners, Hessians and Saxons had either lined up on opposite sides during the many European wars of the last hundred years or adhered to differing religious doctrines. Most of them also spoke diverse dialects of German, which hindered easy communication. As if these inherent issues were not enough to discourage unity, geographic particularism within and among the various urban German communities (often called "little Germanies") and political partisanship joined the mix to complicate everything. Despite these centrifugal forces, a spirit of "Deutschtum," or pan–German American consciousness, began to sweep across the country as the 1850s progressed.[1]

As the crisis over slavery in the territories came to a head late in the decade, German Americans also found themselves being increasingly drawn into the sectional debate. Although 90 percent of them lived in the north, they divided sharply between the Democratic and Republican Party based in part on which organization they perceived offered the most protection from nativism. Unfortunately, both parties waffled back and forth on this salient issue so that by April 1861 the Germans of the North were hard pressed to find a political home that truly satisfied the majority of their concerns. As Stan Nadel argues, many began to look increasingly toward each other, toward a loose-knit sense of Deutschtum as a means to secure both their unique ethnic culture and political rights. Another scholar put it more succinctly: "The nativist crisis of the fifties, followed by the crisis of slavery and the Civil War . . . created the hyphen by making the Germans in America first of all conscious and then self-conscious as a foreign group in American politics," whereas before they had simply been isolated, squabbling enclaves of German-speaking immigrants. Enthusiastic home-front support of the newly enlisted German troops and ethnic leaders like Franz Sigel proved that the North's German American communities had clearly begun to raise their ethnic consciousness well before the fateful spring of 1863.[2]

Immigrants, Nativists, and Antebellum Politics

Starting in the 1830s, and continuing up to the war itself, wave after wave of immigrants from Ireland, Germany, and, to a lesser extent, Scandinavia, set sail from their homelands in Europe and emigrated to the United States in search of political freedom, economic opportunity, and cheap western land on which to build their new lives. By 1860 there were over four million of them, composing thirteen percent of the American population. Most of them landed in the major port cities of the northeast and remained there, joining the great German and Irish neighborhoods of New York, Philadelphia, Boston, and Baltimore. A sizeable number, however, found their way to the Midwest and either congregated in that section's booming cities or in small, rural communities, often ethnically segregated. Many realized their dreams of owning their own land, thanks to federal and state government incentives that made property in the backcountry affordable to those with a few dollars in the bank. The mid- to late 1840s and early 1850s saw a marked jump in immigration, mainly as a result of the Irish Potato famines and the suppression of the democratic revolutions in Germany in 1848–49. The Irish immigrants were frequently poor, hungry, and Catholic. The German immigrants were usually not as poor, but a good number were Catholic, and a minority of them were radical democrats (the so-called forty-eighters) or their immediate followers who came imbued with the spirit of liberalism and, in a few cases, socialism. It was the Catholic, radical, and poor components, in descending order, of these immigration waves that bothered the better-established Anglo Americans the most. The Germans and the

Irish also had a natural fondness for alcoholic beverages, another trait that aggravated many Anglo Americans as the temperance movement gained momentum and began to merge, in many states, with nativist agendas. Americans looked with apprehension at their cities, now bulging with the foreign-born, replete with entire sections where English was not the dominant tongue, if spoken at all, and storefronts boasted signs in a foreign language. It did not take long for paranoia, fear, and, eventually, a political backlash to develop.[3]

As Dale Knobel has shown, nativist beliefs and nationalism among antebellum Anglo Americans were frequently linked. With the multitudes of foreigners entering the country with their strange ways, strange religion, strange tongue, and their "immoral" poverty and drinking habits, it was easy to find an inviting "un-American" target. At first, the criticism was mild and the protests local, unorganized. By 1852, however, the anti-immigrant crusade had grown in intensity, organization, and political power. Secret lodges of "patriotic Americans" blossomed all over the mid-Atlantic in particular, their members sworn both to secrecy and political war on the immigrant. When members of these secret political societies were accosted on the street and asked what activities they were engaged in, they allegedly responded, "I know nothing." Hence their colloquial name, the Know Nothings. In reality, these individuals were nothing but unadulterated nativists, and the political party that grew directly out of their efforts, the American Party, had as its primary planks strongly restrictive naturalization requirements (up to twenty-one years in some cases), anti-Catholic declarations, and pro-temperance laws. The Party's goals and strength varied from state to state, but by 1856 the Americans controlled a number of state legislatures and had elected a good number of national Congressmen. It was well on its way to becoming the second great political rival to the Democrats.[4]

The Know Nothings' meteoric rise to political prominence was followed by an almost equally fast political collapse. Unable to reconcile northern and southern members over the growing problem of slavery in the territories and plagued by gross mismanagement and corruption in certain states, the Party had crashed to its doom by 1857. The problem for the Germans of the North was that most of the old Know Nothings became Republicans by 1860 and, although their new party officially espoused no anti-immigrant beliefs—indeed, it tried very hard to attract the German vote in the presidential elections of 1856 and 1860 (Lincoln especially professed pro-German sympathies)—their own nativist predilections never went away. Indeed, the famous Two Year Amendment of the Massachusetts state constitution, which passed at the polls in 1859 under Republican shepherding, shocked German Americans across the country and "was as much of an outrage to the Germans as John Brown's raid was to the Southerners," according to one chronicler. The amendment stated that no naturalized citizen could exercise the franchise or hold political office in the Bay State until after another two years of probationary residency. Democrats howled that the Republicans were, after all, the enemies of the immigrant, but their heretofore good reputation with the Irish and the Germans had also been recently sullied by anti-immigrant rhetoric emanating from the Party's southern wing. Senator Andrew Butler of South Carolina, for instance, had gone on record that he would rather have slavery in Nebraska territory than "emigrants from the land of the Kraut," a quote that flashed across the nation's newspapers and unsettled immigrant readers. Unsure which party they could really trust, the Germans of the North nonetheless chose political sides, hoping that their party was the best one for their ethnic interests and that the overwhelming slavery issue would subsume lingering nativism in the critical election of 1860. Their hopes were temporarily realized, but only for a while.[5]

The German American vote in the 1860 election has been hotly debated for the last three decades. The so-called ethnocultural thesis, developed in the 1970s, still remains a convincing explanation for ethnic voting behavior during the election, but more recent studies have added substantially to the complex milieu that constituted German voting motivations. These motivations, in turn, reflected the multitude of issues that confronted the German-born throughout the country, as well as the geographic differences between East and West and rural and city-dwelling immigrants.[6] Despite commonsense appeals from the Republicans about free labor, free land, and antislavery legislation, the majority of the Germans still voted Democratic in 1860, especially in the East. A lingering fear of nativism definitely played into Democratic hands there, notably in Pennsylvania and New York, where the old Know Nothings had been strong. The original ethnocultural thesis minimized the role of nativism in ethnic voting behavior and maintained that conservative religious denominations, such as Catholics and Lutherans, tended to vote Democratic whereas the more "reformed" churches, like the German Reformed and German Methodists, likely voted Republican. Later studies have argued that this interpretation, while mainly correct, is too generalized, and that German voting behavior was also affected by local political and social concerns, old-world loyalties and backgrounds, and most importantly, nativistic tendencies among Anglo Americans. In Pennsylvania, for example, the Republican-proposed tariff proved attractive to some German voters in Philadelphia who worked in local industries that would benefit from such legislation; others voted Democratic simply because they were members of clubs composed of southern German immigrants who felt compelled to vote differently from rival organizations, composed of northern Germans.[7]

Yet the issue of nativism proved even more salient in the minds of Philadelphia's German Americans in 1860, and they were certainly not alone in their concerns as they cast their ballots that year. In Pittsburgh, Baltimore, New York, Milwaukee, Cleveland, and a host of smaller cities with sizeable German immigrant populations, the residue of the Know Nothings left a sour taste in the mouths of ethnic voters and compelled them to think twice before voting Republican. Lincoln was clearly a preferable candidate on a personal level because he had gone down on record as early as 1855 as an antinativist in Illinois politics. The Democratic alternatives, Stephen A. Douglas of the Northern Democrats and John C. Breckinridge of the Southern Democrats, were not especially enticing to German American voters because of anti-immigrant invective emanating from southern politicians. But the Democrats on the whole offered urban-dwelling Germans nationwide more peace of mind than the Republicans did, and Lincoln's personal preferences—and the stump-speaking of famous forty-eighters like Carl Schurz—could not outweigh state and local nativist influences, especially where the Republicans had absorbed strong American Party machines (as in Pennsylvania). In the end, the Republicans received less than half of the German vote in 1860.[8]

With Lincoln's election in 1860 the majority of southern states seceded and, after the firing on Fort Sumter in April 1861, the war began. German-, Irish-, and, to a lesser extent, Scandinavian-born volunteers flocked to the colors in the towns and cities of the North just like Anglo Americans. The Germans enlisted in both ethnic and nonethnic regiments in numbers beyond their proportion in the overall population and participated heavily in many of the early skirmishes and battles of the war, especially in the West. The Teutonic residents of St. Louis especially did the Union a service by remaining loyal when most of their neighbors clamored for Missouri's secession, and probably secured the city for the northern cause by capturing en masse a rebel encampment outside of the city. A myth quickly developed, however, that they alone had kept the entire border state in the Union, a myth stubbornly adhered to by postwar German-American writers. At Mill Springs, Wilson's Creek, Carthage, Pea Ridge, and at First Manassas the ethnically German regiments nonetheless distinguished themselves for their courage under fire and their reliability. Ethnic generals who had earlier seen service in Europe, such as Franz Sigel and Ludwig Blenker, happily stepped into the national spotlight and skyrocketed in the estimation of the German American public. Sigel was hailed as the savior of Wilson's Creek and the victor of Carthage and Pea Ridge. Blenker became the hero of Manassas to his ethnic countrymen for the performance of his all-German brigade while covering the retreat of the routed northern army. But much of the significance of these battles and the German leaders lay more in how they rallied German American support for the war than in outright contributions to Union victory. And by making the Germans of the North perceive that they were strongly aiding their adopted homeland, they simultaneously raised ethnic pride and consciousness. The Germans began to believe that their efforts on behalf of the Union were the mightiest of them all. Nativism appeared forever vanquished by their deeds on the early battlefields. How more shocking it would be, therefore, when a contrary reality dawned on them after Chancellorsville.[9]

"They Have Spattered Their Blood upon the Earthworks": Early War Soldiers' Relief and Home Front Ethnicization

Home front support for the newly enlisted German soldiers was strong among the northern German communities and was inextricably entwined with their ethnic consciousness. Charitable contributions of individuals and societies, support of soldiers' families, and articles in the German-language press were especially attuned to the needs of German soldiers and citizens—as opposed to northerners in general—and constituted conscious, public displays of specifically German support for the war. New York, Philadelphia, and to a lesser extent, Pittsburgh Germans created an ethnically German soldiers' relief movement that paralleled that of the greater northern home front. Although strongly supportive of the war (at least until Chancellorsville), and thereby unified with the bulk of the northern citizenry, German American civilians were not necessarily Americanized by their efforts to support the troops. If anything, their contributions to Union victory through distinctly German media enhanced their awareness of their own ethnic identity.[10]

In New York City, where many of the nation's German immigrants first stepped onto American soil and where the North's largest German community resided, the city's German Society found itself stretched to the limits of its philanthropic abilities by the end of 1861. The "Patriotic Central-Assistance Association" of the society "took over the responsibility of supporting all German families, whose providers serve in the armies of the United States, until the city authorities could take over their care." On Saturday afternoons, hundreds of needy Germans lined up at the society to receive food, medicine, and clothing from the association's members. The sick and the very poor received first consideration, but the society committed itself to taking care of all families whose primary male breadwinner was away in the armies. It was estimated that "12–15,000 Germans from the city of New York ha[d] gone to the war," and "most of them in the following pure German regiments: the 7th, 8th, 20th, 29th, 41st,

42nd, 45th, 46th, 54th, 58th." "Additionally, at least 4000–5000 Germans [joined] departed American regiments." The German Society was convinced that because most of the city's German volunteers had joined ethnically German regiments, it was fitting and proper to assist their families.[11]

As the city with the third largest German immigrant population and the oldest continuous German community, Philadelphia's myriad long-established German societies also provided a solid base of support for the families of the volunteers early in the war. The German American Unterstützungsverein (relief organization) was originally founded to assist newly arrived immigrants in beginning a new life in their first weeks in Philadelphia. In 1861 this society pledged to aid financially "the families of members who join the army," and President Andreas Leitinger of the German American Workers' Unterstützungsverein, a competing group, promised his society's support of the families of any member who enlisted in April 1861. As in New York, the task was challenging for the ethnic charitable associations. Four German regiments marched forth from the City of Brotherly Love: the 27th, 73rd, 75th, and 98th Pennsylvania Infantries, and during the late spring and summer of 1861 the classifieds of both the *Philadelphia Demokrat* and *Freie Presse*, the most prominent daily newspapers, were literally bursting with German societies' boasts to assist the loved ones of newly enlisted soldiers. Like the formation of the German regiments themselves, the civilian societies were competing with one another in a frenzied display of ethnic pride. Most of the members of the Philadelphia Turnverein, a national German American gymnastic society, enlisted in the 29th New York immediately upon the outbreak of the war, so this group suspended regular activities during the war. Worker's clubs, immigrant settlement societies, fraternal lodges, and the various German singing and theatrical groups, however, pledged support of the troops and their families at home, the latter staging German plays for the benefit of soldiers' families in the middle years of the war. Even the conservative and long-established German Society of Pennsylvania was not immune from this fervor: it, too, provided funds to support the families of German volunteers throughout the conflict (after most of the other societies' treasuries ran out of money) and donated regularly to other war-related charities. The Society's proudest moments came in the last two years of the war, when its public protests against the illegal importation of immigrants from Germany to serve as "cheap draft substitutes" for several northern cities were heard by the authorities in Washington. The importations were stopped.[12]

German hospitals sprung up in the major northern cities in the early days of the war to care for wounded German soldiers, and in cities like Philadelphia where no specific facility yet existed, philanthropic individuals volunteered to provide for their countrymen. A Pastor C. Boehringer of Philadelphia did his part by organizing a small group of Germans, composed of invalid soldiers, widows, and wives of soldiers at the front, to tend to the wounded lying in military hospitals. An advertisement Boehringer placed in the *Freie Presse* on 12 August 1863 clearly stated his purpose and appealed to German pride:

> An Appeal for the Benefit of Wounded and Sick German Soldiers: German countrymen! Do not forget your German brothers who languish sick or wounded on the rim of the war in hospitals. They are your people, your blood, your language! They have either spattered their blood upon the earthworks and threatened their lives for the adopted Fatherland, have endured unspeakable physical strain and are now sick, or have become partial cripples in the various battles and lie suffering in the hospitals. It is nothing more than our humanitarian and religious duty to ease their situation, to revive them or console them.

Pastor Boehringer also accepted donations of money, medicines, food, and "good German books." Heinrich Bokum, chaplain of the Turner's Lane Hospital, which cared for both German and Anglo American soldiers, similarly appealed to the German citizens of Philadelphia to donate books in the German language, as "the libraries of our hospitals are only slightly equipped with German reading materials." In the same advertisement he specifically thanked editor Friedrich W. Thomas, "in the name of our German sick and wounded," for his daily donation of the *Freie Presse* and urged others to follow his lead. Another man of the cloth, Lutheran pastor Adolph Spaeth, traveled the city's hospitals to assuage the pain of the German wounded with a dose of religion. "How many a crippled German from the Union army did I seek out in those months, to bring him a word of comfort from the Gospel!" he wrote. "How hard these visits often were to the young beginner in the pastoral care of souls!"[13]

In the recently founded "German colony" community of Egg Harbor City, New Jersey, the membership of the governing Gloucester Country and City Association decided to "step forward as German American patriots and humanitarians to their countrymen in the army," and offer a section of their town as a rehabilitation center for incapacitated German officers. Named the "Sigel Institute," this collection of brick buildings, adjacent to a "sparking lake" and gardens, would provide "a friendly asylum" for the invalid officers "for the rest of their days." The general agent of the Association even solicited the support of none other than Franz Sigel himself, the darling of German America and victor of Pea Ridge, who pledged to be involved in its maintenance and leadership after the war.[14]

Two German ladies' aid societies were the primary organizations whereby Pittsburgh's German soldiers and their families received most of their wartime relief in the first year of the war. Formed almost simultaneously in April and May 1861, these societies remained officially nameless, although editorials and advertisements describing the "Ladies' Committee of Allegheny City" or "German Ladies Society" appeared throughout the 1861 issues of the Pittsburgh *Freiheitsfreund*. Seeking "to unify German women and girls in the support of our brave soldiers," the ladies of one society claimed in April 1861 "that in this time of danger the female sex must remain helpful and useful." The other argued in the same issue that "the German ladies of Pittsburgh and the surrounding region" needed to unify in a common organization specifically to support their "husbands, sweethearts, and brothers" because "an American organization, composed of English-speaking ladies, has already formed for the same reason." On 22 April 1861, this particular group met in the Smithfield Church in downtown Pittsburgh for its inaugural meeting. Attended by "over 200 ladies," the assembly voted in a Frau Umstädtler as president and selected six separate vice presidents. Each ward of the city was also assigned a committee to oversee and coordinate the activities of the society within its jurisdiction, and potential members were invited to attend the next meeting, scheduled for the next day.[15]

The practical effects of the two women's groups were clearly revealed in a letter from First Lieutenant M. Hechelmann of the strongly German, three-month 5th Pennsylvania, published in the *Freiheitsfreund* on 30 May 1861: "In the name of the men and boys of Company B, 5th Pennsylvania regiment, it is my duty to express our heartfelt thanks to the honored ladies of Allegheny for the various pieces of clothing they have sent. Their untiring, unselfish activity, which they undertake on a daily basis on our behalf, is further proof that they are with us and our good cause, freedom and Union forever." So many articles of clothing had been forwarded to the men, he continued, that "we are now richly provided for in all areas, and require further provisioning only if new companies are sent to us." Hechelmann ended his letter with an appeal to the societies to turn their attention "to the relief of our dependants at home." Should the ladies "allow their noble spirit and industry to help them [the families], it would be a blessing." Several letters had recently arrived in camp from wives of soldiers in need, and anything that could be done to ease their burden would proportionately assist the soldiers in doing their duty, he claimed.[16]

Not surprisingly, at least one of the German ladies' aid societies responded to Hechelmann's request. Recognizing that the soldiers had received enough support for the time being, the ladies resolved to assist the soldiers' families "with money and foodstuffs." Publishing their new mission on 9 May 1861, the goals of the "undersigned Ladies' Committee of Allegheny City and its Environs" were clearly directed toward the relief of specifically German soldiers' families:

1. To visit at their homes those German families which have sent away at least one freedom-fighter, to become familiar with their personal situations, and to care for them particularly in times of sickness so that they do not want what is necessary.
2. To seek out such families in case of their need, and advise them to come for help to the ladies' committee in charge of the area in which they live.
3. To compile lists of the German freedom-fighters of Allegheny City and its environs, according to their various companies, so that the Committee may best fulfill its responsibilities.[17]

Unfortunately for Pittsburgh's German soldiers and their families, the ladies' aid societies stopped their philanthropic activities in the late fall of 1861. Money probably ran out, or perhaps the membership of each dropped too low. Whatever the reason for their dissolution, the absence of these groups was keenly felt by the soldiers in the field. Sergeant Heinrich Hirsch of the German 74th Pennsylvania, encamped at Hunters Chapel outside Washington, D.C., wrote a letter to the editor of the *Freiheitsfreund* explaining how the suffering of their families would adversely affect the men. "Letters have arrived from home," he said,

crying that the support of our families will soon cease. This news alone was enough to plunge the stoutest patriotic heart into depression. . . . We have not forgotten our wives and children. Recently several men have received letters claiming that they had to send all their pay home or see their respective families go into the poorhouse. "Certain people" have suggested that our wives become washerwomen to support themselves, or told them that "your husbands were bad enough to leave you hanging." These are the sayings of people who have neither heart nor understanding.

Hirsch then blamed these anonymous citizens for the disappearance of the "promised support of our families" and invited them to "join us in sleeping on the wet, cold ground" and "catching rheumatism" in defense of the country. If support for their families did not materialize soon, Hirsch feared "heaven will soon see our children," and a "fearful judgment" would be passed upon those who allowed this to happen. Sadly, no substantial, organized German relief organization was created, as editorials in the winters of both 1862 and 1863 bemoaned the "poor soldier's wife, the half-naked child on her lap crying for bread that the mother cannot give him." The editor of the *Freiheitsfreund* pointed out examples of city boroughs that had created familial support societies, and urged his readers to "follow their example," but by the end of the winter of 1863–64 no similar organizations had been created among Pittsburgh's Germans.[18]

The enthusiastic support of New York's, Pittsburgh's, and Philadelphia's German societies for the German volunteers and their families—even if it slackened—indicates more than simple patriotism. The existence of purely German soldiers' relief organizations was a result of the antebellum growth of *Deutschtum*, in which the German immigrant's ethnic identity became entwined with that of the greater German community in his particular city. In the prewar period, old, regional allegiances to the bickering German states in Europe began to give way in immigrants' minds to a sense of unity among German-speakers as a whole, particularly within the confines of a specific geographic area, such as the city. It is not surprising that the antebellum German organizations in Philadelphia turned their efforts to the support of the German troops and their families when the war came, because to do so was not only patriotic but also reflective of German unity and pride. Likewise, the creation of Pittsburgh's ladies' aid societies, however short lived they may have been, indicates that the German speakers in that city had also begun to see themselves collectively as Germans, with particular interests and ethnic concerns dissimilar from those of the greater American population.[19]

More importantly, the existence of this parallel universe in soldiers' relief organizations, especially among the Germans of the eastern cities, meant that their participation in similar Anglo American organizations must have been severely limited. Why would the average German civilian donate to them when the ethnic associations (advertising in the newspapers he read) promised to utilize his hard-earned funds and energies for the well-being of people who were probably his relatives, friends, and neighbors? Immigrant Germans, like northerners everywhere, fulfilled their self-interests by supporting the charities that would most likely benefit those they knew and loved. In this sense Americanization would have been stymied to at least some degree by the activities of the German soldiers' relief societies. Additionally, the ethnically distinct German neighborhoods in the cities of the North would not have assisted in the intermingling of German and Anglo American soldiers' support groups. The fact that there were well-known German wards in these cities supports the argument that Anglo Americans viewed these neighborhoods as somehow separate from the rest of the urban population.[20]

Franz Sigel, German American Icon

Editorials in the immigrant press also promoted separation between ethnics and Americans by exhorting readers to support the soldiers as Germans first and Americans second. Throughout the first two years of the war the editors of the primary German-language papers repeatedly singled out purely German contributions and concerns. Articles praising the bravery of various German regiments and their leaders dotted the pages of these papers: Illinois Colonel and former forty-eighter Friedrich Hecker, Colonel Augustus Willich of the 32nd Indiana, and the famous 9th Ohio were all favorites, especially as the western Union armies marched from victory to victory in 1862. The latest exploits of Franz Sigel received particularly close coverage, as did the deployments of General Louis Blenker's "German division." Of course, the enlisted men in the various German regiments were given special attention as well; during the spring and summer of 1862, for instance, scarcely an issue of the Philadelphia *Freie Presse* failed to contain at least one published soldier's letter from either the 73rd, 74th, or 75th Pennsylvania. Some issues contained as many as three letters from the field. Although each newspaper, regardless of its geographic location, also carried copious coverage of the national war news, the sheer number of German articles and letters in the first half of the war was proof that the German Americans interpreted the war through the eyes of their ethnic soldiers and their leaders.[21]

One particular episode highlighted in the press is an excellent case in point. Franz Sigel's resignation from the Union Army on 31 December 1861, prompted by a perceived insult from General-in-Chief Henry W. Halleck, created massive outrage among Germans throughout the North. As Stephen Engle and Earl Hess have shown, Sigel was viewed as the preeminent leader of German America and a symbol for Germans of their commitment to the Union cause. A forty-eighter, Sigel had led the Badenese revolutionary forces on a successful retreat into Switzerland in 1849, losing almost no men or artillery on the way. The legend that grew out of this feat became much greater than the actual deed itself, and Sigel's early leadership of German American regiments in Missouri in 1861 only increased his aura among his countrymen in the United States. Despite his questionable generalship at Wilson's Creek, "I fights mit Sigel" became the watchword of German volunteers in the Union armies by 1862, whether or not they had actually fought with him. Thus they and their loved ones at home received news of his resignation as evidence that their overall contributions to the war effort were not appreciated. For months readers of the major German-language dailies read of the hypocrisy of the federal government in accepting the aid of thousands of German soldiers from across the North but not allowing their leader to attain a respectable command. More ominously for German and Anglo American cooperation, the editors blamed Sigel's demise on the nativism of Halleck and a clique of West Pointers prejudiced against foreigners. Tensions rose dramatically among German Americans throughout the northern states as pro-Sigel rallies, some with thousands in attendance, multiplied across the Union.[22]

The *Louisville Anzeiger* of 10 January 1862 carried a bold title on its front news page: "The Resignation of General Sigel." All other news was secondary, and would continue to be for the next several weeks. After explaining why, in his opinion, Sigel had resigned, the editor exclaimed, "The insult that has been done to Sigel is simultaneously an insult against all Deutschtum and indicates just what the Germans can expect from the 'Herren Amerikanern' in return for their spirit of sacrifice and glowing patriotism, namely kicks in the face!" The influential and widely read Chicago *Illinois Staatszeitung* declared, "We will do our duty! . . . From all over German Americans are sending petitions to the President in hopes of persuading him to promote General Sigel to major general and giving him independent command of his own army corps." Another important paper, the Columbus *Westbote*, announced on 16 January that "this fresh disrespect of the Germans, now taken to extremes, has naturally infuriated the tempers of all German officers and soldiers here." When the clocks struck midnight on 1 January and cannon boomed to welcome in the new year, Germans in Columbus raised their glasses not in celebration but "in bitterness about the enraging cheekiness of the decorated American liberty lady [Columbia] that reached a new level every passing minute!" The editor predicted that all German officers would immediately resign if no apologies—or a reinstatement of Sigel—emanated from Washington. Editorials in the Philadelphia *Freie Presse* also emphasized the negative effect Sigel's resignation would have among German soldiers if allowed to stand, and argued that the Germans deserved better. One said, "we cannot possibly accept that our American colleagues should be so stupid not to realize that the odious wrong committed against Sigel must provoke in the breast of every German adoptive-citizen, regardless of political party, the deepest indignation." Sigel's name alone had compelled "thousands of our young Germans to answer the call to duty." His retreat to private life at the instigation of ungrateful federal authorities "will make a fearful impression" on these soldiers, who "justly perceive it as a shamefully deliberate insult to the Germans." Claiming Sigel's misfortune signaled a new rise in nativism, editor Thomas forecasted a clearly anti-American theme on 13 January: "If [the Germans] are rewarded with kicks [in the face] for their patriotism, they know what they have to do. They will not lift one more hand to preserve the authority of the star-spangled banner if it has ceased being the symbol of freedom and equality."[23]

A large pro-Sigel demonstration took place in New York City's Cooper Institute the night of 16 January, which was supposedly attended by five thousand people. The speakers rehashed Sigel's military accomplishments with great hyperbole and unanimously called for the general's reinstatement. Nativism also dominated many of the speeches, and both Halleck and West Point received their full shares of condemnation. A whopping 113 vice presidents were elected, and a special committee of three, comprised of forty-eighter Friedrich Kapp, Weil von Gernsbach, and Andreas Willmann, was charged with the responsibility of delivering the rally's resolutions to President Lincoln. Similar but smaller demonstrations were also held in Milwaukee, Chicago, and Buffalo, and the Wisconsin legislature passed a series of resolutions endorsing Sigel's war record and recommending his reinstatement.[24]

In the end, Lincoln caved in to German American political pressure and recommissioned Franz Sigel as a major general in March 1862. It had taken some time and considerable effort, but the Germans had shown they would not take insults to their ethnic honor—as personified by Sigel—lightly. German-language newspapers rejoiced in the victory. The *Louisville Anzeiger* crowed, "Despite all the machinations of the West Pointers and the nativists, Sigel has been nominated for major general. It took a lot of work to achieve this satisfaction for him. The nativists . . . namely, the military ones, appeared to be unilaterally foresworn to prevent his promotion." But in the end they had failed, and German Americans prevailed. That did not mean the nasty ordeal would be forgotten. For Germans throughout the Union, the perceived insult created by Sigel's resignation was only the first of several steps that ultimately stalled Americanization during the Civil War. Yet Sigel's resignation and the outrage that followed was representative of the preoccupation of the German-language press with distinctly German issues, especially those that dealt with supporting German soldiers. This continued focus—which lasted through the summer of 1864—did not enhance assimilation.[25]

2

Before Chancellorsville: Sigel, Blenker, and the Reinforcement of German Ethnicity in the Union Army, 1861–1862

Although Civil War soldiers everywhere collectively shared many things—the drudgery of drill, sickness, hunger, the terror of battle, and a yearning for loved ones at home—ethnicity undoubtedly influenced the experiences of German American soldiers in the eastern ethnic regiments and inspired in them different reactions and experiences from their Anglo American comrades. Recruited into regiments that boasted memberships entirely or mainly German, performing daily tasks among German comrades, and routinely hearing and speaking the German language, these soldiers could not escape the fact that they were different. Some relished their ethnicity and used it as a means to move up the ranks, eliminate non-German adversaries, and improve the quality of life in their regiments. Others failed to acknowledge their ethnicity in any way. Whatever their reactions to their own Germanness, urban-immigrant soldiers enlisted in both ethnic and regular regiments, encountered and dispensed ethnic prejudice, and lived and fought among other Germans in the camp and field in the first two years of the war. While these areas of focus do not compose the entire early war experience of these men, they are the ones in which the influence of ethnicity was most evident, and thus offer the greatest opportunity to explore its function in their lives before the battle of Chancellorsville.

"All Good Men are Happy to Fight for the Laws of Our Homeland": Enlistment, Motivations, and Promotions

Thousands of books compiling the letters and reminiscences of Civil War soldiers and officers adorn the shelves of most major libraries. Leading historians, such as Bell Irvin Wiley, James M. McPherson, and Reid Mitchell have succeeded in interpreting this vast amount of literature and provide a deeper understanding of various subjects concerning soldiers' lives: why they enlisted and kept fighting, how they dealt with the monotony and hardships of camp, how they perceived their enemies and allies, and how they experienced battle. Very few of these historians, however, have specifically analyzed the lives of ethnic soldiers, and in the few instances in which they do treat this subject, dwell primarily on the Irish. German soldiers, who were collectively the largest ethnic group in the Federal service, have been almost forgotten. Who were these men and why did they serve in the northern armies?[1]

For years most historians have agreed that the majority of Civil War enlisted men were between eighteen and twenty-one years old. The armies of volunteers from both the North and South in 1861 were not only inexperienced in the ways of war, but were almost literally composed of boy soldiers, in many cases, fresh off the farm. The men who enlisted in the German regiments from the east were, however, considerably older than this stereotype. They also came from extremely diverse walks of life, enlisted for reasons somewhat different from their Anglo American comrades, and represented nearly every German state and province. Prussians and Badeners, Hessians and Bavarians buried their European prejudices against one another and enlisted jointly in the same companies. To serve in a German regiment was apparently more important to them than fostering old animosities.[2]

Close scrutiny of the descriptive lists of five companies drawn from each of the primary Pennsylvania German regiments reveals the average age of the recruit in 1861 was 29.90 years, perhaps due to the fact that many of these individuals had immigrated to America as teenagers or young adults in the late 1840s and 1850s. Men in their early forties were as common, if not more numerous, than youths in their early twenties. While men born in the southern German states of Baden, Württemberg, and Bavaria dominated the ranks, each company also included sizeable percentages of men from northern Germany, Prussia in particular. Pennsylvania and Ireland were also listed as the place of birth for several soldiers, indicating not all in the German regiments were German-born. The majority of soldiers were day laborers, shoemakers, farmers, tailors, bakers, and smiths, in descending order. The list of less popular prewar professions was diverse, ranging from two jewelers in the 74th Pennsylvania, to five sailors in the 27th, to three tobacconists in the 98th. Despite the number of common laborers (fifty-seven) which topped the list of occupations, however, the overwhelming majority of men in each of the companies surveyed were skilled artisans.[3]

The inferences gleaned from these statistics portray an image of the Pennsylvania immigrant German volunteer at variance with the typical portrait of the Civil War soldier. He was substantially older than the average Union recruit, more skilled, and enlisted in regiments containing men from extraordinarily diverse occupational backgrounds.[4] Also unlike the American volunteer, who usually enlisted in a regiment composed of men not only born in his home state, but often from his home county, the Pennsylvania immigrant German joined regiments filled with men born throughout Germany. Although they currently lived in Pittsburgh or Philadelphia, these men still remembered their ties to the old German states and had associated with Germans from similar backgrounds in the antebellum period. The German provincial origins of these troops were thus markedly diverse and boded intraregimental conflict; in the old country, for instance, no self-respecting Bavarian would or could enlist in a Prussian regiment. In Civil War–era America, however, the old rivalries between the German states vanished. The bad feelings engendered between Prussians and southern Germans, particularly Badeners and Württembergers, as a result of the failed 1848 revolutions in Europe, must not have played a major role in decisions to enlist. Perhaps some of these men had come to America before 1848, but based on the average age of the troops it is highly unlikely that more than a minority in each regiment had. Hence, the free mixture of men from every major German state indicated that German particularism had succumbed to a joint identity of Germanness among at least Philadelphia and Pittsburgh Germans. The volunteers of the Pennsylvania German regiments clearly wanted to go to war in the company of other Germans, and were willing to allow former rivalries to fall by the wayside in order to support the cause they believed in.[5]

Germans enlisted for a variety of reasons. Like most northern men who volunteered, defense of the flag and the federal laws were common themes, and membership in a prewar militia group made joining up all the easier. Private Jacob C. Kappler was a member of the Lancaster Rifles, a group composed mainly of newer German immigrants living in Lancaster, Pennsylvania. When Lincoln called for 75,000 volunteers to quell the rebellion, the Rifles promptly traveled to Philadelphia and enlisted as Company D of the 99th Pennsylvania Infantry. Kappler wrote his wife from camp on 13 June 1861, "all good men are happy to fight for the laws of our homeland." First Lieutenant Alphons Richter of the non-German 56th New York also answered the president's call to arms, and although he would have rather returned to Germany, believed his honor was on the line to "uphold the oath I took for the rights of the Northern American states, and I will remain true to my oath."[6]

Members of the three-month 5th Pennsylvania, a regiment containing large numbers of Germans who later reenlisted in the ethnic 74th Pennsylvania, published a newspaper throughout June 1861 called "The Pennsylvania Fifth." It contained both an English and a German section, and many of the articles in the German half were not merely translations of their English counterparts. Editor Charles Zinn wrote an editorial on 17 June clarifying the reasons why he and his German comrades had enlisted: "to defend federal property as well as the federal capital, and to bring back to recognition and enforce the disgracefully violated federal laws in the rebel states." Private Joseph S. Johnson, a German speaker in the 96th Pennsylvania, also wrote, "all are ready to give selfless support to [President Lincoln] and the Administration until each remnant of this accursed rebellion is swept from the floor of the Union." Zinn and Johnson firmly believed the war was about the preservation of federal authority and the upholding of the laws. It had "not the slightest to do with slavery," Zinn added. A soldier in the German 27th Pennsylvania, who signed his initials "C. B. A.," agreed. In three months' worth of letters published in the Skippackville *Neutralist* from June to August 1861, not once did he specifically mention his reasons for enlisting, but several times he disputed perceived southern fears that northerners were waging war to free the slaves.[7]

Later in the conflict, after emancipation had become a real issue, some immigrant Germans, both soldiers and civilians, echoed "C. B. A." by loudly protesting the new war aim. Not surprisingly, most of them were Democrats. Henry Kircher of the German 12th Missouri vehemently denounced emancipation and the advent of black troops in his famous diary, and privates Wilhelm Brecht and Alfred Pretz, both of the half-German 47th Pennsylvania, lamented the new reality. Brecht claimed, "we desire and require no black 'kriegskameraden,'" and if the restoration of the Union demanded the same, "we will fight it." Pretz lamented, "it'll be a bitter pill for our boys to live aside of the niggers, I'm afraid." Yet other Germans, especially those imbued with the idealism of the failed 1848 revolutions, believed strongly in the goal of bringing freedom to the slaves, even before the Emancipation Proclamation. Sebastian Mueller enlisted in the nonethnic 67th New York almost immediately upon arriving in Brooklyn, and unabashedly proclaimed in early 1862, "all of America must become free and unified and the starry banner must fly again over the New World. Then we also want to free the slaves, the slave trade must end, and every slave should in time be put on his own two feet." Martin Oefele has convincingly shown that a high percentage of future officers in the United States Colored Troops originally hailed from Germany, indicating that not a few German immigrants must have supported emancipation and black freedom early in the war. As with nonethnic soldiers, partisan affiliation probably played a role in such support along with any lingering democratic tendencies from the old country.[8]

Practicality dictated the decision to enlist for most Germans. Musician Franz Schwenzer of the 47th Pennsylvania clearly enlisted for the steady income he believed the army would provide him. Like many newly emigrated Germans, Schwenzer was eager to move up on the socioeconomic ladder but had few resources at his disposal. The outbreak of war provided an avenue for employment that would ensure his young family's economic survival in Allentown,

Pennsylvania. On 9 October 1861 he wrote them from Fort Ethan Allen, Virginia:

> I must now conclude my writing to my dearest wife and dear little daughter. Also I greet you with all my heart, never forgetting that it is for your welfare that I have gone into this war so that you can keep your lives. I am not fearful of death. Living would be difficult for us without my going to war. To move forward could not have been thought of. When I, however, have served a number of months, then we will be so far as to be able to say that the house is ours, which $200 it would have been [otherwise] difficult to make up.[9]

Schwenzer's economic motivation probably lay under many of his German comrades' additional reasons for enlisting. Letters so frankly stating the pecuniary purposes for joining the army, however, are rare even in the English language, so it is difficult to gauge just how critical the lure of "steady" army pay was for German volunteers. Few soldiers would ever admit that money was at the root of their patriotism.

One other major reason served to inspire Germans to enlist in the Union army, and especially in ethnic regiments: a belief that they had to prove their loyalty and gratitude to their adopted fatherland. George M. Schneider of the German 9th Ohio wrote, "we Germans are second to none in loyalty and patriotism, for we love this country as we love a mother; we are ready to offer our blood and our treasure for her free and matchless institutions." Adolph Frick of the 17th Missouri, another German unit, proclaimed he would not leave the army if given a choice, because "it is a disgrace for any able-bodied man to leave his adopted fatherland—which has guaranteed him protection and aid—in the lurch in the moment of danger." Sergeant Albert Krause of the 116th New York agreed, writing his parents and sister, "I am going with courage and enthusiasm into battle. The [United] States took me in, I have earned a living, and now that they are in trouble I should not defend them with flesh and blood?"[10]

The ethnic regiments held out a special appeal for German immigrants living in the North's major cities. As several scholars have previously shown, most Germans in urban areas clustered together in ethnically distinct neighborhoods and spent their days immersed in the German language and surrounded by other German Americans. Their contact with Anglo Americans was limited and, depending on the locale, it was even possible to live and die in a "little Germany" without ever needing to leave its protective confines. It made good sense for young men living in this prewar environment to enlist in ethnically German regiments. They would not only serve with friends, neighbors, and relatives—a desire they shared with most Civil War soldiers—but also continue to be surrounded by people who shared their cultural background and spoke their language. In nearly every case, their officers would also be German and command them in their native tongue. The traditional estimate regarding how many Germans served in ethnic regiments versus nonethnic or mixed regiments nationwide rests at about one to four. But this proportion may be inaccurate, and certainly does not reflect the percentage of German immigrants from the Union's principle cities who enlisted in all-German units. If one takes just the example of New York City, which sent more ethnically German regiments to the war than any other urban area, an 1862 estimate from the German Society of New York places the ratio of enlistment in ethnic to nonethnic regiments at three to one. That is a figure at great variance with the idea that the bulk of the North's German volunteers served in nonethnic units. The question that really begs to be answered, but cannot be without a systematic statistical analysis of all Union regimental muster rolls, is what proportion of German immigrants lived in cities in 1861 versus small towns and the countryside. Based on the New York example, it appears unlikely that the majority of urban-dwelling Germans fought in "American" or ethnically mixed regiments. And nearly all of the German regiments that campaigned in the eastern theater of war came from the great cities: New York, Philadelphia, Chicago, Milwaukee, and Pittsburgh. Nearly all of them in turn would be first clustered together in Ludwig Blenker's German division and later in the Eleventh Corps. For the thousands of German immigrants in the North's cities, where the pulse of German America beat the strongest and most noticeably, their experiences in the Civil War would be inextricably intertwined with and defined by the fate of the German regiments in the east. Many would have agreed with the editor of the Belleville, Illinois *Belleviller Zeitung*, who wrote on 1 August 1861:

> The German is a born soldier. He can achieve great things during a war, if he has able leaders and if his heart is in the cause for which he fights. . . . This the Germans proved again at Carthage and Manassas. But it is only proper that they see their achievements acknowledged and publicized effectively in the light of the still growing prejudices of the nativists. . . . The German adopted citizens can only hope to reach this goal if they get together in their own regiments and special German corps under German officers.[11]

The peculiarities of Union recruiting methods and the politics related to the formation of the volunteer regiments early in the war ensured that even the most ethnically German regiments contained smatterings of non-German troops. Sometimes an extra company or two was needed to numerically fill up the regiment and ensure its acceptance into the federal service; occasionally non-Germans enlisted—or were recruited—into German units to fill up specific companies. However many of these non-Germans marched off in any given ethnic regiment, they had to face the reality that they were now in the minority and as such could face prejudice, ironically from members of an ethnic minority itself. The records of the 27th Pennsylvania are especially rich with examples exhibiting this sort of reverse prejudice.

In some cases, especially early in the war, letters of complaint written to Governor Andrew Curtin from disaffected Anglo Americans in the 27th revealed what could only be described as ethnic favoritism, in which the Germans blatantly attempted to bar the advancement of non-Germans through prejudicial means. The officers of the regiment appeared particularly guilty of this practice. Acting Lieutenant R. B. Goodman of Company B, recently promoted but not confirmed in his new rank, wrote Curtin on 30 November 1861, complaining that he had received the pay of his old first sergeant's rank: "Pay day comes and I am paid off as first sergeant, for the reason that the officers list of Compy. B had been made complete by the transfer thereto of a 2d. Lieut. by the name of Charles Westhoff, who cannot talk a word of English, and by a first Lieut. by the name of Herman Meiser, with a broken leg, a man who will never again be able to do the least duty." Goodman had served in the army before the war, and was infuriated that "a Lieut. position is denied me, while officers are taken into the Regt., who are only two or three months from Europe." His former sergeant's position already filled, Goodman was effectively out of the army. He asked to be reinstated, but not in the 27th, stating "I should like it best [if] I could be transferred to another regiment."[12]

Irishman Charles Galagher was even more pointed in his complaint. Writing Governor Curtin on 23 August 1861, he claimed he was denied the second lieutenancy of his company in the 27th, "the only company in the Regt or in the Brigade that does not understand the German language," as a result of Lieutenant Colonel Charles Angeroth's intrigues. Angeroth insisted on examining all the newly elected officers "for the purpose of having some of them rejected to place some of his sons in their place," and Galagher failed the test. It was necessary for Curtin to override Angeroth and appoint Galagher because he felt he and his men "are greatly the sufferers in many ways—we had one company of Irish and Americans mixed that wouldn't stay with the Regt they are now in Washington on special duty." Galagher's company was the only remaining non-German company in the 27th and needed an English-speaking officer. If Curtin could not reinstate Galagher, he said, "I humbly crave of you to have me examined by officers that will not be prejudice to me."[13]

Ethnicity on a Daily Basis: Camp Life in the German Regiments

German immigrant soldiers outnumbered the Irish in the Army of the Potomac by more than two to one, and at one point were gathered together in a division almost entirely made up of Germans. Men of remoter German ancestry may also have composed as much as a quarter of the army at any given time. Considering the large numbers of ethnically German soldiers in the primary Union army in the East, the lack of scholarly attention given to them is puzzling. Ella Lonn devoted sections of chapters to them in her landmark *Foreigners in the Union Army,* but a meaningful analysis of the actual lives of German soldiers—what they experienced in camp, felt on the march, and believed important on a daily basis—eluded her. Wilhelm Kaufmann's *The Germans in the American Civil War* is indispensable to the scholar studying the Germans, but again a detailed discussion of the life of the German soldier in the Army of the Potomac fails to emerge. William Burton partially succeeded in explaining important aspects of the lives of ethnic soldiers, such as political motivations and ethnic pride and rivalry, but like the other two authors never presented a clear picture of life in a German regiment. Burton's discussions of ethnic politics, recruiting, and the service records of the various regiments also focused strongly on the Midwest and Missouri, providing only basic information on the Germans in the eastern theater, where the majority of ethnically German regiments served and where the attention of the north's German population tended to focus. Wolfgang Helbich's and Walter Kamphoefner's recent collection of German-American letters from the era provides copious primary source material, but the authors' analysis of those letters is limited. The question, therefore, still remains: Were German immigrant soldiers significantly different from their Anglo American comrades?[14]

Once in the field, German regiments in the Army of the Potomac were surprisingly like the so-called American regiments in almost every way. German soldiers and officers drilled, complained, gambled, got sick, fought in battle, deserted, and died. They suffered the cold of winter and the blazing sun of summer, wore blue uniforms, carried more or less the same rifles and equipage, and slept in the same drafty shelter halves at night. From a distance to an uninformed observer, the German American regiments looked exactly the same as all the other infantry units in the federal service.

A closer examination, however, would have revealed differences that specifically addressed the regiments' ethnicity. Unquestionably the most significant characteristic of a German regiment was the language in which the officers and men communicated. Throughout all of 1861 and much of 1862 nearly all of the orders transcribed in the order, letter, and endorsement books were written in

German script. Orders from brigade headquarters, were, in some instances, still being copied down in German as late as the early spring of 1863. That the written language even switched to English at all was probably due to the fact that the German regiments no longer all served together in entirely ethnic brigades by that point in the war, and had had several Anglo American regiments sprinkled among them. It was undoubtedly easier to correlate and classify brigade-level orders if they were all written in the same language. The Americans could not read German, so the language by default became English.[15]

Whether or not German was spoken as the official language is more difficult to determine, but much evidence supports this inference. Early in the war German was typically the language of drill (itself conducted after German standards), command, and conversation. Lieutenant Colonel Adolphus Buschbeck of the 27th Pennsylvania wrote Governor Curtin an assessment of his regiment's condition in November 1861 and said "the intercourse between officers as well as men is German." A civilian visitor to the camps of the 73rd and 27th Pennsylvania concurred, claiming "the German language is the prevailing one." A Lieutenant Wagner of the 27th testified in a court-martial of one of his men in February 1862 that he had orally translated the articles of war into German and then posted them, "so that every one could understand them." Even on the divisional level, most oral orders were issued in both German and English throughout 1862. When Brigadier General William S. Rosecrans temporarily assumed command of Brigadier General Louis Blenker's German division in April 1862, he wrote a congratulatory message to the men of the division for their diligence in the late march over the Virginia mountains, stating, "this order [will] be translated into German and published in both languages, at the head of each regiment and company of the command." After the battle of Cross Keys in June, Major General John C. Frémont also issued "congratulatory orders" to his command, which included the German division. Claiming they had displayed "the steadiness of veterans," he directed that the orders "will be read before all regiments in the English language as well as in German for the regiments of the German division." Further, company commanders were to ensure their men understood the order.[16]

The German language was not the only ethnic trait infusing the daily life of German American soldiers. Most of the regiments were well supplied with beer—considered a necessity of life by Germans everywhere—in the early days of the war, although this practice was frowned upon by both civil and military authorities and completely eliminated in May 1863. Long before then, however, the beer wagons had been steadily disappearing from the camps of the eastern German regiments. It was discovered that non-German soldiers, who were never allowed the privilege of beer in their camp, would somehow find their

May 21: Bought a Loaf of Bread for 90 cts.
May 23: Paid up 1.10 cts. for a Loaf

It had been even worse for the men the week before in Franklin, where a small supply train and sutlers had finally caught up to the hard-marching division, but were forcibly separated from them because of high water. According to Otto Heusinger of the 41st New York, the starving troops had to stand idly by on their side of the river and watch the teamsters cook beefsteaks and eat heartily while their fare consisted of boiled newspapers and old rags, sprinkled with salt, and accompanied with "empty coffee sacks thrown into boiling water, in order to glean a weak resemblance of coffee flavor." The regimental dogs "had vanished from the camp, all of them slaughtered," and a half loaf of moldy bread reportedly sold for over three dollars in gold. The men received at best one-half piece of hardtack each per day, if that. As one soldier put it, "Our proud, beautiful division—what has become of it!"[23]

The march to join Frémont, costly to every German regiment in Blenker's command, proved especially deadly for the 75th Pennsylvania. The Philadelphia Germans suffered an unexpected tragedy on 15 April, when 48 men of companies K and I drowned while crossing the rain-swollen Shenandoah River in a top-heavy boat. According to various accounts, Colonel Henry Bohlen knew the river was still too dangerous to cross and the boat too overloaded. Several officers pleaded with him to wait. Unconvinced, he stubbornly ordered the boat to get underway. About halfway across, it began to sink, and the men panicked. Many men of the German division witnessed this horrible event and it affected them deeply. From the shore, Leonhard Schlumpf of the 45th New York watched "the unfortunate victims screaming for help, endangering each other by holding and clinging to each other in the water. Even if it had been possible for some soldiers to save their lives, they were pulled underwater by their helpless frightened comrades." A soldier in the 41st New York was appalled at the sight of his comrades, "laden down with knapsacks, all their gear, and rifles, losing their footing and springing into the water. It was a performance terrible to see." The news of this disaster rippled through the other German regiments like a shockwave, prompting many to question whether their own German officers cared about them. It had already become clear to most that the authorities in Washington did not, or, they perceived, more and better provisions would have been sent to alleviate their suffering on the terrible march. The soldiers began wondering if their command was cursed by both prejudice and bad luck.[24]

What was really the purpose of this forced march that had caused so much suffering? Private Ulrich Helmcke of the 27th Pennsylvania summed it up as a "crap trip, as anything else I cannot, with even the best intentions, call our marching affair." He confessed doubt about the utility of sending the German division so far into Virginia's wilds, but still wrested a ray of hope from all the misery. Helmcke hoped that the extreme privations and sacrifices endured by his countrymen would show a questioning northern public that the German soldier was committed to his cause: "I say, not without patriotic pride we look back—let it be recognized [we] prove[d] to our adopted Fatherland that we are not unworthy of him, but as true offspring of the great German nation . . . feel a piercing obligation of gratitude and reverence toward our old and new homeland, [and] are ready and willing to present treasure, blood, and life as a sacrifice to the altar of honor."[25]

Helmcke was not alone in his sentiments. Despite the tragic experiences of the march, once under Frémont's command most soldiers agreed that the ordeal had been worth it. They believed their dogged determination to do their duty would be well received by the northern public, both German and non-German, and remove any shadow of doubt about their soldierly qualities and important role in the war. Unfortunately, reports of Ludwig Blenker's earlier ostentatious lifestyle and lavish entertainment in camp back near Washington had begun to ripen in the Anglo American press, and his division by association automatically received its first tarnish. Further, accounts of excessive foraging by soldiers of the German division both near the capital and on the recent march had also filtered back north, and in this early period of the war plundering civilians was considered bad form. The Confederate press had a field day portraying the "bloodthirsty Dutch" and their rampages among "helpless" Virginia civilians. Soon the northern press, especially the *New York Herald*, followed suit, albeit in a less abusive manner. The Union high command became embarrassed.

The newspapermen and generals failed to note, however, three important considerations: first, the German division was harassed on its way to Romney by Confederate bushwhackers, which prompted some harsh measures against local civilians; second, General Frémont clearly witnessed the plight of the troops under his command and turned a blind eye; and third, the soldiers were literally starving in the field. For his part, Blenker sympathized with his suffering soldiers and dispatched official foraging parties into the countryside. Leonhard Schlumpf admitted in his diary that wholesale looting occurred, but explained why: "We are forced in order not to starve to death to find our own food in farms, sometimes 4–5 miles out of our way. When we find such a farm we plunder it for what is edible." Such explanations never made it to the Anglo American papers. Instead, condemnation began to rain down on the Germans, and a new verb, *to blenker*, was created in army parlance, meaning "to plunder." Otto Heusinger thought he knew the basic reason behind all the uproar: "one damned the German troops for their foraging of cattle and property because the soldiers were German . . . because the German officers were militarily trained and more talented than the Americans . . . because we were 'Dutchmen.' "[26]

After the incredible hardships endured on their way to participate in the hoped-for capture of Stonewall Jackson's army, the Germans' battle with one of his divisions under Richard S. Ewell at Cross Keys on 8 June proved indecisive. In this, their baptism by fire, the soldiery of the German division performed well, but some of their officers did not. Frémont's brigades arrived on the field in piecemeal order, an oversight that could have been easily corrected by the commanding general, and were thrown into battle separately without any real plan of attack. Blenker, at the rear of his division as it moved up, was never really on the field during the action, and Brigadier General Julius Stahel, who made the advance on the Union left against Isaac Trimble's hidden Confederate brigade, failed to keep his five regiments together. The result was that one lone German regiment, the 8th New York, walked into Trimble's carefully prepared ambush and met its destruction. The 27th Pennsylvania and 41st New York somehow fell out of line with the 8th, and the 45th New York inexplicably never fully engaged. With no skirmishers out front, bereft of its sister regiments, the 8th "came marching across the clover field in a beautiful line, carrying their guns at 'support arms.' The Colonel walk[ed] backwards in front of them, seeing that they preserved a perfect alignment just as though they were simply drilling," one Confederate observer wrote. But this was no drill. As they marched up a small incline toward a fenced-in treeline, the unaware Germans had no idea of what was to befall them. Suddenly, in one gigantic explosion, a crashing volley from over 1300 rebel muskets rent the air. The 8th New York simply disintegrated. "The poor Germans fell all across each other in piles," reported one horrified eyewitness. The surprise had been so complete, and the destruction so overwhelming, that the survivors of the 8th immediately broke and ran. Over 180 of their comrades were left dead or wounded on the bloody field, and 74 more would be captured (out of slightly more than 500). In their very first battle and in one brief moment, the 8th New York suffered one of the worst regimental casualty rates of the Civil War.[27]

The decimation of the 8th New York essentially decided the battle. Trimble counterattacked, but Blenker's artillery checked him, as did the musketry of the 27th Pennsylvania of Stahel's brigade and the 54th New York and 74th Pennsylvania of Bohlen's brigade. Casualties were light among the other German regiments. Anglo American regiments on the Union right fought bravely but failed to push the Confederates back. Frémont's attempt to smash through Jackson's rearguard at Cross Keys had failed, garnering little but 800-odd dead, wounded, and missing.

Despite the defeat, the northern press, both Anglo and German American, reported favorably on the performance of the German division. *The New York Times*, unaware of Stahel's bungling, claimed "the part taken by Gen. Stahl [*sic*], and his brigade of Germans, is the theme of general commendation. He has won the popular favor among American as well as foreign officers." The soldiers had done their duty, argued the *New-Yorker Criminalzeitung und Belletristisches Journal*, "but the general opinion in the German Division is that Frémont made the monstrous error of splitting up the division." The Philadelphia *Freie Presse* exclaimed of Cross Keys, "The German Division has gloriously fulfilled the high expectations of its war-readiness and bravery." After suffering "forced marches . . . barely clothed . . . and half-starved," the soldiers "had also bravely passed the fiery test" of battle against Jackson's forces. The result of the battle, it appeared, was not nearly as important as how well the German troops had conducted themselves. Of his regiment's performance, Theodore Sander of the 27th Pennsylvania said "the murderous fire of our new Enfield rifles, which we just recently acquired, convinced [the rebels] that the Pennsylvanians were not prepared to run away." His regimental comrade, L. B. Paul, agreed, stating, "I will never forget, as long as I live . . . how we charged with a thundering hurrah against the foe, and, after a stubborn, half-hour battle, repulsed the enemy." Perhaps Sergeant Major August Horstmann of the 45th New York summed up the feelings in the German division the best: "many brave sons of the German fatherland are already dead on the field of honor and more beside me will fall!" Yet the sacrifices were not in vain. "If I should fall in the struggle of freedom and the preservation of the Union of this, my adopted country, you may rest easier," he told his parents. Both the newspapers and the soldiers clearly believed it was enough that they had done their duty. They thought they had proven that the Germans could fight. The campaign and battle of Second Manassas would reinforce that opinion.[28]

After Cross Keys the German regiments witnessed several changes to their command structure. The embattled Ludwig Blenker resigned his post, finally yielding to the invective emanating from the radical German press (especially the Boston *Deutsche Pionier*, edited by the fiery forty-eighter Karl Heinzen, who personally despised the general), informal charges of misconduct at Cross Keys, and quite probably, political intriguing from officers within his own ranks. Captain Gustave Struve of the 8th New York, himself an old forty-eighter, lamented that Carl Schurz, who had just resigned as minister to Spain, lay behind the ministrations to oust Blenker and conspired with high-ranking German American civilian and military leaders to remove the general. Colonels

Adolph von Steinwehr and Alexander Schimmelfennig undoubtedly played a role also. A dejected Ludwig Blenker bade farewell to his beloved division and left for "vacation" in Washington, where he was formally shelved. He would hold no further commands in the war, and mustered out of the service in March 1863, dying a broken man later that year. Schurz, who had repeatedly written Lincoln and prominent Republicans from Spain requesting a military appointment, was waiting in the wings and, with Blenker removed from the picture, got his chance. His brigadier generalship confirmed by the Senate, Carl Schurz, the self-appointed political spokesman of German America, joined the German division as it retreated northward after the battle.[29]

Not long after Schurz joined the army, Lincoln completely reorganized his scattered forces in Virginia and consolidated them into one, unified command. Franz Sigel, whose resignation had caused such indignation among German Americans at the beginning of 1862, was transferred to the east and replaced Frémont, to the joy of the German-language press. Also brought east, ostensibly to bring order out of chaos, was Major General John Pope. Pope, a westerner who had seen some success on the rivers earlier in the year, was given command of the new Army of Virginia, which consisted of Frémont's old army and those of several other generals who had failed to bring Stonewall Jackson to bay. Combined with some divisions then in Washington and en route from Major General George B. McClellan's Army of the Potomac (disembarking from its failed Peninsular Campaign), Pope's new army was to cooperate with McClellan in protecting Washington and crushing Robert E. Lee's Army of Northern Virginia. To assist in that task, Pope restructured his divisions into three corps, giving Sigel command of the first. The old German division was officially broken up and distributed throughout Sigel's First Corps, which consisted of three divisions under the command of Brigadier Generals Robert C. Schenck, Adolph von Steinwehr, and Carl Schurz. About two-thirds of the soldiers in Sigel's corps were German, with the majority serving in Schurz's division; many of the regiments and leaders that would later fight at Chancellorsville in the Eleventh Corps experienced their first major battle in the coming campaign. As July gave way to August 1862 most in the ranks felt confident because their beloved Sigel had finally come to lead them. Thoughts of the sacrifices made during the infamous mountain march and at Cross Keys faded. "Since Sigel assumed command, a completely different spirit has settled over all of the corps, and the German troops in particular," one newspaper correspondent observed.[30]

The operations that culminated in the battle of Second Manassas, fought on 29 and 30 August, began in late June. For over a month Pope and Lee skirmished, maneuvered, and attempted to outflank each other along the Rappahannock River. In one of those episodes, at Freeman's Ford on 22 August,

Schurz's division played a significant role, and both general and enlisted men performed admirably despite long numerical odds. The 74th Pennsylvania distinguished itself during this fight, attacking the onrushing Confederates in a holding action while its sister regiments withdrew intact across the river. One soldier of the Pittsburgh German regiment wrote, "the drums rolled the sound for the charge, the flags waved, and under the personal leadership of our brave colonel Schimmelfennig the regiment forcefully attacked the enemy. March! March! Hurrah! Hurrah! onward it went and like chaff in the wind the rebels fled in disorder before the German bayonets of the 74th regiment." But soon rebel reinforcements compelled the 74th to retreat, leaving approximately 25 percent of its effective strength dead or wounded on the other side of the river. Freeman's Ford was "a glorious and honorable day" for the regiment. Not so for Brigadier General Henry Bohlen, leading the 74th's brigade, who, according to Otto Heusinger, was shot out of his saddle from behind by members of his old 75th Pennsylvania, who blamed him for the drowning of their comrades back in April.[31]

After Freeman's Ford, Lee dispatched Stonewall Jackson and his half of the Confederate army on a wide flanking movement that ultimately placed him squarely astride Pope's line of supply and communications with Washington. Jackson's men dug in along an abandoned railroad cut just west of the old battlefield of First Manassas and north of the village of Groveton. It was a strong defensive position, and Pope did exactly what Lee and Jackson hoped he would do: attack. Pope ordered Sigel to determine Jackson's dispositions and, if possible, pierce his line on 29 August. Most of the rest of the Union army was not yet on the field, so Sigel would operate alone at first, and, to make matters worse, when Sigel was later promised the assistance other troops, that aid failed to materialize because of the prejudice of an Anglo American general who disliked Sigel. Unfortunately the troops who paid the price for this mismanagement were mainly Carl Schurz's.

About eight o'clock in the morning of the 29th, Sigel gave the order for several of his brigades to advance against Jackson. The heavily German brigades of Colonel Wladimir Krzyzanowki (containing the 54th and 58th New York and 75th Pennsylvania) and Colonel Alexander Schimmelfennig (containing the 74th Pennsylvania, 61st Ohio, and 8th West Virginia) moved forward south of the Sudley Church and into the thick woods where Maxcy Gregg's South Carolina brigade waited. An intense firefight ensued, with men shooting from behind trees toward shadowy images in the thick smoke that they thought were the enemy. Only the bright orange flashes of musket fire revealed the foe's position. The South Carolinians surged forward, putting severe pressure on the New York Germans, then were flanked by the 75th Pennsylvania on their right,

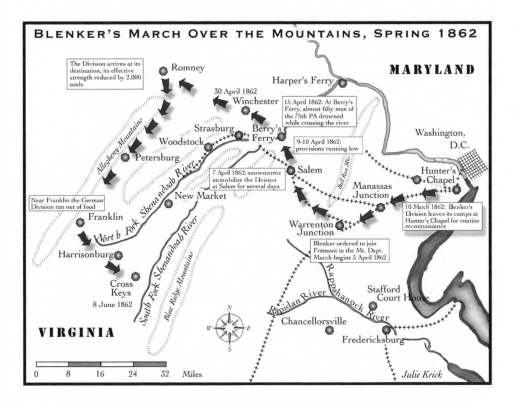

BLENKER'S MARCH OVER THE MOUNTAINS, SPRING 1862

The Division arrives at its destination, its effective strength reduced by 2,000 souls.

Romney

Harper's Ferry

MARYLAND

30 April 1862
Winchester

15 April 1862: At Berry's Ferry, almost fifty men of the 75th PA drowned while crossing the river

Strasburg   Berry's
Woodstock   Ferry

9-10 April 1862: provisions running low

Washington, D.C.

Petersburg

7 April 1862: snowstorms immobilize the Division at Salem for several days

Salem

Manassas Junction

Hunter's Chapel

Near Franklin the German Division ran out of food

New Market

10 March 1862: Blenker's Division leaves its camps at Hunter's Chapel for routine reconnaissance

Franklin

North Fork Shenandoah River

Warrenton Junction

Blenker ordered to join Frémont in the Mt. Dept. March begins 5 April 1862

Harrisonburg

South Fork Shenandoah River

Blue Ridge Mountains

Cross Keys
8 June 1862

Allegheny Mountains

Rapidan River

Stafford Court House

VIRGINIA

Rappahannock River

Chancellorsville

Fredericksburg

0   8   16   24   32   Miles   *Julie Krick*

fell back, and, attacked again. This time, they broke through, pushing Krzyza-nowki's men back in "utter confusion." Schurz hastily sent forward his reserve, the 29th New York from Colonel John Koltes's brigade, which fired several stiff volleys into the charging Carolinians, but to no avail. The 29th also fell back, and for a moment, it appeared that Schurz's line would be breached. At the last minute, a Federal battery belched canister and brought the southern advance to a halt. The rebels, surprised by the intensity of the fire, retreated. Schurz then reformed his New York regiments, shouting "Never mind boys! Such things may happen to the best of soldiers. Now forward with a hurrah!" Krzyzanow-ski's brigade, in tandem with Schimmelfennig's, surged forward, crashed through the woods, and found the South Carolinians again near the railroad cut. One Confederate officer recalled that the Germans "poured in upon us a deadly fire," and in return, "volley after volley was poured into them, but still they stood." Schimmelfennig's men even gained the railroad embankment. At that critical moment, Jackson's defensive line could have been punctured, but the absence of Major General Philip Kearny's division, which was supposed to have simultaneously advanced to the right of Schimmelfennig, stymied the Germans' success. Where was Kearny? Sigel had given him an order to cooperate with Schurz and launch his division against Jackson's far left. That order had been corroborated with and agreed to by Major General Samuel P. Heintzelman, Kearny's superior.[32]

According to the leading historian of the battle, Kearny held a grudge against Sigel because he had earlier obtained and published a rather nasty letter written by Kearny in which he cast prejudicial aspersions on the fighting qualities of German soldiers. Anxious to defend the honor of his countrymen, Sigel believed Kearny's nativism needed to be publicly reprimanded. Indeed it was, but the result was that Kearny's disdain for Sigel and his troops only grew deeper, and it is believed that he purposefully withheld his support of Sigel that hot August day. That he did so indicated the lengths to which some Anglo Americans would go to vent their anti-German predilections, even to the point of jeopardizing the Union cause. In that light, nothing could excuse Kearny's behavior. He would never come under official scrutiny for this action because he was killed at Chantilly only days later.[33]

After fighting Gregg's South Carolinians and other Confederates for more than eight hours, Schurz was permitted to withdraw his tired, dirty, and badly depleted regiments on the 29th. But his troops were not yet out of the fight. The next day, when Confederate General James Longstreet launched his half of Lee's army against Pope's left, Sigel noticed the danger and dispatched first Koltes's brigade and then Krzyzanowski's to Chinn Ridge to bolster the heroic stand made by Colonel Nathaniel C. McLean's badly outnumbered brigade. McLean's Ohioans and Captain Michael Wiedrich's New York German battery, struck by overwhelming force, put up a herculean fight, but were ultimately compelled to withdraw. Koltes's all-German brigade arrived just in time to be badly mauled by the onrushing Confederates, and Krzyzanowski's regiments could do little to stop the rebel assault, but both brigades did manage to delay the enemy, buying Pope time to create a strong defensive line on Henry House Hill. In fairness, most of the credit was due McLean's men, but Koltes was killed leading his soldiers, and the 41st New York fought stubbornly, suffering 75 dead, 116 wounded, and 93 missing. Sigel, Schurz, and the German regiments finally conducted a skillful retreat, keeping good order and discipline, even as they passed panicked and disorganized units from the rest of the army. When it was all over and blame began to be assessed they received little criticism for their performance on the fields of Manassas. Other, Anglo American officers became the official culprits for the debacle, but as the ever observant Otto Heusinger of the 41st noted, recognition of the Germans' hard fighting and blood sacrifice would go largely unnoticed by the greater northern public: "Unfortunately the deeds of the German regiments at Bull Run, like so many others, went unrecognized; we remained as before 'the damned Dutchmen.'" That realization must have unsettled Germans like Heusinger who were acutely aware of their ethnic identity, and boded ill for the future.[34]

After Second Manassas, most of Sigel's battered corps went into camp near Fairfax Courthouse, where it remained, licking its wounds, during the subsequent Antietam campaign. Shortly thereafter, the First Corps was dissolved as an organization and the German regiments consolidated into a new army corps, the Eleventh, composed of both German and Anglo American units. Sigel retained control of this new corps, but complained both privately and publicly that he deserved a greater responsibility. The men under his command did not seem to mind the organizational change, enjoying the relatively easy life of guarding Washington's western approaches. Germans and non-Germans alike wrote home about everyday life in camp, complained some—but not much—about mingling with each other (good-natured jibes about "dutch colonels" and "dutch cooking" appeared in some Anglo American letters), and scrawled their names and regiments on the attic walls of Blenheim, a mansion that served as a hospital for the corps. For many in the German regiments, the halcyon days of fall 1862 would be remembered as among the most pleasant in the war. All too soon their memories would acquire a more bitter aftertaste.[35]

3

The Battle of Chancellorsville and the German Regiments of the Eleventh Corps

"All Were Astonished at the Grand Appearance of the Dutch"

In the months prior to Major General Joseph Hooker's spring campaign of 1863, the veteran German American regiments of the newly formed Eleventh Corps moved from their encampments at Fairfax to winter quarters at Stafford Court House, north of Fredericksburg. Arriving at the scene of battle too late to have taken part in Ambrose Burnside's calamitous frontal assaults at Marye's Heights in early December, the men in the New York and Pennsylvania regiments nonetheless participated in the ill-conceived and frustrating "mud march" that occurred afterward. Although letters home from this period were filled with complaints about the weather and bungling on the part of the generals, the men generally considered themselves fortunate to have avoided the slaughter at Fredericksburg and looked forward to the spring under the leadership of Major General Franz Sigel. They also welcomed ethnic comrades from several new regiments assigned to the corps. Two of them, the 82nd Illinois and the 26th Wisconsin, hailed from the Midwest and were posted to the eastern command because of their ethnicity. The 82nd was recruited from Chicago's German-speaking wards, and was led by the fiery forty-eighter Friedrich Hecker. Many men who had seen European service filled the ranks of the 82nd, a fact that would serve the regiment well later in the battle. Composed of Milwaukee Germans and other Teutonic immigrants from the Badger State, the newly raised 26th was as yet untested in battle but its men were hankering for a fight. Also joining the corps was the 119th New York, a new, predominantly German regiment led by Elias Peissner, supposedly the illegitimate son of the King of Bavaria, and the nine-month 153rd Pennsylvania, an amalgam regiment with both German American and Pennsylvania Dutch recruits from Lehigh and Northampton counties.[1]

The winter of 1863 was not as grueling as the previous one, but German American politics proved just as troublesome. Suffering from poor health, chafed by the smallness of his corps compared to others in the Army of the Potomac, annoyed by the lack of promotions of fellow German officers (for which he believed Army Chief of Staff Henry W. Halleck responsible), and deluded by his own inflated sense of importance, Franz Sigel resigned command of the Eleventh Corps on 11 March. Both Abraham Lincoln and Secretary of War Edwin Stanton were enraged at his arrogance and refused to give him back command of his old corps when Sigel reconsidered his action in April. Instead, they appointed Major General Oliver Otis Howard, a West Point graduate and an evangelizing New Englander, as new commander of the Eleventh Corps, with Brigadier General Carl Schurz taking temporary command until Howard reached his charge. The beloved Sigel, darling of Germans nationwide, never again commanded German troops in the Army of the Potomac.[2]

The realization that Sigel would not be with them for the coming spring campaign unsettled many Eleventh Corps soldiers, both German and non-German. Captain Theodore Howell of the 153rd Pennsylvania wrote, "I would rather fight under Sigel than any other Gen'l in the army as he tries to save his men and don't go in blind." Private William Charles of the 154th New York lamented, "I heard yesterday that Gen. Sigel had resigned. For one I am very sorry for I believe him to be a very good General and one that wishes to put down this Rebellion." Sergeant Otto Heusinger of the 41st New York recalled that "the news surprised us very much," and blamed it on "miserable politics, that sore spot in American military history." Sigel "had the gift to make himself beloved among the soldiers," especially with the Germans. Who could replace him? Many believed he would succeed in being reinstated, but in the event Sigel failed to get his old command back, Lieutenant Colonel Alwin von Matzdorff of the 75th Pennsylvania predicted another German officer from within the Eleventh Corps would replace him: "in this case Genr'l Schurtz will probably take command of the corps." But neither Schurz nor any other German received the coveted permanent position. Instead, the teetotaling, one-armed Howard, a tested Anglo American veteran of the Army of the Potomac who had never before served with Germans, rode into camp. Baron Friedrich Otto von Fritsch, special aide to the 74th Pennsylvania's former colonel (now brigadier) Alexander Schimmelfennig, remembered escorting Howard to Schurz's headquarters to take formal command of the Eleventh Corps. Upon his arrival, "the Generals turned out to salute the new Commander and then made very long faces. It was a surprise to everybody. General Schurz had hoped to succeed General Siegel if the latter should resign."[3]

Riding through the camps of the German regiments after nightfall, von Fritsch noticed that the "piety" of Howard along with their natural affection for Sigel prejudiced the troops against the new corps commander. "I heard various exclamations in the tents: 'Boys, let us pray.' 'Tracts now, instead of Sauerkraut.' 'Oh Jesus!' 'Oh Lord!'" According to von Fritsch, Schimmelfennig himself "prophesied that the troops would not like the new commander." The baron also correctly noted that "not quite half" of the Eleventh Corps was composed of non-Germans, who might receive Howard's religious inclinations more favorably. But even they, apparently, were unhappy with him. The new commanding general perceived the dissatisfaction among his troops, and recalled in his autobiography, "I soon found out that my past record was not known here; that there was much complaint in the German language at the removal of Sigel . . . and that I was not at first getting the earnest and loyal support of the entire command. But for me there was no turning back."[4]

Not all the events preceding the battle of Chancellorsville boded so negatively for the German American regiments. In early February, the regimental commanders of the Eleventh Corps submitted status reports to their brigade commanders. The news was very good. Both the 27th and 75th Pennsylvania, for instance, were in excellent condition, numbering 449 and 355 effectives, respectively. Few men were sick in either regiment, their drill and discipline were good, and their morale high. Colonel Mahler of the 75th mentioned the "flattering remarks made on several occasions by our esteemed Brigade Commander, Col. Krzyzanowski," about the precision in drill of the regiment. Later, on 10 April near Brooks Station, Abraham Lincoln and other notables from Washington reviewed the Eleventh Corps as it paraded by at the salute. Lieutenant Colonel von Matzdorff called his regiment's performance "brilliant," and remarked "that all were astonished at the grand appearance of the Dutch!" Private Adam Muenzenberger of the 26th Wisconsin boasted to his wife that his regiment was the largest in the Eleventh Corps, and "also the cleanest and the neatest." When it marched past the reviewing stand, Carl Schurz's daughter reportedly asked him which regiment it was, to which he answered, "that is the 26th Wisconsin." Then she said, "That is the finest looking regiment in the army." With flags flying and bands playing, the German regiments paraded by crisply at the eyes right, and a smile reportedly pursed Lincoln's lips. Colonel Wladimir Krzyzanowski's brigade, containing both the 26th Wisconsin and the 75th Pennsylvania, was universally acclaimed as the "best drilled and most soldierly" of all.[5]

Governors of various states also visited the camp of the Eleventh Corps at Stafford Court House that spring and remarked favorably. Pennsylvania Governor Andrew Curtin, for example, arrived in late March and extensive preparations were made to receive him. In the camp of the 153rd Pennsylvania, "triumphal arches, with appropriate inscriptions, devices, and festoons greeted the august visitor in great profusion." The camp looked like a "fairy land" to one observer. Curtin reviewed the regiment, addressed the men "in a neat and appropriate manner" and left amid "hearty cheers." Two days later the governor visited the 75th Pennsylvania "and made an excellent speech to our troops," von Matzdorff wrote. Afterward, "he stopped in my tent, and placed himself upon my bed—took some wine—in fact he was very pleasant." The German American governor of Wisconsin, Edward S. Salomon, paid the 26th Wisconsin a visit on 19 April. Adam Muenzenberger was jubilant about the occasion in a letter home to his wife. He noted the camp had been "decorated . . . with green boughs and festoons," and that the governor praised the 26th and felt honored by it. That night members of the Milwaukee Sängerbund serenaded Salomon and his guests, including Carl Schurz. The camp echoed with the harmonies of the old German songs, "In der Heimat ist es Schoen" and "Das treue deutsche Herz," and the governor was so moved that he exclaimed, "In my whole life, I have never before been so proud of my German descent as I am now." Three cheers for the Union and the governor followed, "but they didn't go so well. . . . But when [Colonel William H. Jacobs] called for three cheers for General Schurz they went! Schurz merely smiled."[6]

Many in the Army of the Potomac had reason to smile that early spring of 1863. The new army commander, Major General Joseph Hooker, had instilled a renewed sense of élan and pride among his troops. Gone was the depression following Fredericksburg, replaced instead by a firm, even cocky confidence in the success of the impending campaign. Hooker's plan was simple: outflank Robert E. Lee's Army of Northern Virginia, stationed at Fredericksburg, by marching the bulk of the Federal army in a wide arc to the west, cross the Rappahannock and Rapidan rivers well upstream, and advance on Lee's rear and flank. At the same time, a smaller segment of the army, under Major General John Sedgwick, was to cross the Rappahannock at Fredericksburg and occupy Lee's attention. Hooker would then close in on the southerners from the west. Lee would be caught in a gigantic northern pincer movement, and, already outnumbered over two to one, be forced to "ingloriously fly" or "give battle" on ground of the Union commander's choosing. It was definitely a good strategy, but much depended on Robert E. Lee's idleness. That was a trait the Confederate leader had not yet shown.

After much anticipation and in high spirits, the Army of the Potomac broke camp in the last days of April 1863 and commenced the campaign that would so affect the course of the war in the East as well as the stature and self-esteem of the North's German Americans. On a rainy and overcast 27 April that belied the happy mood of the men, the Eleventh Corps left its winter quarters, assembled by regiments, brigades, and then divisions, and marched south toward Kelly's Ford on the Rappahannock River. It was in the lead because it was the smallest corps in the army, and thus supposed the fastest, but by some bungling on the part of O. O. Howard or his staff, the entire train of the corps accompanied it, including herds of cattle to be slaughtered later for food. All of the extra baggage delayed the progress of the corps and those marching behind it, but in the end it made no difference. Two days of marching saw the Eleventh, Twelfth, and Fifth Corps safely across the ford. Carl Schurz remembered that "officers and men seemed to feel instinctively that they were engaged in an offensive movement promising great results. There was no end to the singing and merry laughter." The men carried at least 60 rounds with them, as well as ten days' worth of rations. Knapsacks bulged with 30 tablespoons of coffee, 15 of sugar, and 80 pieces of hardtack, and five pounds each of salt pork, beans, rice, and potato meal followed each soldier in the trains.[7]

Philadelphian Adolphus Buschbeck, former colonel of the 27th Pennsylvania (now in command of a brigade in Adolph von Steinwehr's division) also gave the men reason to laugh. Buschbeck and his brigade, sent out in advance of the main Eleventh Corps column, were settling down for a hard-earned rest when suddenly very loud barking was heard from a nearby cabin. The noise was so loud that the men could not fall asleep, so the colonel sent his aide to take care of the problem. When the aide returned, obviously unsuccessful in his mission, Buschbeck knocked on the door of his cabin and confronted the owner himself, exclaiming, "Hullo dere wy you not stop dem dogs bark?" The "old rebel" replied, "I can't make them quit barking," to which Buschbeck blurted, "Git up and ketch dem dog or I burn your house down right away!" The discussion ended there; the dogs were duly silenced by their owner and Buschbeck's regiments slept through the night. For his efficient quelling of the rebellious dogs the German colonel was praised by the editor of the *Pittsburgh Gazette*: "When this officer is surprised in his camp, or fails in the discharge of his duty as a soldier, there will be reason to doubt all men, and to trust none." Just how well these words applied to Buschbeck's performance at Chancellorsville, and how quickly they were forgotten in the anti-German prejudice that followed, is uncanny.[8]

On rainy 29 April the Eleventh and Twelfth Corps marched to Germanna Ford on the Rapidan River. The water was high—about four feet—and flowing swiftly. Most of the men held their rifles and cartridge boxes over their heads as they crossed late in the evening, but a few regiments had the advantage of a hastily built and jerry-rigged footbridge constructed by the 123rd New York. Regardless of the method of crossing, however, everyone got wet. Sergeant William H. Weaver of the 153rd Pennsylvania wrote that it rained hard that night, and since the men were tired and worn out, they just "lay down there in the mud and rain" until ordered to cross. Lieutenant Karl Doerflinger of the 26th Wisconsin described that night "as a short sleep in the mud or water between the corn hills of a level field." The next day the rain-soaked troops of the Eleventh Corps arose early, cooked their coffee and breakfasts, and marched to within ten miles of Chancellorsville. On 1 May—May Day to the Germans—the regiments encamped directly to its west along the Orange Turnpike. It was a "splendid" day according to one soldier, the sun shining for the first time since they embarked on the campaign. The German troops were in a festive mood. They could finally dry out, rest for a whole morning, and enjoy themselves. One man remarked that he and his comrades were "cheerful" and "happy." But on that same day, Joseph Hooker, whose plan to outflank and surprise Robert E. Lee had so far succeeded brilliantly, relinquished the initiative to the Confederates. After running into rebel resistance at the Zoan Church, west of Fredericksburg, the army commander decided to adopt a defensive position in the deep woods around Chancellorsville. When asked about this curious change of posture by one of his generals, Hooker replied, "It is all right, Couch; I have got Lee just where I want him; he must fight me on my own ground." He knew he had numerical superiority and wanted to consolidate his army before pressing on. If Lee attacked, all the better. He also thought he had time on his side. The problem for Hooker, and very soon for the Eleventh Corps, was that Lee would not sit idly by and await the Federals' next move. He and Stonewall Jackson had to act immediately to prevent a southern disaster, and in so doing, they scored their greatest victory.[9]

"A Queer Jumble of Sounds"

The Eleventh Corps occupied the extreme right flank of the Army of the Potomac on 2 May 1863. Why exactly it was positioned at the far right end is puzzling. It may have been the result of pure circumstance, the corps having marched in from the west behind the Twelfth Corps. Some historians have argued that the Eleventh was still considered the unwanted stepson of the Army of the Potomac, a vestige of Major General John Popes's Army of Virginia, defeated at Second Manassas the year before. Others have claimed that the number of new regiments in the corps, eleven out of twenty-seven, prompted Hooker to place it in an area where it would likely see little action should Lee attack. Then, too, the high percentage of German troops in the corps still aroused suspicion among Anglo American veterans in the high command. Over half of the organization's 12,000 men were German-born or of direct German lineage. Although many of these soldiers were themselves veterans and had fought hard on previous battlefields, their reputation for plundering civilians, service under unsuccessful commanders like Frémont and Pope, and perhaps most importantly, their foreign language and customs rankled many Yankee officers. A combination of all of these reasons probably obliged Hooker to deploy the Eleventh Corps as far as possible from what he thought would be the heart of his operations—the center of his line near Chancellorsville.[10]

German and non-German regiments alike spread their camps out facing south along the Orange Turnpike and in the clearings just to its north, in expectation of an attack by or against the rebels in that direction. At the extreme right of the Eleventh Corps' line, bivouacked in the forest, were the regiments of Colonel Leopold von Gilsa's brigade of Brigadier Charles Devens's First Division. Von Gilsa's men were nearly all German Americans or of German decent. Three of the regiments (the 41st, 45th, and 54th New York) as well as their commander were tested veterans, having first served under Blenker in his German division around Washington in 1861–62. They took credit for stemming the Federal rout after First Manassas and participated in the grueling march over the Virginia mountains to join Frémont, fought at Cross Keys, Freeman's Ford, and Second Manassas, and were now ready to fight again. The fourth regiment, the 153rd Pennsylvania, composed primarily of Pennsylvanians of direct German decent (Pennsylvania Dutch), was new to the army, but eager to show its mettle. Howard had ordered von Gilsa to place the camps of the 54th New York and 153rd Pennsylvania perpendicular to and north of the turnpike, a token nod to the possibility of an attack from the west. He then deployed the second brigade of Devens's division, under the command of Brigadier General Nathaniel McLean, directly to the east of von Gilsa and just north of the road in the Talley House clearing. McLean and his men, mainly Ohioans, were nearly all Anglo American and also battle tested, with the exception of the 107th Ohio, which was a veteran German regiment. Carl Schurz's Third Division came next in line along the turnpike, with a few regiments of Krzyzanowski's brigade, including the 26th Wisconsin, positioned north of the road in the Hawkins Farm/Wilderness Church clearing. Finally, at the end of the mile-and-a-half-long Eleventh Corps line near Dowdall's Tavern, Adolph von Steinwehr's Second Division made camp. Howard decided to make the tavern his headquarters. As he fell asleep there on 1 May, he rested with the knowledge, passed down from Hooker himself, that Lee would either retreat or attack the Union army in its center. The scrub pines, tangled vines, briars, and thick shrubbery of the wilderness to the west ensured that his right flank, "hanging in the air," could not possibly be assailed.[11]

The men in all the regiments had spent the afternoon of 1 May preparing for an assault from the south, digging entrenchments, felling trees in a makeshift abatis, and positioning the artillery in key locations. Brigadier General Francis C. Barlow's brigade of von Steinwehr's division had partially dug some shallow rifle pits in a line running north to south at Dowdall's Tavern, but other than a few even more incomplete breastworks near the Wilderness Church, no other earthworks were ordered dug to meet a potential assault from the west. Early on Saturday morning, 2 May, General Hooker rode out along the Eleventh Corps line and, cheered by the men, acclaimed the position secure. But shortly thereafter, signs began to appear that the Confederates were up to something.[12]

Union lookouts at Hazel Grove, a clearing in the forest to the south located about halfway between Dowdall's Tavern and Chancellorsville, had climbed some trees around nine o'clock and observed rebel infantry moving to the west. They were about a mile and a half distant. Hooker received this news at his headquarters after returning from his inspection of the Eleventh Corps' positions. He was puzzled. Were the southerners retreating, as he had hoped? Or could it be possible that Lee and Jackson were trying to outflank him? Hooker played it safe, and at 9:30 issued the following order to Howard and Major General Henry Slocum, commanding the neighboring Twelfth Corps:

> I am directed by the major general commanding to say the disposition you have made of your corps has been with a view to a *front* attack by the enemy. If he should throw himself upon your flank, he wishes you to examine the ground, and determine upon the position you will take in that event, in order that you may be prepared for him in whatever direction he advances.
>
> He suggests that you have heavy reserves well in hand to meet this contingency.
>
> J. H. Van Alen,
> Brig. General and a.d.C.

> We have good reason to suppose that the enemy is moving to our right. Please advance your pickets for purposes of observation as far as may be safe in order to obtain timely information of their approach.[13]

About the same time as Hooker issued the order, Carl Schurz was alerted to the possible danger by some of his men, who had spoken to soldiers in Devens's division claiming they had seen gray infantry moving off to the west about a mile away. Schurz argued with twenty-twenty hindsight years later that "it flashed upon my mind that it was Stonewall Jackson, the 'great flanker' marching toward our right." He recalled immediately riding to Howard's headquarters at Dowdall's and trying to convince the corps commander that precautions had to be taken, but that "he clung to the belief which, he said, was also entertained by General Hooker, that Lee was not going to attack our right, but was actually in full retreat toward Gordonsville." Whether or not Schurz actually foresaw Jackson's flanking movement at this point in the day is debatable. It is ironic, however, that about the same time as Hooker became alarmed at the possibility of being flanked, his corps commander on the very flank in question was convinced nothing was amiss. To Howard's credit, he independently sent off a letter to Hooker at 10:50 informing him of the discovery Devens's pickets had made, indicating "I am taking measures to resist an attack from the west," but in reality Howard did nothing except move the corps' reserve artillery behind Barlow's rifle pits and change the location of a signal station. According to Schurz, Howard soon settled down for a nap, and asked to be awakened if any important dispatches arrived.[14]

Not long after Howard fell asleep, Schurz awakened him, Hooker's 9:30 dispatch in hand. Schurz claims that he read it in full to Howard "and put it into his hands." A few minutes later a second dispatch arrived from Hooker with the same message. The German division commander and his New England corps commander proceeded to have a lengthy discussion about the prudence of preparing for a possible assault from the west. Schurz pleaded to realign the corps. Howard declined. Schurz then asked to simply change the front of his division. Howard again refused.

Did O. O. Howard willfully disobey his superior's orders? After the war, Henry M. Kellogg of the 55th Ohio swore an affidavit in front of a notary public that he had been assigned to Colonel T. A. Meysenberg, Howard's assistant adjutant general, and "had charge of the records and files of letters, telegrams, and orders received" of the Eleventh Corps. All of the official correspondence addressed to and from Howard went across his desk so that he could write duplicate copies for the corps' files. "There was not among these papers the famous and all important order of May 2nd, 9:30 a.m., from headquarters of the Army of the Potomac at Chancellorsville House, from General Joseph Hooker," Kellogg affirmed. Later, however, on 30 June during the Gettysburg campaign, "within 48 hours following the departure of General Joseph Hooker from the said army as its commander," Meysenberg entered Kellogg's tent and handed him a field order, saying "There is a very important order relating to the Chancellorsville campaign; you will file it in its proper place, among the papers of that campaign, and record it in your book, giving it the proper date, May 2nd." Kellogg read the order "with amazement and astonishment and immediately made a copy of the order from the original, which for two months had been concealed and kept from the files until General Hooker had been relieved from command." Filing the original in "its proper place," the clerk said nothing until his 1897 deposition, where he noted that the original had now mysteriously "disappeared from the files in the War Department."[15]

Howard claimed after the war in *Century Magazine* that he never received the famous 9:30 order. But the evidence from both Schurz and Kellogg indicates that he almost certainly did, even allowing for discrepancies created by memory and damaged egos. Meysenberg would have had no reason to keep the order away from his general on 2 May, so it is unlikely he simply pocketed it. Schurz would not have made such a punctilious effort of documenting his conversation with Howard about the order on the same day if he did not receive it. What most likely happened is that Howard got the order and ignored the spirit of it, firm in his belief that the Confederates would not, could not, attack his flank through the thick underbrush. His commanding general shortly reinforced this belief by reversing his earlier cautionary concern about a possible flanking movement, allowing Major General Daniel Sickles, commanding the Third Corps, to pursue what was believed to be a retreating foe at Catharine Furnace. Sickles was adamant that Lee was retreating, and even if not, he thought he could strike him before the rebels struck the Union army. Hooker convinced himself that Sickles had to be right and could do the job. Ultimately he gave him nearly all of the Third Corps and most of the Twelfth Corps—the very troops that connected the Eleventh Corps with the rest of the army—and, around 4:00, Barlow's brigade of von Steinwehr's division. Thus, the Eleventh Corps not only became isolated from the rest of the army at one fell swoop, but also lost its only infantry reserve, sent away on a wild goose chase that would result in only a few bagged enemy prisoners. Howard accompanied Barlow on this ill-fated expedition, and therefore the corps also temporarily lost its commander. Stonewall Jackson's flanking march would proceed undeterred. But it would not go undetected by the rank and file of the Eleventh Corps.[16]

The first soldiers in the corps to notice that Confederates were moving around them and massing on their right belonged to Devens's First Division. Germans and Anglo Americans of multiple regiments reported numerous times that they had either seen the rebel column approaching or actually bumped into Jackson's battle line forming up. The picket line of the 55th Ohio, for instance, had started sending in status reports of the rebel movements as early as 11:00, and continued throughout the afternoon. Devens ignored them. Lieutenant A. B. Searles of the 45th New York, on picket well in front of the flank, heard a "queer jumble of sounds" to his front, including what he thought were commands being shouted "and bugles sounding the call to deploy." His report made it all the way to Howard, but was dismissed with a warning that "Lieutenant Searles must not be scared of a few bushwhackers." Major Owen Rice of the 153rd Pennsylvania and in charge of von Gilsa's picket line, actually witnessed Jackson's men lining up for the assault about 2:45. His report was emphatic: "A large body of the enemy is massing in my front. For God's sake make dispositions to receive him." Von Gilsa was convinced, and personally brought the dispatch to Howard, but the corps commander rebuked him. By this point in the day, thanks to reports from Sickles that he was driving the rebels, Howard was so certain that the enemy was in retreat that he simply closed his mind to any contrary idea. His division commander on the flank was even more recalcitrant, and could not even plead Howard's myopic excuse. Three of Devens's veteran regimental commanders reported to him at the Talley House with clear evidence from their scouts that Confederates were massing on the right, and Devens did nothing except castigate some of them for being scared. Colonel William Richardson of the 25th Ohio, Colonel John C. Lee of the 55th Ohio, and Colonel Robert Reilly of the 75th Ohio all came to their division commander at various times during the afternoon and were brushed off. Devens said to Lee, "You are frightened sir," and angrily told their brigade commander, General McLean, that his "western colonels" belonged with their regiments rather than constantly coming to him. The most unfortunate aspect of this failure in command is that most of the men in the ranks of at least McLean's brigade knew they were going to be attacked and had not been adequately prepared. Skirmishing with the enemy earlier in the afternoon had put them ill at ease, and camp rumor had fully circulated the reports of the pickets. Colonel Lee later wrote, "we sent all our non-combatant material to the rear. The opinion throughout our brigade was general that we would soon be attacked from our right flank."[17]

Von Gilsa received a last-minute report from a picket in the 41st New York, his old regiment, and again rode to Howard, recently returned from his foray with Sickles and Barlow, about 5:00. An interesting exchange ensued. Von Gilsa: "General, I must have reinforcements." Howard: "With the help of God, you have to keep this position." Von Gilsa: "The Devil! Of what use is God's help—I must have soldiers!" According to one account, the first Confederate shells began to fall at that very moment.[18]

Stonewall Jackson's 26,000 Confederate veterans, organized in 70 regiments, began springing forth from the underbrush about half-past five on 2 May 1863. Their appearance was preceded by frightened animals, deer, rabbits, and birds, which scampered in fear through the camps of Devens's division. Most of the men were alert to the possibility of danger from the west but had been ordered to continue preparing dinner. Their beef still boiling in cooking pots, the hungry soldiers at first found the traveling feast of game a source of great amusement. That mood abruptly changed as artillery shells suddenly exploded in their midst and the unmistakable, spine-tingling sound of the rebel yell reverberated through the forest. The 8,500 men of the Eleventh Corps were about to fight their most infamous battle.

"We Held Firm as Long as We Could"

The Germans of the 153rd Pennsylvania and 54th New York were the first struck by Jackson's onslaught, specifically the Alabamans of O'Neal's brigade.

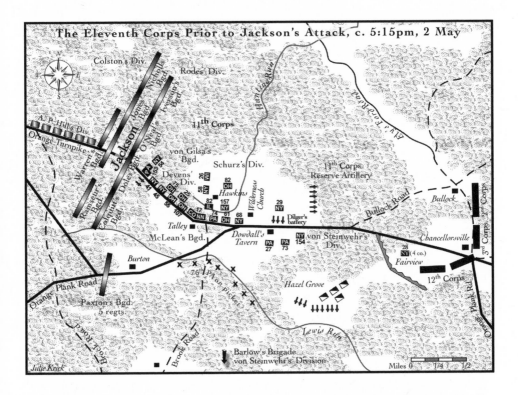

The Federal pickets barely escaped back to their own lines, followed by the steady tread of "a perfectly solid mass of men" and an especially shrill-sounding rebel yell. Major Eugene Blackford of the 5th Alabama remembered, "we moved on about 1/4 of a mile in silence and then suddenly came upon the Dutchmen cooking in the woods. . . . With a yell we reached in." The Confederates fired a devastating volley that brought the leaves of the trees "fluttering down upon us as though a thunder storm had broken loose," said one Pennsylvanian. Leaves were not the only things falling. "Here and there a soldier dropped," Private Francis Stofflet of the 153rd wrote. He could not yet see the enemy, "but fired into the thicket, others did likewise, reloaded and fired again." The regiment, in this unexpected baptism by fire, somehow managed to form a makeshift battle line, but within minutes the Southern vanguard had converged on it and that of the 54th New York, surrounding them on three sides. Captain Theodore Howell of Company D of the 153rd realized an immediate withdrawal was imperative: "I know if our regiment had stood 3 minutes longer we would all have been cut to pieces." The Confederates got so close that "they struck some of the men with the butts of their rifles." In the end, the Northampton and Lehigh County men managed to fire four or five volleys before being overwhelmed. No records or personal accounts exist for the 54th New York, but it appears they did likewise. Colonel Charles Glanz of the 153rd wrote a month after the battle that even after the neighboring 45th and 54th New York "were in full retreat," "I stood with 7 companies of brave Pennsylvanians, fighting as old veterans for the honor of their state and their country." Withdrawing at first in good order, the regiment's cohesion broke down as the men realized running was the only alternative to capture.[19]

The soldiers of the 41st New York, one of the most German of all the regiments in the Eleventh Corps, found themselves especially disadvantaged because their regiment was encamped in close quarters along the Orange Turnpike, right at the bend in the "L" of von Gilsa's brigade, and literally perpendicular to the Confederate battle line when it hit. Sergeant Otto Heusinger made no apologies: "A panicked fear overcame us, how crazily we plunged away, the rest of the division running with us." Sergeant William Burghart of Company A, 45th New York, was distributing rations to his men when "a terrible fire from front and right and rear" crashed into the regiment. "We could not see a rebel," he exclaimed, but "the boys did not wayt for the distribution of the balance and run, nobody knew where to." His comrade, Luis Keck, wrote his wife that "we had them at our back and in the front," and then added, "if the rebels had not been so drunk, there would not have been more than 500 of our men left" in the entire corps. These supposedly "drunken" Confederates attacked as if they "wanted to completely annihilate us, the Eleventh Corps, those damn Dutchmen! We sure had to suffer for it!" Keck probably took the attack on his regiment and his corps a bit personally, but his words reveal the sudden nature and ferocity of the rebel assault. Like the 41st New York, the 45th was encamped in close quarters along the turnpike, hemmed in by the thick woods on either side. Not only was there no time to change front and face the enemy, but there also was no space to execute such a maneuver. Individual soldiers in the 41st and 45th probably got off a few shots, but beyond that, the regiments' resistance was negligible. The gunners manning two pieces of Captain Julius Dieckmann's New York battery, stationed at the edge of the 41st, managed to fire only two rounds before being overrun.[20]

As Von Gilsa's regiments collapsed, fragments from them immediately streamed into the formations of McLean's brigade. Because many of the commanders of these Anglo American regiments were certain of the impending attack, they had their men up and ready as much as possible, but most had not yet changed position and faced west. They were waiting for official orders from Devens to do so. The orders never came. Instead, the Confederates of Doles's Georgia brigade came charging, right on the heels of von Gilsa's skedaddling soldiers, and rolled up the Ohio regiments like clockwork. Staff officer Charles

T. Furlow of the 4th Georgia wrote, "the men gave a yell which shook the very earth under them and charged forward at a run. . . . We came into an open field where the enemy had constructed breastworks and here they endeavored to make a stand but it was no use, they could not resist the impetuosity of our charge." The 25th Ohio hurriedly tried to change front and fired off three volleys; the 55th reportedly got off two. The 75th Ohio, acting as brigade reserve, successfully changed front and held for about ten minutes, but the refugees from other regiments continually broke its lines and disrupted its cohesion. Soon, it, too, joined the rout. Private Luther Mesnard of the 55th remembered, "we stopped the rebs in our front for a moment, but there was a perfect hail of lead flying, a perfect mass of rebs not twenty feet away, the man on my right and left both fell." When the enemy "surged ahead," Mesnard "ran toward our left flank, and how I did run." Private John Lewis of the 17th Connecticut, the lone Yankee regiment in McLean's "Ohio brigade," also ran: "We got most of the regiment together but the Rebbles came down on us with such great numbers that we broke and fell back." Lewis ran so hard and so far that he became "completely exhausted" and hid behind a pine tree. Jacob Smith of the German 107th Ohio correctly noted that "the losses were enormous" in Devens's second brigade, "the battle [having] assumed the character and appearance of a massacre." The 107th stood as long as it possibly could, but it, too, quickly disintegrated under the extreme enemy pressure and joined the rout.[21]

Jackson's veterans pressed onward, driving the panic-stricken survivors of the First Division before them. The regiments in Major General Carl Schurz's Third Division, next in line along the Orange Turnpike and in the Hawkins Farm/Wilderness Church clearing directly above it, were alerted to the imminent danger by the sounds of fighting directly to their west, but many of the officers and men had suspected a Confederate attack was coming since the early afternoon. Brigadier General Alexander Schimmelfennig had sent out numerous scouts who returned with reports of Confederates massing to the south and west, and Captain Hubert Dilger of the 1st Ohio Light Artillery had actually discovered the Confederate battle line forming up about two o'clock. Narrowly escaping capture by rebel cavalry pickets, Dilger frantically rode to Hooker's headquarters, where he was rebuffed by a "long-legged major of cavalry" who advised him to "tell his yarn" at Eleventh Corps headquarters. Reaching Dowdall's Tavern, he was even more discourteously received, lampooned for having made his unauthorized reconnaissance, and told that Howard had gone off with Barlow to the south. Dejected and "crestfallen," Dilger then reported to Schurz, returned to his battery and prepared it for action, even refusing to allow his horses to be watered. Schurz had long convinced himself the attack was coming, and after the ill-starred conversation about Hooker's 9:30 a.m. order, tried once again to persuade Howard to change front and face west. According to his 1907 recollection, Schurz stood with Howard about three o'clock on the porch of Dowdall's Tavern and mentioned that an assault from the west would "crush Gilsa's two regiments," deployed to "protect the right and rear" of the Eleventh Corps. He asked Howard if von Gilsa would have any chance to resist, to which Howard supposedly replied, "Well, he will have to fight." Riding away, Schurz claimed, "I was almost desperate," and on his own volition ordered the 26th Wisconsin and 58th New York of Colonel Wladimir Krzyzanowski's brigade to fall into line, face west, and send out skirmishers. The 82nd Ohio was encamped just south of the other two regiments and was also ordered to turn to the west in support. "This was all, literally all, that was done to meet an attack from the west," Schurz lamented. "I was heartsick."[22]

Schurz's men were nearly all German. Only two regiments out of nine in his division—the 82nd Ohio and 157th New York—were composed primarily of Anglo Americans, and even so there were Germans among them. By five o'clock, some of his soldiers were already prepared to fight, rifles in hand or close by, eyes facing west. Those who belonged to regiments not repositioned had still been uneasy as the afternoon wore on. Like some of their Anglo American comrades in Devens's division, the men had known something was afoot. Rumors from the various scouting parties filtered about, proliferating camp gossip. Rifles were stacked, but the soldiers sat near them. Campfires still cooked some of the freshly slaughtered beef, but the men ate quickly. When the rabbits, deer, and birds frightened off by Jackson's advancing columns ran through their camps about 5:45, they were not greeted by whoops of joy and hilarity. Schurz's men knew what was coming behind the animals, and could already hear the approaching battle.[23]

Soldiers in the 75th Pennsylvania (in Vladimir Krzyzanowski's brigade), most of whom were on picket duty in the woods south of the main Eleventh Corps line, may have discovered the Confederates' game long before Jackson actually launched the attack. During the early afternoon, Private Jacob Ullmann and Sergeant Charles Mehring both reported that they watched helplessly as "the enemy appeared and marched quietly along in our front. They were so close that . . . any ordinary marksman could have taken aim and pick[ed] away the leading officer." This account is a bit suspect, doubtless clouded by the fog of memory, but Ullmann and Mehring were not the only members of the 75th to remember seeing the flanking Confederates. Ullmann's brother, Private John Ullmann, also supposedly spotted the rebels that afternoon, and noted that "the sun was about to set when [we] heard firing in [our] rear." Most of the pickets hesitated only a few minutes before retreating in the direction of Hazel Grove. Assembling at "the headquarters of the pickets" in a small clearing in the forest, the Ullmann brothers, Mehring, and their comrades prepared to deploy in line of battle. Lieutenant Colonel Alwin von Matzdorff gave the order, "but found such at the next moment impossible, as the enemy appeared in sight with their customary indianlike yell." Cut off from their comrades by the advancing Confederates, "nothing more was left our men than to take to their heels." In the end, most soldiers of the 75th did manage to elude capture, like many in Devens's First Division, by first retreating at the double-quick and then literally running. According to Sergeant Hermann Nachtigall in a postwar letter, a good portion managed to find sanctuary among the Union batteries posted at Hazel Grove, but their journey there through the dense underbrush and over streams and fences was far from easy. Hotly pursued by the rebels, some of whom were screaming "Give it to the damn Yankees," the Philadelphia Germans did not even have time to unsling their knapsacks to ease their escape. Importantly, however, a sizeable percentage of the 75th regained order after its flight and even rejoined the battle as infantry support for the Federal artillery at Hazel Grove.[24]

Immediately after hearing the first crashes of musketry directly to their west, the company and regimental officers of the 61st Ohio, 68th New York, and 74th Pennsylvania jumped into action, barking commands in both English and German, trying desperately to form the men up by company before the tempest broke upon them. Yet for these regiments posted along the Orange Turnpike there was just not enough time, not enough space because of the thick woods, and far too much chaos. First the fleeing soldiers, wagons, mules, and artillery from the broken regiments of the First Division crashed into their ranks, and then the Confederates themselves appeared, screaming the rebel yell and rushing on with a sort of wild abandon that Union survivors remembered years later. In his official report, Carl Schurz wrote that "the officers had hardly had time to give a command when almost the whole of General McLean's brigade, mixed up with a number of Colonel von Gilsa's men, came rushing down the road from General Devens's headquarters in wild confusion." Along with the wave of frightened men came the batteries of the First Division, which "broke in upon my right at a full run. This confused mass of guns, caissons, horses, and men broke lengthwise through the ranks of my regiments," making it "an utter impossibility to establish a front at that point." On top of that, Schurz continued, the enemy had followed right on the heels of the fugitives, and succeeded in firing into the backs of the 74th Pennsylvania, some companies of which could not turn about-face to meet them as a result of the confusion caused by Devens's skedaddling survivors.[25]

The Pittsburgh Germans of the 74th Pennsylvania (in Alexander Schimmelfennig's brigade) were just about to settle down for the evening when the bugles and drums suddenly sounded the call to arms. Hearing the din of battle grow-ing louder by the minute, and assaulted by the first groups of First Division refugees, the men nonetheless attempted to form up and resist the onslaught. Schimmelfennig was everywhere, exhorting the troops of his old regiment to rally to the colors and stand firm, but the chaos wrought by the fleeing human and animal flotsam steadily grew worse and severely hampered his attempts. Lieutenant Colonel Adolph von Hartung reported that "the different regiments on our right were in a few minutes all mixed up with the Seventy-Fourth." He claimed that "a restoring of order was an utter impossibility." Private Martin Seel wrote his brother that "there was no more time to . . . change the forma-tion of the front line. Bullets came from somewhere behind us. The rebels took advantage of the confusion, they charged ahead with all their might." The 74th simply could not form a proper regimental line in its current position, and, according to Seel, Schimmelfennig's entire brigade "could not even fire off any bullets so as not to hit our own people." For the first time in the war the disci-pline and good order of the 74th broke: "everyone scattered apart in a wild rout." But the battle was far from over for most of these Germans. They would fight again, and soon. Retreating by companies, groups, and individuals through the woods to their east, the men of the 74th joined those of the 61st Ohio and 68th New York, regiments that had also been shattered along the road, and fell into a quickly growing battle line in front of the Wilderness Church.[26]

The 119th New York, also of Schimmelfennig's brigade, found itself in only a slightly better position than the 74th Pennsylvania. Posted at the intersection of the Plank Road and the Orange Turnpike, its ranks were not as badly broken by the fleeing soldiers of the First Division, but surgeon Carl Uterhard nonethe-less told his family that "thousands of people suddenly burst forth from the woods in wild flight," creating confusion in the New Yorkers' ranks. Colonel Elias Peissner still managed to form the regiment into line while under heavy enemy fire, and had succeeded in holding it for several minutes when he was suddenly shot dead. Along with eight other men of the color guard, flagbearer Joseph Carter also fell, mortally wounded, at the feet of his father. In 1864, Cap-tain Charles Lewis remembered the incident in his diary, writing that "Old man Carter" took the flag from his dying son's hands and began to wave it back and forth, shouting "Poor Joe, poor Joe, I'll save your flag." The sight was "truly dramatic, and did more, I think, than any other one thing to keep the line steady and firm during these awful moments when we were exposed to the full fire of that line of Jackson's." Exactly how long the 119th held firm is unknown—it could not have been more than twenty minutes—but it paid a high price in blood for its stand against Doles's Georgians. So did Hubert Dilger's Ohio battery, which had deployed behind the 119th and 61st Ohio and fired over their heads until the infantry withdrew. For several minutes thereafter Dilger's artillerymen and their six cannon stood alone as the only Federal forces still resisting west of the Wilderness Church. Sweeping "his entire front with charges and double charges of canister," Dilger did his best to hold up the rebels, but as gunner Darwin Cody observed, "such yelling I never heard before as the Rebs made. . . . [They] soon commenced to charge on our battery," and were determined "to get one of our guns." Dilger shouted the order to retire, but it was too late to salvage the gun the Confederates had aimed for. He ended up leaving it to the triumphant enemy but miraculously saved the other five amidst repeated calls to surrender. Evading capture with the help of a small boy who picked him up after his horse was shot, Dilger and his battery retreated beyond the Wilderness Church and resumed firing.[27]

Positioned just north of the Orange Turnpike close to the Hawkins Farm, the Chicago Germans of the 82nd Illinois, commanded by forty-eighter Friedrich Hecker, had a bit more time to react, but were still in the process of forming up when the battle erupted upon them. Private Frantisek Stejskal, a Czech serving in the 82nd, had to leave his supper of coffee, rolls, and beef to grab his musket. "We vainly tried to defend ourselves" he noted, "but the stronger forces of Jackson forced us to retreat." Sergeant Friedrich Kappelman wrote his parents that "our regiment would have stood its ground better, but the attack came unforeseen, and we were caught down." The official regimental report was a bit more optimistic, claiming the regiment had already fallen into line when the rebels attacked. Then it "marched in good order to the top of a little hill" in the immediate rear of its original position and turned to face the enemy. Their ranks continually broken by fleeing First Division soldiers, the men of the 82nd still managed to retain their regimental cohesion and fired "at least six rounds" from the hill. But the Confederates were "fighting like tigers," according to Kappelman, and quickly closed in to the front and right, creating a veritable "hailstorm of grape and musketballs." The regiment could not stand such punishment for long, and finally Schimmelfennig rode over to Hecker and ordered him to fall back. Retreating only 15–20 yards, Hecker stopped his regiment and grabbed the national colors, cheering on his men to make a charge, but soon realized such an act of suicidal heroism would avail him or his men nothing. Returning the flag to the colorbearer, Hecker was then shot in the thigh and fell from his horse. Major Rolshausen, who ran to his side, was also quickly wounded, and command passed to Captain Greenhut of Company K. His colonel and major down, the regiment surrounded on three sides, Greenhut led the bulk of the 82nd "in good order" to the Wilderness Church, ordering several halts to fire at the closely pursuing rebels. These halts cost the regiment dearly in dead and wounded, but preserved its integrity and bought valuable time for other Eleventh Corps units further back to mount an organized defense. Along with sizeable portions of Schimmelfennig's other regiments, the 82nd joined the growing line of Third Division regiments forming at the church.[28]

The 58th New York and 26th Wisconsin, regiments Carl Schurz had ordered to change front late in the afternoon, were ready and waiting, side by side, at the western edge of the Hawkins Farm clearing. They occupied the northernmost positions in the entire Eleventh Corps deployment, and were under the direct command of their brigade commander, Colonel Vladimir Krzyzanowski. Although many of the men sat around campfires "boiling coffee," eating, or relaxing in the late afternoon sun, they were also vigilant, rifles by their sides. Their skirmishers were deep in the forest ahead of them, eyes alert and muskets primed. Lieutenant Karl Doerflinger was among them. Suddenly a cannon boomed—presumably one of Dieckmann's two guns at the end of von Gilsa's line—and the young officer heard "the rattle of musketry in a Southwesterly direction." He and his comrades were tense, unsure of what was about to ensue. Then, through the gloom of the scrub pines and brambles, his eyes picked out human forms "skipping from tree to tree," and "later the grey uniforms" of the advancing Confederate picket line. Behind them came a wall of gray and butternut, Iverson's and O'Neal's men, who soon let loose with a heavy volley. Doerflinger and his comrades replied in turn. When the order arrived for the skirmishers to retreat, Doerflinger gladly obliged, and dashing back through the woods, emerged opposite the line of the 58th New York. "We then and there annihilated all our previous records for 75 yard runs," the Milwaukee German remembered. He safely made it back to his regiment.[29]

As the Confederates charged out of the woods right behind the skirmishers, the 58th New York and 26th Wisconsin, well-deployed in battle lines a bit further back into the clearing, began firing by volley. Corporal Adam Muenzenberger of the 26th described the scene to his wife: "They came out of a bluff in great numbers and outnumbered our regiment seven to four. As we were back of a small hill it was hard for them to hit us but every round our regiment fired mowed down rows of southerners." Private Frank Smrcek agreed with his comrade that the 26th, in its baptism by fire, held its own against the superior numbers of the enemy. "The enemy wallowed from the forest throwing in our lines the deadly fire. We paid them back in their own coin. At first it seemed as if the rebels were giving in, but then they attacked us so violently that we could not hold against their attacks. Three times we retreated and then faced them again." The 26th fought the Confederates in the Hawkins Farm clearing approximately twenty minutes, first standing toe to toe against their numerically superior foes, then refusing their right flank when the rebels outflanked them, and finally by stubbornly retreating a few paces, turning about, firing, and retreating again. As the historian of the regiment put it, "it was an unequal battle of hundreds against thousands," but the men seemed intent on proving their courage. Karl Wickesberg noted that even as dear friends and comrades fell all around them, "[we] stood there coldbloodedly and shot at the Rebs."[30]

The Wisconsin Germans were not alone in their valor on this part of the field. To their south, in a loose order of battle that became known as the "Wilderness Church line," fought the 58th New York, 82nd Ohio, 82nd Illinois, 157th New York, and large fragments of the 74th Pennsylvania, 61st Ohio, and 68th New York regiments, which had been shattered along the turnpike further west but now reformed and rallied at the church. The 119th New York and Dilger's battery made their stand at the southern end of this Federal line, but were somewhat isolated from their comrades. Indeed, the total number of Eleventh Corps defenders numbered close to 5,000 along the Wilderness Church line, and proved a welcome sight to some of Devens's fleeing soldiers. Lieutenant A. B. Searles of the 45th New York, falling back through the woods south and west of the Hawkins House, clearly remembered emerging into the clearing and seeing "Schurz's line of battle, with its flags waving right toward us. . . . Round came his line like a top, swinging sharply as though upon a pivot. . . . Their front was to the west—in unbroken line, shoulder to shoulder, to stem that oncoming torrent of men." Searles probably saw the 26th Wisconsin and 58th New York, which did stand closely together, but gaps between other regiments' battle formations, combined with the continuing confusion caused by Devens's fleeing soldiers, rendered the Wilderness Church line less effective than it could have been. Private Benjamin Carr of the 20th North Carolina in Iverson's brigade recalled that "their line . . . was formed across a field . . . and was about 400 yards from the woods from which we emerged charging with a yell." The Yankees ultimately retired, "firing only a few shots at us." Nonetheless, the resistance here—certainly more than "a few shots"—did stall the relentless southern advance for at least twenty minutes and bought precious time for most of the corps baggage train, cattle, and reserve artillery to escape. Martin Seel of the 74th Pennsylvania claimed "we fired[d] ferociously and stopped their quick advance from continuing." Most importantly, German bravery at the Wilderness Church and Hawkins Farm allowed Buschbeck's brigade adequate time to prepare a defense at Dowdall's Tavern, and that action proved critical for the survival of the Eleventh Corps and, arguably, the Army of the Potomac. Friedrich Hecker, lying wounded on the field near the Hawkins House, probably summed it up best when he observed that the German regiments, and Krzyzanowski's brigade in particular, "fought as long as possible against superior numbers that would have snuffed out resistance from any other troops."[31]

The makeshift line at the Wilderness Church finally collapsed under the overwhelming pressure of four Confederate brigades, outflanked on both sides and penetrated in various points in between. The Eleventh Corps regiments fighting along it withdrew one at a time, some of them conducting fighting withdrawals and others simply double-timing it back through the woods and over the Orange Turnpike. Intermingled with them were the last refugees from the First Division. General Howard, astride his horse on the road, supposedly attempted to stop the retreat at this point, believing it a continuation of the earlier rout. Recent historians disagree about when the corps commander supposedly grabbed a stand of abandoned national colors, placed it under the stump of his right arm, and tried by sheer heroics "to arrest the tide." Based on contextual primary-source evidence, it appears likely that the event occurred between the stand at the Wilderness Church and that at the Buschbeck line. In any case, there are also conflicting accounts about Howard's personal bearing during this episode: one soldier from Schurz's division asserted that the general behaved like a child, crying, "Halt! Halt! I'm ruined, I'm ruined! I'll shoot if you don't stop!" Another claimed he recognized Howard "on his horse in the roadway, as cool as if on parade, but urging and insisting and entreating the flying men to go slower." Whichever version of the story is true, it is likely that the corps commander did all he could to direct his men and contain the damage once the battle had opened. He did not want for courage, and may have even admitted his terrible error in not preparing for the flank attack when he wrote his wife, "I felt . . . that I wanted to die . . . but that night I did all in my power to remedy the mistake, and I sought death everywhere I could find an excuse to go on the field." In the end, death would not find Oliver Otis Howard at Chancellorsville, but controversy and accusations of incompetence would. Perhaps he was thinking about that very possibility as he wheeled his horse around and hurried to the next axis of resistance, literally right in front of his headquarters at Dowdall's Tavern. It was half-past six.[32]

That resistance was formed along what historians have subsequently titled "the Buschbeck line." This shallow and unfinished line of breastworks, hastily constructed the day before by Barlow's now departed brigade, fortuitously faced west, intersecting the Orange Turnpike at Dowdall's. The regiments of Brigadier General Adolph von Steinwehr's Second Division had originally made camp along the turnpike on either side of the tavern, facing south, just like their sister units in the now wrecked First and dissolving Third Divisions. When the Confederates attacked, the Second Division found itself blessed by its rearward location and the proximity of the breastworks but cursed by the departure of half of its fighting power. The earlier detachment of Barlow left only the four regiments of Colonel Adolphus Buschbeck's brigade at von Steinwehr's disposal. The division commander himself was also initially absent from the field, having accompanied Barlow and his men in their hapless march to assist Sickles, but Colonel Buschbeck quickly took stock of the precarious situation. Buschbeck had been educated in the military schools of Germany and knew his tactics. After a minimal delay, he ordered the German 27th and 73rd Pennsylvania and 29th New York and (non-German) 154th New York to file into line behind Barlow's shallow entrenchments. The officers and men, their ears filled with the sounds of approaching battle, moved fast, and had rifles cocked and ready when the first retreating elements of Schurz's and Devens's divisions reached them. Right behind them came the rebels.[33]

The scenes that confronted the men of Bushbeck's brigade must have been at once awe inspiring and unsettling. Scrambling back to them by whole regiments, partial regiments, companies, and lone individuals, their comrades in blue presented a motley appearance; some retreating doggedly and in good order, even turning and firing on their pursuers, others running for their lives. Gun teams and single horses from the remnants of Dieckmann's First Division Battery and Michael Wiedrich's Second Division Battery thundered past on the road. Most of Devens's men, either panic-stricken or completely fought-out, refused to stop and rally at the Buschbeck line—although Hamlin indicates that some did—but the majority of Schurz's soldiers heeded their officers' calls to halt and quickly filled in the line north of Buschbeck's regiments. There was precious little time to reorganize and prepare—the enemy was literally only minutes away. Elements of six Confederate brigades—Doles's, Iverson's, Nicholl's, Colquitt's, O'Neal's, and Ramseur's—began to emerge out of the woods to the west and southwest of the Dowdall clearing and advanced at the double-quick, flushed with victory and confident that this last Yankee line would be crushed like the others before it. Other men in gray tramped through the woods to the north of the clearing, already overlapping the short Federal line. The rebel yell resounded over the open field and through the forest as the sun began to set.[34]

Numbering slightly over 4,000 men, of whom approximately 2,000 hailed from Carl Schurz's regiments, the Buschbeck line stretched for a thousand yards behind rifle pits that barely shielded the soldiers' knees. The men were badly crowded and had no artillery support except for one gun of Captain Hubert Dilger's Ohio battery. The powerful Eleventh Corps artillery reserve, which had previously occupied the narrow stretch of cleared land between the breastworks and the treeline, had been ordered out to save it from presumable capture. Although the gunners would have been sorely pressed to operate their pieces efficiently in such close conditions, their absence deprived the Buschbeck line of much-needed clout and staying power. Nonetheless, the men crouched behind Barlow's old entrenchments girded themselves for the onslaught, confident they could give as much as they got. South of the Orange Turnpike, the 154th New York anchored the position, with the 73rd and 27th Pennsylvania to its right, followed by loose companies of soldiers from Schurz's and Devens's divisions. On the road itself, Hubert Dilger placed his remaining cannon under his personal command, flanked by two companies from the 61st New York. North of the road, the New York and Philadelphia Turners of the 29th New York were first, followed in line by more loose companies from Schurz's and Devens's commands and then the intact 82nd Illinois, 82nd Ohio, 58th New York, and 26th Wisconsin. As a general reserve, Buschbeck ordered the 157th New York to take position behind the 82nd Illinois, on the edge of the treeline.[35]

Carl Schurz and Alexander Schimmelfennig joined Buschbeck behind the hastily formed Eleventh Corps line and desperately worked to reorganize the regiments and partial regiments of the Third Division. Schurz wrote that he and corps commander Howard also "made every possible effort to rally and reorganize" a "confused mass of men belonging to all divisions" that milled around behind the regiments manning the rifle pits. But time had run out. The Confederates were upon them.[36]

Schurz took the initiative, gathered a number of the non-aligned men around him, jumped the rifle pits, and with a "hurrah" led them on a counterattack. They followed him a few steps, but were "dispersed by the enemy's fire." Nonplused, Schurz "tried the experiment two or three more times, but always with the same result." The 82nd Illinois also charged the enemy, to the point of entering the woods to the right of the Union line, but soon fell back, hopelessly overpowered by Iverson's advancing North Carolinians. Unlike the previous hour's fighting, the Confederates of Iverson's and Nicholl's brigades had outstripped the progress of their comrades in gray to the south, and now exerted incredible pressure on the northern half of the Buschbeck line from front and flank. Private William Clegg of the 2nd Louisiana wrote his cousin, "the musketry was very heavy and continuous. They seemed to make a determined stand behind some rifle pits, but were soon routed from them." The 82nd Ohio, 26th Wisconsin, and 58th New York fought for as long as humanly possible, but already badly depleted from their earlier stand near the Wilderness Church, were forced to withdraw and abandon the line. They retreated in good order through the woods to their rear. Jacob Smith of the 107th Ohio, fragments of which also joined the northern end of the line, recalled the ferocity of the fight on this sector of the field, claiming that "the resistance was desperate, but without change of front could avail nothing against the advancing hosts of the enemy." John Haingartner of the 29th New York, occupying a position just north of the turnpike, also termed the fighting "desperate" as his regiment and others tried to "check the impetuous attack of a victorious foe." Haingartner "fired 14 shots" from behind what he called "mere dugouts," but then was struck by a piece of shell in the right leg and put out of action. Like many wounded men in the Eleventh Corps that day, he knew his fate was in his own hands and would be determined by how quickly he moved to the rear. "Between excruciating pain and fear of being captured by the onrushing foe," the Philadelphia German managed to find one of the last remaining corps ambulances and survived his stand on the Buschbeck line. Many of his German-speaking comrades, especially those south of the turnpike, did not.[37]

At close to seven o'clock, around the time the northern end of the Buschbeck line began to unravel, Adolph von Steinwehr reigned in his frothing horse behind the southern end of the line. He had ridden to the sound of the guns from Barlow's brigade under his own prerogative, and was pleasantly surprised to find his other brigade already in line and repelling the rebel onslaught. Buschbeck and his men were holding—for now:

> When I arrived on the field I found Col. A. Buschbeck, with three regiments of his brigade (the Twenty-Seventh and Seventy-Third Pennsylvania and One Hundred and fifty-fourth New York), still occupying the same ground near the tavern, and defending this position with great firmness and gallantry. The fourth regiment (the Twenty-ninth New York) he had sent to the north side of the road. The attack of the enemy was very powerful. They emerged in close columns from the woods . . . Colonel Buschbeck succeeded in checking the progress of the enemy, and I told him to hold his position as long as possible.
>
> The men fought with great determination and courage. Soon, however, the enemy gained both wings of the brigade, and the enfilading fire which was now opened upon this small force, and which killed and wounded nearly one-third of its whole strength, soon forced it to retire.[38]

Private Adolph Bregler of the 27th Pennsylvania wrote that "our division did not have enough time to correctly deploy before the running rebels hurled themselves at us, but we still held firm as long as we could, and pushed them back hard several times." Lieutenant Colonel Adolph von Hartung of the 74th Pennsylvania of Schurz's division, whose regiment had partially rallied on the southern end of the Buschbeck line, reported that "we were . . . furiously attacked, but the enemy was handsomely checked and driven back. The men stuck to their colors and fought bravely, but renewed attacks of superior forces

and flank movements of the enemy made all the troops on our left fall back."
Private James Emmons of the 154th New York, the non-German regiment on
the southernmost edge of the Buschbeck line, told his parents that "we would
mow a road clear through [the rebels] every time but they would close up with
a yell and come on again." There was no stopping the Confederates. As
Emmons put it, "before we run we g[ave] the rebs enough." Emmons may or
may not have run, however: Buschbeck and von Steinwehr claimed they over-
saw an orderly retreat and filed at least their four badly mauled regiments onto
the Orange Turnpike, stopping now and then to turn and face the enemy. Captain Dilger and his single gun covered Buschbeck's retreat, stubbornly firing
canister and solid shot by prolong as they followed the infantry up the Orange
Turnpike toward Chancellorsville. Still accompanied by the stalwart companies
from the 61st New York, as well as Generals Howard and Schurz, Dilger kept
firing until there were no more Confederates to fire at. The resistance at the
Buschbeck line had broken some of the impetus of Jackson's attack, forcing the
rebels to pause and reorganize before pressing forward.[39]

    Accounts differ regarding how long the Buschbeck line held. Some veterans
of the fight remember holding for nearly an hour, others for about twenty min-

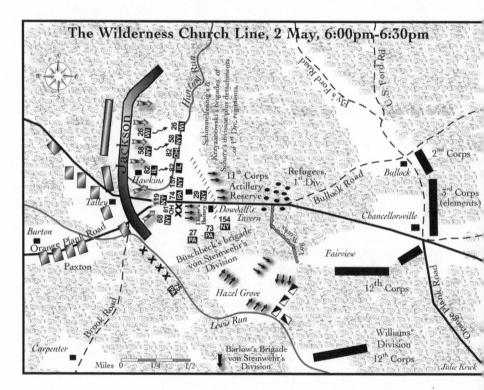

The Wilderness Church Line, 2 May, 6:00pm–6:30pm

utes, whereas most Confederate reports completely disregard this last effective stand of the Eleventh Corps. Realistically, the line probably held up the rebel advance for about twenty-five minutes. What is most important to consider, however, is not exactly how long the line held, but *who* held it and what the blood sacrifice of its defenders bought. If Hamlin is to be believed, a good half of the Eleventh Corps, which had supposedly already fled in panic, formed up with Buschbeck and put up a stout defense. This is important by itself when contemplating the later vituperations and complaints emanating from Anglo Americans who claimed the entire Eleventh Corps had broken "and fled like sheep" at the first shots of the enemy. Based on a number of firsthand accounts from soldiers of the First Division, quite a few men in that organization did, apparently, run after only firing a round or two. Most probably did not reform and fight at the Buschbeck line. But the historical record is rife with evidence attributing to the stand of Schurz's Third Division German regiments first around the clearings near the Hawkins Farm and Wilderness Church, and later with Buschbeck. Although some doubt exists regarding how complete Schurz's regiments were when they held the line north of the turnpike, and how long they may have fought there compared with Buschbeck's men, it is clear that these predominantly German American soldiers had fought. In Buschbeck's own command, all but the 154th New York and two companies each of the 27th and 73rd Pennsylvania were German-born or the offspring of German immigrants. Perhaps the Anglo American 154th was the last in its brigade to retreat, but that hardly impugns the courage of its immigrant sister regiments. In the end, the noble stand at the Buschbeck line leaves little doubt that a high percentage of German soldiers in the Eleventh Corps had indeed stood and fought, many paying the ultimate price for their courage. Their sacrifice, however, had not been in vain. In official reports after the battle and in numerous postwar accounts, the delaying action at the Buschbeck line was credited with allowing the artillery reserve and baggage trains of the Eleventh Corps to escape and permitting the rest of the Army of the Potomac to react to the Confederate flank attack.[40]

Throughout the night of 2 May and into the early hours of 3 May, the German Americans of the Eleventh Corps reorganized their shattered regiments, fully expecting to be hotly engaged at any moment. By nine o'clock, about one-half of the corps' survivors, approximately 3,200 to 3,500 men, had been successfully rallied at the western end of the Fairview clearing, near Chancellorsville.[41] With the last ounces of their energy, Howard, Buschbeck, Schurz, and Steinwehr managed to establish yet another defensive line, this one mightily protected by artillery and joined, after a short while, by Major General Hiram Berry's division of the Third Corps. As more Union reinforcements arrived to shore up the Federal position, the Eleventh Corps was ordered to retire behind the Chancellor mansion (Hooker's headquarters) and continued the process of reconstitution. Soldiers who had earlier skedaddled returned to their regiments, comrades who had been separated in the confusion and smoke of battle found each other and embraced, thankful to be alive, and many simply collapsed in exhaustion among the trees. In the wee hours of the morning the men were roused and marched into line along the Mineral Springs Road, near the Union left. There they would remain for the rest of the battle. Baron Otto von Fritsch got little chance to sleep, however, as he helped Alexander Schimmelfennig regroup his brigade and align it closely with neighboring troops.[42]

Fritsch was undoubtedly among the first to feel the stings of the nativist backlash. Word had quickly spread among the other corps of the Army of the Potomac about the so-called "flight" of the Eleventh. Encountering the colonel of the regiment bordering his brigade, Fritsch reported that a gap existed between his German brigade and that particular regiment (which, based on the location of Schimmelfennig's brigade, probably belonged to the Second Corps), and asked if the colonel would assist in doing something about it. "We are comfortable enough here," was the reply, "fill it with runaway Dutchmen." Angered, Fritsch shouted "I will not stand this! I am no more of a Dutchman than you are, but I have no doubt that you are uneducated enough to believe that Germany is a province of Holland; besides let me tell you that the Dutch were always honorable and brave men." The situation grew dangerous. Rising with his hand on his sword hilt, the American colonel appeared ready to finish the argument through a duel, but Fritsch wisely mounted his horse. Just before riding away, he exclaimed, "I am sorry that I addressed a Colonel who is not a gentleman!" Fritsch obviously plugged the gap, however, because the following day Schimmelfennig's brigade, indeed the entire Eleventh Corps, held their positions firmly as they skirmished with enemy snipers. In a fit of hyperbole, the Philadelphia *Freie Presse* stated that "the German division fought bravely, as if it were aware it had to make amends, and the enemy was repulsed with great loss." The fighting was over for these troops at last.[43]

"Literally Cut to Pieces"

Considering the poor tactical situation in which they found themselves at the start of the battle, the Eleventh Corps had fought reasonably well at Chancellorsville. As private Charles E. Davis of the 13th Massachusetts wrote years later, "not Napoleon's Old Guard, not the best and bravest troops that ever existed, could [have] held together in such a case." The casualty rates speak for themselves. The corps as a whole lost close to 2,500 men, about 25 percent of those engaged; of that number, just under 1600 were killed and wounded. Twelve of 23 regimental commanders were casualties. Moreover, the Confederates paid for their success on the evening of 2 May with approximately 1,000 dead, wounded, and missing.[44]

An analysis of casualties suffered just by the Pennsylvania German regiments indicates that Jackson's Confederates certainly did not simply "stampede" their foreign-born adversaries.[45] In Schurz's division, the already small 75th Pennsylvania lost 24 percent of its total strength, 59 men, with its lieutenant colonel, adjutant, surgeon, and two captains prisoners of war. While 51 of these casualties were captured, the 75th Pennsylvania had little chance to resist thanks to its low numbers, the vast numerical superiority of the enemy in its position on the field, and its poor position. Some companies lost over a third of their men. The 74th Pennsylvania, a larger regiment, had suffered 52 casualties, approximately 15 percent of its total strength, but 22 killed and wounded. It, too, had been plagued by its unlucky original position, but fought well on the Buschbeck line, losing as prisoners two captains and its major. The 73rd Pennsylvania of Buschbeck's brigade in von Steinwehr's division suffered grievously. The colonel, lieutenant colonel, major, and four captains were casualties, one captain mortally. Almost the entire color party was killed or wounded, and over a third of the regiment's sergeants were hit. A total of 74 dead and wounded and 29 missing reduced the number of effectives by 24 percent. The 73rd Pennsylvania would never recover its numbers lost at Chancellorsville. In the words of Samuel H. Hurst, a private in the 73rd Ohio, Buschbeck's brigade had been "literally cut to pieces," losing just shy of 500 men, over a third of its total strength.[46]

The 27th Pennsylvania had fared somewhat better, but its stand on the Buschbeck line had been costly, too. Of the 345 men engaged, 56 were lost, a casualty rate of 16 percent. Of that number, 37 were dead or wounded. The nine-month 153rd also had substantial casualties: 85 men out of approximately 700 effectives, or 12 percent, evenly distributed between captured and dead and wounded.[47]

The losses of the Pennsylvania German regiments taken as a whole present a mixed picture reflecting that of the larger Eleventh Corps. Those regiments which had some time to prepare themselves for the rebel attack, such as the 27th and 73rd Pennsylvania, fighting on the Buschbeck line, appear to have suffered a higher number of dead and wounded compared to their sister regiments. Standing up to a superior foe in a full-fledged shooting match naturally produced more deaths and wounds than firing a few volleys and retreating. Units that did that, such as the 75th and 153rd Pennsylvania, though they had good reason to flee because of their closer position to the point of attack, had higher numbers of captured. Colonel Adin B. Underwood of the 33rd Massachusetts observed, "every old soldier knows it to be true, that if soldiers, even the best of them, are put in a position where there is not a living chance for them, or for anybody, they will not fight." As if in reply to Underwood, Captain William Saxton of the 157th New York noted that even if the entire Eleventh Corps had stood and fought, "Stonewall Jackson with his 33,000 men would have soon had them all killed, wounded, or prisoners." Saxton exaggerated the size of the Confederate force, but considering the overwhelming numbers that struck the regiments of the Eleventh Corps, particularly those on its right flank, it is a wonder any of them stood and fought at all.[48]

Compared to the losses of other Eleventh Corps regiments, the Pennsylvanians fell about in the middle. Among the Germans, the stalwart 26th Wisconsin and 82nd Illinois were shattered. These two regiments paid dearly for their valor at Hawkins Farm, the Wilderness Church, and the Buschbeck line, losing 204 and 155 men, respectively, many of them killed and wounded. Their casualty rates approached 40 percent. Yet the 54th New York suffered only 42 casualties and the 41st New York, 61. These regiments were positioned next to the 153rd Pennsylvania, and like the 153rd received the initial hammer blow of Jackson's assault. Most of their casualties were captured.[49] The casualty rates in the American regiments of the corps also ran the gamut. In Brigadier General Nathaniel McLean's brigade, also positioned near the western edge of the Eleventh Corps' line, the 17th Connecticut suffered 111 casualties and the 25th Ohio, 152, many of whom were captured. The 61st Ohio of Schimmelfennig's brigade, a mixed Irish American regiment, lost 60 men. The 154th New York, however, was decimated fighting on the Buschbeck line, losing 240 men, or 40 percent of its strength. It suffered the highest loss in the Eleventh Corps.[50]

Overall the casualty rates of the Eleventh Corps portray a corps whose regiments stood and fought when possible and retreated and ran when necessary. According to the figures, the Germans had done their duty. Beyond the grisly statistics, however, lay the courageous reality. Hamlin, perhaps, put it best: "For an hour and a half the nine thousand men of the Eleventh Corps, attacked in rear and flank, and in detail, without any assistance from the rest of the army, had endeavored to stay the impetuous march of Jackson's determined battalions." Those attacking "battalions" outnumbered the defending Eleventh Corps by three to one, and many German American soldiers recognized the long odds against which they fought. Private Adolph Bregler certainly did. "I know this much," he wrote, "it has been the ugliest battle of the war, and again many people have been killed." Second Lieutenant Wilhelm Roth of the 74th Pennsylvania probably summed up the feelings of most German troops immediately after the battle: "The last few days, from 26 April to 4 May were the most difficult of my life. We had to march or fight day and night and had little to eat. The rebels will long remember this attack." Very soon Roth and his comrades would themselves remember Chancellorsville, not only for the battle and the losses suffered there, but also for the resurgence of nativism that it spawned.[51]

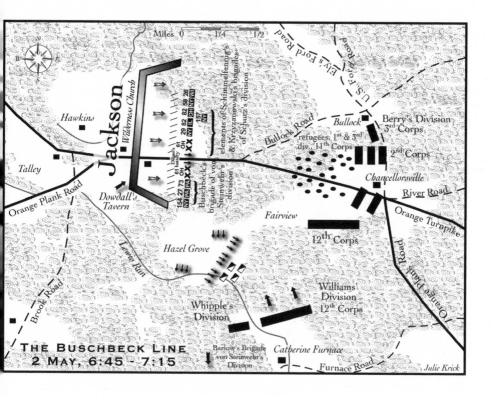

4

"Retreating and Cowardly Poltroons": The Anglo American Reaction

J ust as the German soldiers in the Eleventh Corps began to recover from the shock of their losses and attempted to reorganize their shattered regiments in the days after the battle, they were attacked again, this time by their own comrades in the Army of the Potomac. Non-Germans in the Eleventh Corps itself railed against the "damn Dutch," but because of their own experiences in the battle and proximity to the Germans many of their vituperations were either qualified or muted. The most vocal denunciations emanated from soldiers of other corps, especially the Third and Twelfth, which had to be hastily thrown in to stem the faltering Confederate advance late on the night of 2 May. A few Anglo American soldiers who knew them well defended the Germans, but the much more widespread name-calling and scapegoating continued right up to the beginning of the Gettysburg campaign. Indeed, the reputation of German American soldiers in the eyes of their comrades in the eastern theater would never recover.

Equally damaging, however, to the morale of the rank and file in the German regiments and even more disheartening to their families at home were the specious reports of Chancellorsville that appeared in the English-language press in the coming weeks. Newspapermen from the major northern papers, some of whom had supposedly "witnessed" the May 2 battle, prepared their commentaries, gathered stories from prejudiced non-German soldiers, and began to transmit their reports back home. The troops of the Eleventh Corps, incorrectly said to be composed only of Germans, were alleged to have all broken and shamefully run in the face of the enemy. These reports of the corps' performance, created almost singlehandedly by correspondents of the New York City press, were widely circulated among smaller newspapers and hence strongly influenced northern press coverage against the Germans.

An analysis of twelve major Anglo American newspapers indicates that the reports published in the *New York Times*, *New York Tribune*, and *New York Herald* were later partially disputed by other important English-language papers, and the blame shifted from the German soldiers to other scapegoats, such as the Lincoln administration. The national prominence of the New York organs nonetheless initially influenced the reports of the others, overshadowed their palliations, and were perceived by the Germans to speak for the nativist north-

ern public as a whole. It was this perception that so angered Germans throughout the North in the weeks after Chancellorsville and caused them to react with
indignance, outrage, and ultimately anti-assimilationist beliefs.

In May 1863 the Eleventh Corps was identified by both German and non-
German soldiers and civilians as "the German Corps" of the Army of the Potomac. Public attacks against it in the press were viewed, whether accurately or
not, as attacks against the Germans. Nearly all of Ludwig Blenker's earlier German division had been absorbed into the command, and Franz Sigel, symbol
of German America, had led its precursor, the First Corps of Pope's Army of
Virginia, in the summer of 1862. Sigel had then actually commanded the corps
for several months before his resignation in February 1863, and Carl Schurz,
that other highly visible spokesman for the Germans, served as its next leader
before Howard took over. Most of the newly raised German regiments of 1862
from both the East and the Midwest had been assigned to the corps, such as
the much-publicized 26th Wisconsin, 82nd Illinois, and 119th New York. Taken
together, these actions ingrained in the northern public's psyche the idea that
the Eleventh Corps was a German organization. Abram P. Smith of the 76th
New York noted in 1867 that the Eleventh Corps at Chancellorsville, "formerly
commanded by General Siegel [sic], was composed chiefly of German regiments. There were in it, however, two or three regiments of Americans." Colonel Patrick R. Guiney of the 9th Massachusetts wrote on 7 May 1863, that "we
would have gained a great victory were it not for the cowardice of the Eleventh
Corps—a German corps that was formerly commanded by Sigel but now by
Howard of Maine. The Dutch Corps ran." Even Second Lieutenant Oscar D.
Ladley of the 75th Ohio, a regiment attached to the Eleventh Corps, remarked
that "the Eleventh Corps is composed principally of New York dutch." On 25
June, Carl Schurz wrote to Sigel complaining about Howard's attempts to
"transfer my German regiments, and in this way to give the Corps a new char-
acter," and even the famous poet William Cullen Bryant described the Eleventh
Corps as German. Writing to President Abraham Lincoln about the chances of
restoring Sigel to command of the corps, Bryant claimed "it [the Eleventh
Corps] is composed of German soldiering."[1]

"They Were Like a Flock of Scared Sheep"

Anglo Americans in the Army of the Potomac harshly blamed the Germans
of the Eleventh Corps for the defeat at Chancellorsville. Carol Reardon explains
that Hooker also came under fire for being "completely out Generalled," as one
soldier put it, and many in the Second Corps particularly pilloried the army

high command. James Biddle of the Fifth Corps' headquarters staff declared, "I attribute the failure with confidence to the want of ability in Gen. Hooker," and certain officers and men in the Eleventh Corps itself criticized their own generals. But the Germans were targeted more frequently, and the complaints against them resounded from practically every corps of the army. Typical were comments like those of Colonel Robert McAllister of the 11th New Jersey, who told his wife the Germans "were panic-stricken and perfectly worthless. But our brave boys heeded them not and treated them with perfect contempt." Private Smith of the 76th New York lamented that the Germans "broke and ran in the most cowardly manner," pushing aside "the brave regiments" in "cowardly waves," and a soldier in the 4th Ohio wrote his son, "every Dutchman was making for the river . . . trying to save his own cowardly body." Within Hubert Dilger's own Ohio German battery, Private Darwin Cody claimed the German infantry supporting his artillery had all "run without firing a gun." Cody blamed the loss of some of the battery's horses and cannon on Germans: "I say dam [sic] the Dutch!" Corporal Francis McCarthy of the Irish 37th New York was even more bellicose in his accusations, asserting that "we were fired upon by our own men—the Eleventh Corps—cowardly dogs who fired and then ran." French American Colonel Regis DeTrobriand probably best summed up the general mood in the rest of the army: "The Eleventh Corps was the object of a general hue and cry, nobody stopping to ask if there were not some extenuating circumstances."[2]

Digging deeper into the mountain of accusatory verbiage, however, a noticeable pattern emerges: Anglo American soldiers in the Eleventh Corps who actually fought with the German regiments on 2 May tended to tone down their prejudicial remarks or omitted them altogether. Those who served with Barlow, and were therefore spared the experience of being flanked and attacked, were more pronounced in their criticisms, whereas men who were most removed from the worst of the fighting that Saturday unleashed the most colorful invective. Especially condemning were letters written by the veteran soldiers of the Third and Twelfth Corps, who felt that their commands were forced to sacrifice themselves to hold back the victorious Confederates late on 2 May and throughout the next day. A few lone voices arose here and there to defend the Germans, but they were drowned out by a sea of angry and self-righteous detractors.

Sharing the horror of Civil War combat and the doldrums of everyday army life, most soldiers serving in the same regiment formed a close bond that could supersede previous differences such as class and ethnicity. Obviously, this process worked to a greater or lesser degree depending on the regiment in question, and in those dominated by a certain ethnic group—especially in the German regiments, as we have seen—prejudice against minority soldiers could easily become an issue. But generally, loyalty to the regiment and to one's comrades was paramount; all other considerations were secondary. Service in the same brigade and even the same corps could also create solidarity among the troops, even between those of different nationalities. Although Anglo Americans in the Eleventh Corps did frequently complain about having to serve alongside the "Dutch," and sometimes exceeded in their vitriol the condemnations of those from without the corps, usually a better understanding bred from familiarity ameliorated their commentary about the Germans. Those who most assailed their German comrades often hailed from regiments newly attached to the corps, or served in Barlow's and McLean's brigades, which had only one German regiment between them. These men thus had little time or opportunity to get to know the Germans as people before the battle—instead, they were simply strange-talking foreigners to them.[3]

The 154th New York had been randomly assigned to Buschbeck's brigade in mid-October 1862 as reinforcements for the new command of Franz Sigel. As the regiment's historian, Mark Dunkelman, explains, the upstate New Yorkers had had a series of altercations and miscommunications with the German majority in their brigade before Chancellorsville, ranging from simple, good-natured catcalling among the soldiers to a court-martial that witnessed one of the privates of the regiment sentenced to three months' hard labor for uttering ethnic slurs and resisting arrest. Tension clearly existed between the Anglo American 154th and the German 27th and 73rd Pennsylvania and 29th New York. Most of it seems to have emanated from the soldiers of the 154th. Some of them even complained about "the awful dutchy look" of their comrades or sung a song that went, "O, I'd better staid at home with the gal I love so much, Than be traveling round the Country with these dam Dutch." One private even lamented guard duty at General Steinwehr's headquarters because he thought himself "in the midst of Dutchdom." Perhaps if the men of the 154th had had more time or opportunity to acquaint themselves personally with the Germans of their brigade, such ethnic commentary would have remained in the realm of the comical. But "contact between members of the 154th and the Germans seems to have been infrequent," and only six months had elapsed from the time the regiment joined the Eleventh Corps to the end of the Chancellorsville campaign. Add these factors to the heavy losses suffered by the regiment during the battle—240 out of 590 engaged—and the stage was set for some of the strongest anti-German invective in the entire Army of the Potomac.[4]

Of the stand along the Buschbeck line, Surgeon Henry Van Aernum argued that "the real fact is the 27th [Pennsylvania] and 29th [New York] both skedaddled without showing fight." He also wrote, "Just now it is a reproach for a man to belong to the 11th Army Corps and the Dutch part of it did behave like slinks." Horace Smith recorded in his diary on 2 May that "the 29th N.Y. of our brigade ran like deer," and a few days later added, "How I would like to give them a volley of musketry from our guns." Private Allen Robbins sent a report back to the local newspaper at home, claiming that the Irish companies in the predominantly German 73rd Pennsylvania were the only ones deserving of praise in the brigade besides the 154th: "Our battalion with the help of those brave sons of Erin, held the ground till every dutch 'sour krout' had retreated to the woods or fallen in the attempt. For my part, I have no confidence in the fighting qualities of the Dutch." Isaac Porter also condemned the majority of the 73rd, who "followed the example of the 29th and 27th," and "shamefully retreated." Although Private Robbins admitted in his newspaper letter that "I am quite sure there was a great lack of generalship in the battle of Chancellorsville on the 2nd inst.," and that "circumstances point strongly to Gen. Howard as one of the delinquents on that (to us) unfortunate day," he was shortly rebutted in the same paper by Sergeant James Mathewson , who found Howard guiltless and blamed the Germans: "The faults were with the men, and not in their commanders . . . they were mostly Germans, and were not satisfied because Sigel did not lead them."[5]

The 33rd Massachusetts was in Barlow's brigade, which not only had just been attached to the Eleventh Corps, but had also not fought with it on 2 May. Private E. L. Edes reminded his mother, "When you read that the 11th army corps cowardly skedaddled remember that the 2nd brigade, 2nd division was not there and have done no fighting and consequently no running." He continued, "everybody is cursing the 11th corps." W. H. Hinds, also of the 33rd, wrote "of course all our ill luck was charged to the 'damned Dutchmen' to use the common expression." The chaplain of the 33rd, who "did not believe in swearing," nonetheless thought certain occasions merited coarse words. Chancellorsville was one of them, "and he would say from the bottom of his heart '*Damn the Dutch.*'" The 134th New York also marched with Barlow to assist Sickles, "whose force did most gallant work . . . rendered of no use by the flight of the Germans." An anonymous soldier of the regiment wrote his local Schenectady newspaper a report of the action on 2 May, and seemed to separate his unit from the rest of the Eleventh Corps by his verbiage: "On returning from the successful completion of our enterprise, we learned, to our disgust, that the Eleventh Corps, to whom was intrusted the defence of our strongly intrenched camp, had ignominiously run like sheep. . . . Our baggage, knapsacks, and much valuable property was taken possession of by the enemy under the retreating heels of the flying Dutchmen."[6]

Equally disparaging, but not quite condemnatory, were the words of Private John Lewis of the 17th Connecticut in McLean's brigade. Lewis warned his wife on 14 May that "you will no doubt hear that the Eleventh Corps broke and run which is so but our Briggade stood firm till outnumbered. The Dutchmen proved themselves cowards." Captain Wilson French, also of the 17th, agreed with Lewis. On 10 May he wrote his wife, "our corp is mostly german and will not fight. It was them that run last Saturday and disgraced the whole corps. *They fight with Sigle so they say* but I would not trust them any where." However, the next day, he penned another letter that placed the blame on others' shoulders: "I hope and pray to God that the blame will rest where it belongs. I would to God that we could send home *General Howard and Devens covered with tar and Feathers*, if I had a corporeal in my company that could not display more Generalship than either of the above I would shoot him." Andrew L. Harris of the 75th Ohio, also in McLean's brigade, questioned the abilities of his commanding officers more pointedly, and even exonerated the Germans in a letter he wrote to a friend:

> If it were known that the enemy were massing their forces on our right and rear, why was not such a disposition made of the 11th Corps as the case demanded to give us a chance to repel the attack? . . . The blood of the hundreds of dead and wounded demand that the blame should rest where it belongs, where ever that may be. The wounded honor of the living soldiers of this corps crys out for an investigation into the facts as they actually existed. We want no covering up of blame by hired correspondents around the genial shades of Head Quarters, who are paid to stave off the blame from the guilty high in power. . . .
>
> I have but little fault to find with the German troops—they did not stand as long as bravery would dictate, but it was certainly as long as it was prudent (much is heaped upon them unjustly and that too to try and direct attention from another locality a little higher up)—They have been very useful tools to help up the reputation of others though at a sacrifice of their own honor, but you know that "murder will out sooner or later" and justice demands it in this case.

Lieutenant William Wheeler of Julius Dieckmann's (German) battery, who had served alongside Germans since the beginning of the war, also defended his ethnic comrades and displayed an uncommon depth of compassion for them: "With regard to the Eleventh Corps, I have heard some say that they would not fight because they did not have Sigel; this is absurd, and yet allowance must be made for the great influence on the men, produced by their losing the man on whom they leaned unreservedly, and whom they would follow to the death, and getting in his place a person unknown, peculiarly uncongenial to the German mind, and considered by them as a parson in uniform." No corps "so scattered, so strung out" could have resisted for any length of time, he insisted to his mother, and "McLean's brigade fought as well as men can fight." As for the culprits behind the disaster, Wheeler, like French and Harris, accused the generals. "General Hooker allowed General Howard to scatter his corps along too great a line, and then allowed the Corps thus scattered to be flanked." He asked his mother to show his letter to any of his friends at home who wanted to know the truth behind the "panic."[7]

Unfortunately, very few Anglo Americans at the time of the battle or directly afterward were interested in learning the truth behind the defeat of the Eleventh Corps. High-ranking officers and enlisted men alike condemned the "flying Dutchmen," and some were better equipped than others to lodge their criticisms.

Brigadier General Alpheus S. Williams, commanding the First Division in the Twelfth Corps, rushed his men to stop the Confederate avalanche after Howard's lines began to crumble. He was certainly in a good position to assess the situation as it probably existed about 7:00 p.m. near the Chancellor House. Yet his perspective, like many others near the commanding general's headquarters, was nonetheless limited by both time and space. He could have only observed the swirling mass of panicked men and animals from the Eleventh Corps' First Division who may have fled to Hooker's headquarters by that time, even though the exact identity of this mob is still not completely known. Hamlin believes it was composed mainly of artillerists and camp followers from reserve elements of the Third and Twelfth Corps that had earlier been posted in the Hazel Grove area and were scared off by rebel pickets. If there were Eleventh Corps soldiers in the mass of men Williams describes, they would have had "three miles to run before reaching Chancellor's," and therefore "must have possessed wonderful strength and endurance." The general's account, moreover, gives no mention of any resistance on the part of the Eleventh Corps, and it is highly unlikely, given his location, that he could have witnessed anything but a scene of despair and disorder:

I rode rapidly to the right near the plank road, where some officers of the general staff had arrested a group of a few hundred men and were trying to get them into order. Lt. Col. Dickinson of Hooker's staff was riding fiercely about, pistol in hand, and occasionally discharging it at some flying Dutchman. Swords were out and flashing in the setting sun. Such a mixture of Dutch and English and oaths! Such a rolling in and out of frightened men . . . ! Such a swinging of arms on the part of their officers, who evidently were quite as much stampeded as the men! I saw at once that all effort to organize such a body of men was fruitless. They were like a flock of scared sheep driven into a corner; not one thought of defense.[8]

Williams was not alone in writing about this perspective of the performance of the Eleventh Corps; indeed, Anglo American soldiers outside of the Eleventh Corps who saw anything would have necessarily *only* seen the results of the initial rout of Devens's division, and thereafter only retreating elements of the Third and Second Divisions. Naturally, they would not have been able to witness the stubborn fighting of regiments like the 82nd Illinois and 26th Wisconsin near the Wilderness Church, or the bitter defense of the Buschbeck line later on. Because all they could see was either panic-stricken men or retreating soldiers, they believed the Eleventh Corps and its Germans had not fought at all. Anglo American officers and soldiers who witnessed these unfortunate scenes talked to others who had not (like newspapermen), and camp rumor took over from there, exaggerating the scope of the Eleventh Corps' defeat and excoriating its members, especially the easily identifiable Germans. A perfect example is a letter written by Thomas H. Elliott, an officer in the Twelfth Corps, to a friend in the Third Corps:

As somebody's account has given you a mistaken idea of the conduct of the Eleventh Corps, let me explain to you truthfully. The corps adjoined our own and I was an eyewitness to their unsoldierly behavior. They had advanced beyond the works, and under pressure from the enemy fell back to them, when they could have offered a resistance that would have baffled three times their numbers. . . . But filled with timidity hundreds through away their arms and fled, and others fired into the air and followed, dropping the colors sacred to their care, and they came panic-stricken into our lines, where our officers tried to rally them but they said 'no, I goes dis way' (to the rear). We called them cowards, etc. but it was of no avail. They did not fire an average of two cartridges apiece—a lasting blot upon the name of soldier. . . . [Howard] wept like a child when he found his every effort could not inspire the poltroons with manliness. They are a wretched party in the aggregate. . . . This is an unbiased statement founded on what I saw. . . . On my conscience I would advise one-half of them to benefit the service by divesting themselves of the livery which none but brave men should wear.[9]

The vague description of the Eleventh Corps' fight—Elliott apparently did not know where it advanced to before it was driven back—coupled with hyperbolic rhetoric about "timidity" and Howard "weeping" make the veracity of this account questionable. The word "poltroon," although much more common in the 1860s than today, was precisely the one used by the *New York Times* in its 5 May report of the Eleventh Corps' discomfiture. Two other clues in this letter raise suspicion: the date, 23 May, long after someone of Elliott's position and education would have had access to the biased newspapers, and a final parting sentence by the author: "No feeling is here manifested, for I am laughing in unassumed merriment while I recollect these unpalatable truths."

Whereas some of the officers of the Twelfth Corps clearly exaggerated their depictions of the Germans in the Eleventh Corps, the enlisted men under their command necessarily had a restricted view of the battlefield and could also fall prey to the lure of ethnic stereotyping. The regiments in Brigadier General Kane's brigade of the Twelfth Corps' Second Division had more experience than most encountering refugees on 2 May, but as both Hamlin and Bigelow explain, only some of these men hailed from the Eleventh Corps. Many belonged to Brigadier General David Birney's Third Corps artillery park, which had just been spooked from its position at Hazel Grove by a few Confederate skirmishers. In fact, the majority of the Eleventh Corps' fugitives had already passed the areas the Twelfth Corps would occupy on the night of 2 May by the time these soldiers had returned from their foray with Sickles to the south. As the shadows of night descended deeply on the woods of the wilderness, however, distinctions between organizations and ethnicities mattered little to soldiers confused by the events of the day and eager to assess blame for a lost battle.[10]

About 7:45 p.m., Kane's men were on their way to their old positions behind the "log works," a substantial barrier of felled trees, just north of Hazel Grove near the Bullock Road. Suddenly, men without hats, knapsacks, and other accoutrements, accompanied by various wagons and cattle, "came running down in the rear of us and seemed terribly demoralized." According to David Mouat of the 29th Pennsylvania, "our brigadier general Kane became so excited at the sight of several officers running that he attempted to kick them, [but] owing to his lameness . . . he nearly fell down." In the end, "we prevailed on a large number of the 11th Corps to fall into line with us" and fight, he wrote, "the firing lasting until midnight." James T. Miller of the 111th Pennsylvania was much less charitable. He declared that the Army of the Potomac would have won the battle if the Eleventh Corps had done its duty, and that its rank and file earlier "had done some good fighting, [but] in the last fight they were panic-stricken and ran like a parcel of scarte sheep." Miller continued, "we think very little of the dutch sons of bitches that used to brag that they 'fight mit Sigel' and I don't know but they might have fought well with [Sigel] but they did not fight worth shit under Howard." Another Twelfth Corps soldier, Sergeant Rice C. Bull of the 123rd New York, was on his way to the log works with his regiment when they ran directly into "the panic and stampede of a part of the 11th Corps." Streaming from the woods to their front and fleeing across the field, "their retreat was headlong; they had thrown away everything that was loose, guns, knapsacks, caps, and many had no coat or blouse. . . . They were crazed and would fight to escape as though the enemy were close to them. We were ordered to stop them but we might as well have tried to stop a cyclone, they dived through our lines regardless of our guns or bayonets."[11]

Not only did Bull automatically assume these were Eleventh Corps soldiers, but he also felt rattled by the experience, adding that "their panic was nerve-wracking to troops new to the service." Luckily for him, he did not witness the shooting of fleeing Eleventh Corps soldiers, which apparently occurred at the Chancellorsville clearing, or he would have been even more disturbed. Darwin Cody of Hubert Dilger's battery wrote, "Gen. Hooker soon ordered the 12th corps to kill every man that run in the 11th. I saw a number of officers and privates shot trying to break through the guard. It served them right." Cody's story was unfortunately corroborated by others, but again the question has been raised by both Hamlin and Bigelow—and ignored by recent chroniclers Furgurson and Sears—whether the majority of the panic-stricken men who burst upon Chancellorsville were indeed from the Eleventh Corps.[12]

Soldiers in Major General Hiram Berry's division of Sickles's Third Corps were the first thrown in to stem Jackson's now disorganized assault after the Buschbeck Line collapsed. Berry had not accompanied Sickles on his earlier advance to Catharine Furnace, and his division was the only one readily available to Hooker when he finally realized the Eleventh Corps had been crushed. It was also Hooker's old division, and the men in it keenly realized that their former general, now commander of the army, had turned to them to save the day when the Dutchmen had failed him. They poured out a waterfall of criticism against the Germans, even though they themselves did not actually stop the Confederate advance—nightfall and the rebels' own disorganization did. What the men of the Third Corps could not have known then—but failed to acknowledge later—was that the Eleventh Corps had delayed Jackson's advance until night made it difficult for the enemy to reorganize.

"When the Rebs made a dash at the 11th corp (Dutch as Hell) and surprised them they came a running in and officers with revolvers out trying to stop them [were] no use," Daniel O. Macomber of the 1st Massachusetts exclaimed. "Such a scampering to get to the rear I never saw in my life," but the officers of the regiment managed to stop "all of the Dutchmen they could and made them fall into our Regt and every one of them happened to get shot." Macomber placed the last comment in parenthesis in his 15 May letter to his friend—could it be that he meant the Germans who stopped and formed up with the 1st Massachusetts were purposefully shot later on? The chaplain of the regiment wrote three years later that "the German regiments fought gallantly for a while," but broke after a charge from the enemy, prompting "the shattered columns [to] stream back to the rear like an irresistible torrent. One might as well have attempted to stop a tornado. The fugitives were panic-stricken and beside themselves . . . jumbling and tumbling things together in indiscriminate and lamentable confusion, and making such a perfect bedlam." A squad of Eleventh Corps Germans were taken in by the 1st, recalled Henry N. Blake, and "repeated the skulker's story, that their commands 'were all cut to pieces;' 'we are all that are left'" and other pleas. Based on what actually happened to many of the regiments of the Eleventh Corps, the "skulkers" may have been telling the truth, but Blake's commanding officer opened a few cartridge boxes and found them still full, thus believing he had put the lie to them. "I should detail some of my good men to shoot you, but they have no ammunition to waste on your worthless carcasses," he said. Blake concluded, "the Germans sought to escape the censure which the whole army justly bestowed upon them by tearing the badges from their caps—for the crescent was recognized as the insignia of a poltroon," but in the end that failed to help them. They could not find a sympathetic ear.[13]

Other men in the Third Corps were equally unyielding when it came to describing the Germans. "The greater part of them ran without fireing a shot, it was the most cowardly thing I ever saw," observed Benjamin Robb of the 26th Pennsylvania, and Quartermaster Sergeant Dennis Tuttle of the 20th Indiana claimed, "Those Dutchmen will fight very well [with] Sigel, but they will not fight well [with] any one else." The Fifth Corps joined in the general derision of the Germans, one soldier insisting that "the Division of Dutchmen in the Eleventh Corps broke and run almost on the first fire of the Rebs," and another observing "Gen. Griffin . . . swearing at the damned Dutch with their chow-chow-chow, and in a very bad humor." The venom in all of these letters was undeniable and the nativist predilections, muted since the mid-1850s, came roaring back with a vengeance. In an age when immigrants were routinely viewed with suspicion, it was entirely too easy to blame the most obvious foreign group for the failure of the Chancellorsville campaign. The Germans had run—had not everyone "seen" it for themselves? The historical evidence indicates that some of them certainly had fled, but for many Anglo American soldiers the temptation to overgeneralize, oversimplify, and find an obvious scapegoat was too great. Major Grotius R. Giddings of the 14th U.S. Regulars summed up the overall feeling of the rest of the Army of the Potomac: "The Germans have disgraced themselves forever in the Army."[14]

"*Somebody* Is to Blame for This Disgraceful Affair"

That perception would, unfortunately, be immediately mirrored in the Anglo American press. Instead of private letters sent home by soldiers, or ethnic slurs and comments spoken in the ranks and kept there, the national broadcast of the Germans' "disgrace" would enter the homes of the northern people and indelibly impress upon them that, indeed, the Dutch were cowards. The rumors spread by the soldiers' letters and camp gossip were confirmed, and the real culprits for federal defeat—Hooker, Devens, and Howard—escaped the public notice.

The 5 May *New York Times* was most vociferous in slandering the Germans, claiming they behaved like "cowards:"

> But to the disgrace of the Eleventh Corps be it said that the division of General Schurz, which was the first assailed, almost instantly gave way. Threats, entreaties and orders of commanders were of no avail. Thousands of these cowards threw down their guns and soon streamed down the road toward headquarters. . . . General Howard, with all his daring and resolution and vigor, could not stem the tide of the retreating and cowardly poltroons.[15]

Only Buschbeck's brigade had resisted the foe for any length of time, asserted L. L. Crounse, the *Times* correspondent, failing to acknowledge how long that actually was and how many other fragments of regiments rallied with Buschbeck. Another unnamed correspondent wrote that the Eleventh Corps, "without waiting for a single volley from the rebels, disgracefully abandoned their positions behind the breastworks, and commenced coming, panic-stricken, down the road toward headquarters." The "panic stricken Dutchmen" were so intent on reaching safety that they fled all the way to the United States Ford, far beyond Hooker's headquarters. "Many members of the staff of Gen. Hooker, and other general officers, placed themselves in the road, and with drawn sabers smote and slashed the cowardly retreating rascals."[16]

L. A. Hendricks, correspondent of the *New York Herald*, was hardly more sympathetic. His report also appeared on 5 May, claiming "the disastrous and disgraceful giving way of General Schurz's division of Gen. Howard's corps (Sigel's old corps) completely changed the fortunes of the day. The men, I am told, fled like so many sheep before a pack of wolves, and the enemy rushed up, taking possession of the abandoned line." T. M. Cook, also of the *Herald*, complained that the German commanders "retreated before their men" and hence set a bad example. Their regiments then "broke in confusion . . . and fled from the field in panic, nearly effecting the total demoralization of the entire army." A report written by an eyewitness published in the 7 May issue of the *Herald* likewise portrayed the Germans in a negative light, exclaiming in a section entitled "The Panic" that "the flying Germans came dashing over the field in crowds" nearly "stampeding through the lines" of Generals Amiel W. Whipple and David B. Birney. They were so intent on escaping the attacking rebels that some swam across the Rapidan River "and are still running yet."[17]

If the *Times* and the *Herald* were the Germans' sharpest critics, their greatest enemy in terms of verbal harshness had to be Horace Greeley's *New-York Daily Tribune*. Greeley called for "swift justice" to "overtake the regiments that broke," suggesting that "if it be deemed too rigid to shoot them all, they may at least be decimated and then dissolved." Greeley soon retracted his incendiary statement, but by then the German-language newspapers had already reported it.[18]

Even worse, The Washington *Daily National Intelligencer*, New York *Evening Post*, Philadelphia *Public Ledger*, Philadelphia *Inquirer*, Pittsburgh *Gazette*, *Pittsburgh Post*, Hartford *Evening Press*, and Chicago *Tribune* all initially published verbatim the *Times* and *Herald* reports of 5, 6, and 7 May, or uncited variations thereof. Hence, the Anglo American public first heard only negative reports about the Eleventh Corps and its Germans at Chancellorsville. The *Pittsburgh Post* claimed the corps "retreated rapidly," before the rebels even fired a shot, and left their breastworks "apparently much panic-stricken." The *Evening Press* argued "they ran without fighting at all," and labeled this "an inexcusable piece of cowardice." As the *Public Ledger* put it, the "losses sustained by this corps, either in killed or captured, could not have been great—they ran too fast for that." The *Inquirer* called the corps' performance "unaccountable and inexcusable," exclaiming that "its position ought to have been held, and *somebody* [emphasis orig.] is to blame for this disgraceful affair." Echoing the words of the other papers, which also exonerated Hooker for the defeat, the *Inquirer* added that only "the superb generalship of the Commanding General" saved the Army of the Potomac from utter disaster. Corps commander Howard had likewise performed brilliantly, the paper reported, and was not to blame for the disaster that befell his men.[19]

After hastily assigning blame to the troops of the Eleventh Corps, however, some of these newspapers reconsidered their original reports and published editorials that deflected some of the odium away from the Germans.

The Chicago *Tribune*, a sheet that frequently circulated among the Windy City's German wards, was among the first to question whether the New York correspondents may have too harshly judged the Eleventh Corps, and the Germans in particular. Its 7 May editorial, entitled "The Germans With Hooker," admitted that the recent reports flooding the Anglo American press were "certainly mortifying" to Germans across the North, and attempted to assuage their injured pride with assurances that the Germans' flight at Chancellorsville, if true, had been preceded in the war by countless examples of cowardice by "Americans and Irish, Scotch and nondescripts." The editor continued to argue that the German regiments' conduct had not yet been precisely determined, and thus "if it is said that the Germans disappointed the expectations based on their valor, and fled just when they should have stood fast, let us hear all the particulars before we severely condemn." It was "unjust" to blame "all men who are of German blood" based on the telegraph reports, since "German soldiers proved their courage more than fifteen hundred years ago" and remained steadfast fighters. Ending his editorial "with perfect confidence, that, when investigated, the case which has provoked these comments will present quite another aspect," the editor urged his "readers of American birth" to judge not lest they themselves be judged: the great Union defeats of the war so far (such as First Manassas) had not, in his opinion, been caused by "cowardly Dutchmen."[20]

The Philadelphia *Inquirer* published an editorial on the same day as the *Tribune*'s, actually extolling the performance of some of the German troops, no doubt because the troops in question were from Philadelphia:

> The conduct of Colonel Bushbeck's Brigade has, indeed, an especial interest for the people of this city, for it contained two regiments of Philadelphia Germans, the Twenty-seventh and the Seventy-third. It was this brigade, composed of the above named regiments and two from New York, all under the command of Colonel Bushbeck, of our old Twenty-seventh, that saved the trains and artillery of the fugitive divisions of the Eleventh Corps from capture by the enemy. They stood before Jackson's impetuous columns like a rock, until the brigade was left alone, and then they fell back slowly, stubbornly, and in good order, with their front to the foe.[21]

Other English-language papers, although acknowledging a general panic among the Germans of the Eleventh Corps, attempted to persuade their readers that the reasons they performed badly had little to do with the fighting abilities of the men themselves. It was the fault of the Lincoln administration, Chief of Staff Henry W. Halleck, and, as if in an afterthought, the Confederates under Jackson. Most of these papers, not surprisingly, aligned with the Democratic Party. The Cleveland *Plain Dealer*, under a headline entitled "Why the Germans Ran," claimed that "we need not go far to discover the reason of the stampede of the Germans in the late battle." Franz Sigel, whom the Germans "followed anywhere," had been removed, and his absence at the head of the

Eleventh Corps allowed the Germans to be routed: "This political administration had dispensed with the services of the hero of Pea Ridge, and his men were led by the squirt Carl Schurz, who received his appointment, not because he was fit for it, but as a reward for his stump speeches for Mr. Lincoln in 1860. This blame does not belong to the Germans, but to the Administration."[22]

The *Pittsburgh Post* argued along similar lines on 12 May, stating that "Sigel has demonstrated his ability as a soldier" and that the country now needed "the services of such officers" desperately. Agreeing with the *Plain Dealer* that Schurz was not the best choice for a general, the *Post* nonetheless explained that "the falling back of the Germans under Carl Schurz we attribute to no want of pluck upon their part; but partly to a want of confidence in their leader [General Howard], besides the fury of Jackson's overwhelming numbers." The Chicago *Tribune* went a step further in its 9 May editorial, claiming Sigel's absence at Chancellorsville and the subsequent rout of the Eleventh Corps "was the work of Halleck, who acts like a bigoted Know Nothing, with a cross of the Copperhead." Halleck's prejudice against Sigel was well known, and it was "the personal malice of this mis-manager" who had set up the conditions for defeat. "Does any man believe the German regiments would have given way had their beloved General been at their head?" The editor clearly did not think so.[23]

Another Anglo American who believed Sigel would have saved the day was poet William Cullen Bryant, who professed to understand the German Americans of New York City and certainly sympathized with them. He wrote Abraham Lincoln on 11 May about the need to reinstate the general, claiming it was "the universal desire of our German fellow citizens that General Sigel should be again placed in command of that part of the army of the Rappahannock which is composed of German soldiery and which has suffered some loss of credit in recent battles." Bryant continued that the president could not "conceive of the strength and fervor of this wish of our German population," and argued that Sigel's return to the Eleventh Corps would be equivalent to the addition of ten-thousand men." Lincoln wrote back three days later, stating that it was now "inconvenient" to reinstate Sigel "without relieving or dismissing some other officer, who is not asking, and perhaps would object, to being so disposed of." Did Lincoln mean Howard here? Perhaps, but in any case the president was unwilling to act, as he put it, because of "how embarrassing" such an action would be. He had grown weary of Sigel's repeated requests to be relieved earlier in the winter, and then finally acquiesced, allowing Halleck to replace him with Howard. To bring Sigel back now might appear as if he were caving in both to ethnic politics (which he had repeatedly done earlier) and Sigel's capriciousness (which he had already done once before). Lincoln believed his hands were tied. He also probably thought that Sigel had gotten what he deserved. No solace for the Germans would come from the White House.[24]

In the weeks to come the English-language press would attempt to assuage the Germans and erase the falsehoods created by its over-hasty reaction to the defeat at Chancellorsville. The *New York Herald* even admitted as early as 6 May that "the Germans have always fought well, and, though they have not generally played so brilliant a part in the field as French, British, and Irish troops, cowardice is not a German characteristic." Yet the damage had been done, and no amount of apology could erase the first impressions created in both German and non-German minds.[25]

"It is always convenient to have a scapegoat in case of disaster, and the German element of the Eleventh Corps have been freely censured and their name a byword for giving way," wrote Private Davis of the 13th Massachusetts years later. According to Wilhelm Kaufmann and Stephen W. Sears, that fact strongly contributed to the restoration of morale in the beaten Army of the Potomac after Chancellorsville. In a time when nativistic beliefs were very strong, mere years after the demise of a political party devoted to the infringement of immigrant rights, it is not surprising that the onus of defeat was placed on the Germans' shoulders. With an identifiable foreign group to pin the badge of disgrace on, the rest of the army could rest easier about the failure in the knowledge that the Germans were at least partially to blame. The Anglo American public could also better come to grips with yet another major Union defeat and explain away the bungling of their generals. The morale of the Anglo Americans would recover, and soon. The morale of the Germans, and their ardor for the Union, would never be the same again.[26]

5

"All We Ask Is Justice": The Germans Respond

Three realizations quickly dawned on the German Americans of the Eleventh Corps even before the battle of Chancellorsville had concluded. The first was disbelief at what had just befallen them. For a day or two most soldiers still suffered from a state of shock, unsure just how they, as a corps, had been overwhelmed, and how as individuals they had escaped becoming killed or wounded. The second, also an entirely human reaction, they shared with soldiers of every time and place: sadness. Many of their comrades had fallen and would be sorely missed by friends, brothers, and relatives. Normally, this feeling of loss would be replaced by a reassurance that their blood sacrifice had not been in vain. If the battle ended in victory, the casualties were explained away as a necessary cost for the greater goal. Even after lost battles, Civil War soldiers could usually rationalize the numbers of dead and wounded in their regiments by claiming they had held their ground and made the enemy pay dearly for his triumph. It was important that this belief be substantiated by soldiers in other units or high-ranking officers. Most of the Germans in the Eleventh Corps, regardless how much they deserved it, received no such vindication. Instead, they became the universal scapegoats for the rest of the Army of the Potomac, were labeled cowards, and suffered nativistic prejudice at the hands of the English-language press. Their morale plummeted. Their sacrifices *had* apparently, been in vain. It became abundantly clear that Anglo Americans, both in and out of the army, blamed them for the defeat. Their German officers, especially Schurz, von Steinwehr, and Schimmelfennig, also felt the sting of prejudice, and did all they could to clear the name of their commands and defend their bravery, but the language barrier conspired with likely nativist and selfish concerns on the part of Anglo American superiors to foil these efforts. Thus the third realization most German soldiers came to was a feeling of helplessness: nothing, save perhaps an exhibition of great bravery in the next battle, could ever free them from the stain of Chancellorsville. They would forever be the "flying Dutchmen."

That did not mean, however, that they and their friends and relatives at home did not attempt to explain the defeat and place the blame where they perceived it belonged. In numerous letters from the field and countless newspaper editorials, the Germans of the North—the entire North—rallied behind the downtrodden Eleventh Corps. Many argued that the Germans had fought well and Americans poorly earlier in the war; why suddenly jump on the Germans for this one defeat? Others declared, through detailed battlefield accounts and reports—sometimes embellished—that even if the Eleventh Corps had behaved badly, the Germans in it had not. Nearly all claimed that Franz Sigel would have led the Germans to victory, and determined that the real culprits behind the disaster were Hooker, Howard, Devens, and, possibly, the Lincoln administration. Howard particularly came under heavy fire.

As May gave way to June 1863, German American soldiers and civilians began to stop explaining and started questioning, even attacking, Anglo American motives behind the criticism of the Eleventh Corps. Many prominent newspaper editors and not a few political leaders believed that nativism was the true reason the Germans had been so badly singled out for blame. The time had come to publicly respond to the outrageous allegations, and several mass meetings were held that clearly expressed a spirit of German American unity and anti-Americanization. The German-language press went a step further in some instances, openly criticizing American society, illustrating the differences between Germans and Americans, and suggesting that Germans were better off remaining German. By the time of the Gettysburg campaign, the Germans of the North, and especially in the east, had begun to seriously question their role in the war for the Union and their future as American citizens.

"The Spirit of This Corps is Broken"

Major General Oliver O. Howard never came close to admitting his culpability in the disaster that befell his corps. In his official report, issued the week after the battle ended, he blamed the rout of the Eleventh Corps on the density of the wilderness, which shielded the enemy from detection, the absence of the reserve brigade under Brigadier General Francis Barlow when Jackson attacked, and a poorly defined "panic produced by the enemy's reverse fire." He said nothing about the multitude of warnings he and Devens received from various scouts, nor a word about the valor of his troops. A few officers received some credit, such as Captain Hubert Dilger, and Howard vaguely admitted that "a part of General Schimmelfennig's and a part of [Colonel] Krzyzanowski's brigades moved gradually back to the north of the Plank Road and kept up their fire." Absolutely nothing addressed the specious accusations directed toward his men. On 10 May he issued a General Order obviously meant to uplift the spirits of his men, but the timing of this dispatch, as well as the tone which it adopted, could not have inspired many at all:

As your commanding general, I cannot fail to notice a feeling of depression on the part of a portion of this corps. Some obloquy has been cast upon us on account of the affair of Saturday, May 2. I believe that such a disaster might have happened to any other corps of this army, and do not distrust my command. Every officer who failed to do his duty by not keeping his men together, and not rallying them when broken, is conscious of it, and must profit from the past.[1]

Howard clearly failed to understand that many of his German troops did believe they "rallied" and fought, and did not blame themselves or their regimental officers, but were crestfallen by the aspersions cast upon them by the Anglo American press and the rest of the army. He was misguided in gauging the feelings of the Germans under his command at the time, and only worsened his plummeting reputation with them by issuing two unpopular orders. The first, dated 12 May, demanded the wearing of the crescent badge on all caps (many of which no longer bore them). By itself, this order was harmless. Following it, however, came the infamous ban on lager beer for all enlisted men.[2]

This order created incredible dissatisfaction. Although beer had never been officially provided to the German regiments by either state or federal authorities, and Ludwig Blenker had discouraged the selling of beer by sutlers in the German division in 1861, the occasional lager barrel still frequented the camps of the Eleventh Corps and had become a much-relished privilege the German troops believed they deserved. When Howard suddenly took that away, it was perceived as an unwarranted punishment. Practically every major German-language newspaper reported his action and the soldiers' reactions. A private in the 26th Wisconsin wrote a letter back home that was prominently reprinted in nearly all the major papers: "We have become Temperance men against our will," he complained. "The beer is gone forever, and now it's all water-drinking for us. . . . This General Howard is a pure Puritan, who not once will find an order good enough to sign on Sunday. Honestly a worse exchange the Eleventh Corps could not have made. 'If we only still had our Sigel!' is the correct and universal complaint." The Philadelphia *Freie Presse* claimed elsewhere in the same issue that the Eleventh Corps was now "completely demoralized." Captain Howell of the 153rd Pennsylvania passed over the beer issue but was certainly not upbeat when he wrote his wife on 10 May that "our last movement did not amount to much and our 11th corp has to bear all the blame . . . I suppose it will be investigated and the blame be putt where it belongs." Howell's comrade, Lieutenant Reuben J. Stotz, reiterated the former's displeasure. He claimed as late as 2 June that "the Eleventh Corps is censured very much, but I know that some regiments fought bravely, and no blame should be put on such."[3]

Howell and Stotz were mild in their descriptions of the despondency that descended over the Germans of the Eleventh Corps. Soldiers in other regiments, especially those that had fought hard and suffered heavy losses, were far more crestfallen. Adam Muenzenberger of the 26th Wisconsin wrote of his regiment's return to its old camp at Brooke's Station: "When we reached our camp again, and pitched our tents, we saw only misery. One-third of the tents in the camp were empty. And why? Because those who had occupied them were no more. Where are they? Dead! In the hospitals. Captured by the rebels. That is the worst thing that could happen to a regiment that was once so excellent." Muenzenberger's comrade, Frederick Winkler, declared on 7 May that "the army, at least our corps, is demoralized; officers talk of resigning and a spirit of depression and lack of confidence manifests itself everywhere; this may be, and I hope is, transitory." The *depth* of the demoralization would improve as the men of the 26th and other hard-fighting regiments came to terms with their losses and put time between themselves and the events of 2 May, but it would not vanish because of the prejudicial criticisms lodged against the Germans from within and without the army. Huge numbers of officers from the German regiments resigned and asked for leaves of absence following the battle, beginning just days afterward and continuing through early June. These actions were not simply the result of losing so many comrades—they had to do with indignance. Officers in the 26th Wisconsin resigned wholesale, but found their resignations unaccepted. In the 119th New York, four company-grade officers resigned and six received a leave of absence. In the 58th New York, the major and three lieutenants tendered their resignations and four other officers went on leave. The 82nd Illinois lost five officers who requested transfers out of the Army of the Potomac and four more resigned, whereas the lieutenant colonel, a captain, and four lieutenants resigned in the 68th New York.[4]

Colonel William H. Jacobs of the 26th Wisconsin went home on a leave of absence but then wrote to Carl Schurz asking to resign. Schurz was adamant in his response. "Whoever fights for a great cause has to consider that one's steadfastness will be crucially tested," he wrote, continuing, "Whoever does not pass the test has no right to claim manliness." He chided Jacobs for wanting to resign now, arguing that "to do such a move after a defeat and to give 'reluctance' as the reason for doing so" would prove the Germans' critics were right. "Even the most disheartened of your men thinks more manly," he said, admitting that "the spirit of your men is definitely better than at the time you left." Apparently, Jacobs wanted to resign as an example of how to counter false charges of cowardice. Schurz was quick to deny the request. "I cannot allow that a colonel serves his men as an example of demoralization." Jacobs ended up staying with his regiment, but the numbers of requests for leave from other officers became so unmanageable that on 27 May Howard issued an order explaining that no further leaves of absence would be granted except for medical reasons and "special circumstances."[5]

By mid-June the demoralization of the majority of the German officers in the Eleventh Corps continued unabated. The Pittsburgh *Freiheitsfreund* printed a letter from a correspondent who visited the camp of the corps. He claimed that a "comprehensive bitterness against Howard is evident that borders on insubordination—as expected, morale is quite depressed, especially among the officers, who without exception feel offended and outraged in the aftermath of the strenuous denunciations from the American press." However, the mood among some of the troops "is much improved than after the infamous affair at Chancellorsville." Music had re-entered the lives of the German rank and file and raised their spirits. "Lusty singing" could be heard at night in the camp of the 82nd Illinois, and even more so in the 26th Wisconsin. A letter from an officer in the 82nd to Colonel Hecker, recovering in a hospital from his wound, supported the correspondent's story about the enlisted men's better mindset. "The change of camp has made a good impression on the men," he wrote. "Instead of living in the middle of many abandoned and empty huts of the old camp that, of course, makes us reflect on the fate of our former comrades, we now live on a beautiful vacant hill." The privates and non-commissioned officers of the 27th Pennsylvania also had regained much of their morale, but still complained about "dirty Virginia water" and the loss of "cognacs, brandies, etc. to higher authorities" who confiscated them.[6]

Despite the improved feelings among the men of some of the German regiments as early as mid-May, an overall mood of depression still lingered, and Carl Schurz correctly ascertained that the reason lay in the inability of the German soldiers to feel vindicated. Their honor had been badly impugned, their ethnicity lampooned, and, indeed, their status as men questioned by the torrent of invective ushering from Anglo Americans. As long as the affronting allegations from the English-language press and the non-Germans of the army went publicly unrepudiated, the German soldiers would continue to feel despondent and, he feared, become unreliable. Singled out for blame for the defeat in certain newspapers, Schurz also keenly felt the sting of nativism himself and embarked on a month-long letter-writing campaign seeking justice for both himself and his fellow Germans.

No Federal military investigation was ever launched into the disaster at Chancellorsville, and that bothered Schurz to no end. As early as 7 May he began to bombard Howard, Hooker, and Secretary of War Edwin Stanton with continual protests about the treatment he and his men were receiving in the press and the army, and requests to publish the "truth" about what had happened. Schurz's individual crusade to exonerate himself and his division bears closer scrutiny than it has previously received. The German's correspondence strongly reveals his growing anxiety and frustration and the correlating collapse of morale among his troops. Howard's and Stanton's replies are also revealing, indicating a desire to keep Schurz muzzled and possibly remove him from the Eleventh Corps.

On 8 May, Howard penned a letter to Schurz expressing his concern about the accusations against him just recently published in the press. "I am deeply pained," he wrote, "to find you subjected to such false and malicious attacks." He admitted to seeing Schurz "rallying troops near the rifle pits upon the ground occupied by our Corps," which must have meant the Buschbeck line. Howard continued, "I do not believe that you could have done more than you did on that trying occasion. The allegations with reference to your division are untrue, since your troops did not occupy the front on the point of attack." The corps commander obviously knew that the reports of particularly the *New York Times* and *New York Herald*, which singled out Schurz for blame and transposed his division with Devens's, were false. He also expressed some personal sympathy for Schurz's unfortunate position, but then closed with a rebuff, no doubt in response to an earlier letter from the German asking for a specific exoneration of his division. "It would be improper for me at this time," the corps commander remarked, "to speak relatively of the conduct of different divisions. My official report will soon be made." Perhaps Howard cannot be blamed for not prematurely discussing the performance of one of his divisions in isolation from the others, but the problem for both Schurz and the Germans under his command was that Howard's brief letter contained almost nothing in it to satisfy German honor. Such hollow verbiage did nothing to assuage Schurz's indignation or that of his fellow Germans.[7]

On 12 May, Schurz wrote a nineteen-page letter (the bulk of which would later become his official report in the *Official Records*) to Howard discussing in detail the actions of his Third Division during the entire campaign, thereby offering further evidence that he and his troops fought as well as they could have. The bulk of the report covered the deployment and action of the various regiments under Schurz's command, and carefully explained the general's own whereabouts and decision-making on 2 May. But in the last two pages the general wrote frankly about his growing exasperation with the nativist press coverage and concern about his men's state of morale: "In closing this report I beg leave to make one additional remark. The 11th Corps, and by error or malice especially the 3rd Division, have been held up to the whole country as a band of cowards. My division has been made responsible for the defeat of the 11th Corps and the 11th Corps for the failure of the campaign." There was the crux of the whole issue—Schurz clearly expressed the truth of the situation facing himself and his fellow Germans, and knew it, pressing his point further. "Preposterous as this is yet we have been overwhelmed by the Army and the Press with abuse and insult beyond measure. We have borne as much as human nature can endure." Here was another very pointed, and very accurate statement. Schurz was aware that the odium now attached to his corps and especially his division was emanating both from the rest of the army *and* the Anglo American press. And he and his men could not take any more of it without serious ramifications.[8]

The concluding paragraphs of the letter demanded satisfaction. Schurz admitted that not every soldier "did his duty" on 2 May, and that the corps as a whole could have done better, but that did not warrant the badge of cowardice. "These men are no cowards. I have seen most of them fight before this, and they fought as bravely as any." That other troops in the army now "affect to look down upon the Eleventh Corps with sovereign contempt" who had earlier "behave[d] much worse under circumstances less trying" was unacceptable to Schurz, and he claimed "that every commander in this corps has a right to a fair investigation of his conduct." He "most respectfully and most urgently" asked for permission to publish the foregoing report, vouching that all the information it contained was "strictly truthful." His last sentence argued, "I deem it due to myself and those who serve under me, that the country should know it."[9]

Howard would not allow Schurz to publish his report, most likely because the corps commander felt he had no authority to grant such permission. No doubt he also did not want to be upstaged—or implicated. So Schurz did what any disgruntled subordinate would do in the same situation: he went over his superior's head. Schurz went to see Hooker sometime between 12 and 15 May and asked his permission to publish the report. Hooker said he had "no authority" to permit its publication, but that the Secretary of War, Edwin Stanton, might allow it. Despite this less than favorable meeting with Hooker, Schurz nonetheless wrote him on 17 May, again asking for the army commander's blessing, this time in the form of an endorsement when the request to Stanton was officially passed back to Hooker for his approval. Schurz prophesied that "the battle of Chancellorsville is not a thing, that happened yesterday in order to be forgotten tomorrow. It will fill a prominent page in the history of this Republic, on which every incident and the conduct of every commander and every command ought to be presented in their true light. This, you will admit, is no matter of small moment." Then he touched upon a more emotional note, just as he had done with Howard:

> You may believe me, General, when I say that the spirit of this corps is broken, and something must be done to revive it, or the Corps will lose its efficiency. Too much humiliation destroys the morale of men. I am not permitted to enumerate the causes which produced the loss of that self-confidence which formerly animated it, but I am sure the bad effect produced upon the men by the sad occurrences of the 2nd May and of the obloquy to which we have been and still are subjected, will be in some measure obliterated by a fair and complete exposition before the country of the real facts in the case. . . . Every private in this command knows and appreciates them as well, that it would be looked upon as the grossest injustice, if they were ignored in official publications. Permit me to suggest that it would have an excellent effect upon the troops if you in your report would notice those whose conduct on that occasion would justly entitle them to credit or at least to an exemption from blame and reproach.

Schurz ended his starkly written letter by asking again for the publication of his report, apologizing if anything in it "might seem objectionable," and claiming that it only purported "to protect the honor of those, whose past career and whose conduct on this sad occasion deserve regard." If Stanton did not grant his request, Schurz spared no words about his next action: "I should [then] find myself under the disagreeable necessity of asking for a court of inquiry."[10]

The same themes, and even some of the same language, appeared in Schurz's letter to Stanton: the Eleventh Corps, and especially the Third Division, was "outrageously misrepresented by the Press throughout the country," and even worse, was still being pilloried within the Army of the Potomac. The men had a right to have "the true circumstances of the case laid before the people" so that they might be fairly judged, because "it is a very hard thing for soldiers to be universally stigmatized as cowards, and apt to demoralize them more than a defeat." The morale of the troops was so bad that only if the "true character" of the events of 2nd May were brought to light would they ever again be in fighting mettle, and Schurz's report would provide the necessary information. If its publication should "seem inexpedient," the general concluded again with the threat of a court of inquiry.[11]

Stanton refused to consider the publication of Schurz's report. He also opened a discussion with Howard, and most likely Hooker as well, regarding the possible transfer of Schurz, with or without his command, to another theater of war. Apparently Schurz's constant heckling, however justified it may have been, had stirred up a bit of personal animosity. The German got wind of the scheme, an idea he admitted he himself had proposed *before* the debacle at Chancellorsville, and now considered it a personal insult above and beyond the refusal of his superiors to publish his report. In a scathing letter to Howard on 21 May, Schurz exclaimed that "the arrangement spoken of between yourself and the Secretary of War with regard to myself is not acceptable under present circumstances." He reminded his superior that he had "anticipated difficulties, which would be apt to place me in a false position," when Howard assumed command of the Eleventh Corps, and had then requested "to leave with my troops." But now, even though the current "state of things . . . justifies my apprehension in a much larger measure than I had expected," Schurz found such a solution completely out of order: "I have been ridiculously slandered by the Press. Ridiculous as it is, I have been made responsible for the defeat of the Corps. If I go now, it will seem as if I were shaken off by the Army of the Potomac. It would to a certain extent confirm the slander circulated about me. To such a thing I can never consent." He stated that he would be willing to "go anywhere" once "the mist that hangs over the battle of the 2nd May is cleared up . . . but till then I consider it a duty I owe to myself and my men to stand right here." Schurz repeated his plea to publish his report—"that is all that I ask for"—but he must have known by this point that that possibility was becoming very remote indeed.[12]

Howard and Hooker were becoming impatient with Schurz's continual barrage of letters and requests, and were aware that Schurz had written to Franz Sigel, then in New York City, regarding the need for his return to the army. The German soldiers—and not a few Anglo Americans—of the Eleventh Corps were crying out for Sigel's return. Schurz, of course, agreed that the "Yankee Dutchman" should return and take command of the Eleventh Corps. Schurz no doubt had personal reasons behind his desire to see Sigel reinstated; he and Sigel were friends and Schurz respected Sigel for both his military abilities and rapport with the troops. Most of all, however, Schurz wanted to see Howard removed. His patience with the evangelizing New Englander's refusal to publish his report had evaporated by the end of May, and with it went whatever might have been left of Schurz's respect for his corps commander. On 27 May Schurz wrote to Sigel, one of many letters he sent his friend in the two months after Chancellorsville, and claimed that Howard had told him he might acquiesce to being a division commander under Sigel. "For heaven's sake, do not consent to such a plan. He is impossible here, with Americans as well as Germans. We have all, with each hour, arrived . . . at the conclusion that he possesses neither ability nor knowledge." The day before, Schurz had ironically written another letter to Howard, expressing his regard "for a man, whom I would always be proud to call my friend," in which he nonetheless told Howard that "your expectation to retrieve your reputation with these troops, rests upon a delusion." This letter, a curious mixture of "friendly" frankness and direful warning, repeated Schurz's estimation that "the spirit of the troops is such, that I would not, under existing circumstances, dare to take any responsibility." They had "no mutual confidence," and because of this "another panic, another disaster, another disgrace, to yourself, to the troops, to all of us" would be the inevitable result. Schurz spared no words in explaining that "this is the true state of things, not with the Germans alone, but it is the same, if not worse, with the American troops. I know it to be so, and whoever may tell you differently, either is deceived or is deceiving you." Then Schurz all but asked Howard to resign: "But what good would it do to you or the troops, if we indulged in, or fostered delusions, the consequences of which might bring disaster and dishonor not only upon us, but upon thousands of good and patriotic men?" Howard had to go.[13]

Ironically, Howard simultaneously thought that Schurz had to go, and had already taken action to that effect. It is very likely that Hooker agreed with Howard in this regard, and based on Schurz's 21 May letter to Howard where he mentioned Stanton's involvement in the scheme, it is amazing that Schurz was not transferred out. Who defended Schurz? Howard did withdraw a request to have Schurz transferred, but it appears to have been made under duress and is not very convincing. Could General in Chief Halleck, perhaps, who had been accused by German Americans everywhere as an enemy to ethnic generals and ethnic concerns in the army, have purposefully kept him with the Eleventh Corps? It is possible that Halleck realized that if Schurz left, the outcry from the German American community would have been tremendous, and coupled with its demand to reinstate Sigel, might have resulted in that general's return to the army, an outcome Halleck probably wanted to avoid. Schurz would have appeared to him the lesser of two evils. Regardless of who kept Schurz in his command position, there is definite evidence that Howard traveled to Washington to see about getting rid of him. According to a 26 June letter from Schurz to Sigel, Hooker had sent Howard sometime between 21 and 26 May to the Federal capital to negotiate Howard's transfer to another command, possibly in conjunction with Sigel's potential re-assumption of command of the Eleventh Corps. But Howard apparently did not behave as intended. Schurz wrote,

I must also tell you, that Howard, whom Hooker had sent to Washington, in order to find a new position for himself, did not look for a new position for himself, but for me. I had, namely, shortly after he took command, and

after our attempts to have your return here, expressed the wish, to be transferred with my division to another department, which did not succeed.
Howard now went and tried to effect my transfer with my German regiments, and in this way to give the Corps a new character. As soon as I heard
this, I at once objected, and Hooker also declared himself absolutely
opposed to the plan. And there it rested. . . . Once more, see that you come
as soon as possible. Under Howard the Corps will go on to new misfortunes,
and later you might bitterly repent having delayed.

Sigel did delay in seizing the opportunity, according to his biographer,
because he had no written proof from Hooker that the commanding general
would support his return to corps command. No doubt Schurz's arguments
about not accepting a command position with Howard still in the corps also
proved somewhat persuasive, and Halleck certainly refused to give Sigel any
undue consideration unless his hand was forced. In the end, Howard retained
command of the Eleventh Corps, to the great chagrin of Schurz, his German
soldiers, and the German American community.[14]

The fact that Schurz believed Hooker was opposed to Howard's idea to give
the corps "a new character," meaning the dilution of its German component,
is interesting. Hooker may have been playing both sides during the intense
behind-the-scenes negotiations after Chancellorsville. Had he indeed sent
Howard to Washington for the supposed purpose of finding himself a new
command, or was that simply what Hooker told Schurz? It is possible that
Hooker, who later went on record in his accusations of the Eleventh Corps, had
actually dispatched Howard to the capital to replace Schurz under the auspices
of the German's earlier request for transfer. In the 26 May letter to Howard,
Schurz wrote that Hooker was receptive to the idea of Sigel's return, and that
he indeed favored it. Then Schurz claimed, "I know for what purpose he
desired you to go to Washington the other day and have good reasons to suppose that the result of your visit disappointed him. He told me that he would
now go to Washington himself in order to look about this matter."

Did this mean that Hooker really wanted Howard replaced, or was it instead
Schurz's impression of a carefully expressed statement from Hooker that
cloaked his true intent? It would not at all have been out of character for
Hooker to tell Howard one thing and Schurz another. For that matter, Schurz
was certainly being disingenuous with Howard, telling Sigel of Howard's weakness as a leader in his 27 May letter, only a day after he had written another
letter to Howard, explaining how much he admired his "character" and valued
his friendship. False pretenses and shrouded intentions were probably at work
on both sides in this case. Indeed, Schurz and the Germans and Howard,

Hooker, and the Anglo American high command had much to gain or lose, depending on who was replaced by whom, and when. In the end, the status quo remained, and Schurz never was permitted to publish his detailed report. Its official publication would have too easily exonerated the Germans and by fiat indicted Howard and Hooker for the disaster on 2 May. Likewise, an official court of inquiry would have probably exposed Hooker's and Howard's incompetence too much. When the Joint Committee on the Conduct of the War investigated Chancellorsville, the members were very careful not to invite Carl Schurz or any other German; interestingly, O. O. Howard also found himself left out of the circle. The Anglo American high command could not risk a change in scapegoats.[15]

Clearly, it was the fact that he could not publish his report that riled Schurz most of all, not only because he honestly believed his men were unfairly victimized, but also because his own ego had been badly damaged. The maneuvers to throw out Howard and bring back Sigel were purely secondary for him. The publication of the report would have gone a long way toward reconciling both the German troops and Schurz personally with their Anglo American leaders and comrades, but Howard and Hooker knew well what the price would be, and so Schurz and his German troops remained stigmatized as cowards. Those who had witnessed Schurz's performance at Chancellorsville never doubted his personal courage. Howard himself published letters in both the English- and German-language press refuting the allegations that Schurz had led his men in running away, and Colonel Friedrich Hecker of the 82nd Illinois, recovering in Washington, wrote publicly that "Schurz led the regiments in the retreat to good defensive positions" and "stood like a man in the rain of bullets and did his duty as soldier and general." He also privately wrote Schurz, trying to soothe his friend, claiming, "the mood in the West is strongly in your favor and you already have satisfaction in the eyes of the people." The false criticism flying about would be "terrible traps for those who lie," Hecker predicted. But these protests and hopeful prophesies could not begin to remove the stain of cowardice that had by now so embedded itself in the Anglo American public's image of Schurz and his Germans. "I fights mit Sigel und runs mit Schurz" became the snide taunt in and out of the army.[16]

The outrage Schurz forced himself to stifle, however unhappily, exploded in his subordinate Brigadier General Alexander Schimmelfennig, who was equally as proud of his German heritage as he was of his German soldiers and the reputation of his "German division." Schimmelfennig had been in the thick of the fight on 2 May, rallying his brigade from the double blow of Devens's fleeing men and the rebel onslaught, and had assisted Schurz in leading as many fragments of his disorganized division to the Buschbeck line as possible. Thanks to timely reports from various scouts, Schimmelfennig had expected Jackson's flank attack and witnessed firsthand the courage of the German soldiers under the impossible conditions in which they fought. Colonel Hecker wrote in his letter that Schimmelfennig had been "in the middle of his troops and did his utmost." It had not been enough to prevent defeat, however, and Schimmelfennig was so depressed after the battle that he remained alone in his tent for days, refusing to talk to anyone, even his favorite aide, Baron von Fritsch.[17]

One day Fritsch "scratched on his tent," entered, and confronted Schimmelfennig with the bad news being printed in the northern press. "Just what I expected," the general said. "Bring me all the papers tomorrow," he told Fritsch, and commenced to read them aloud in his tent one night, adding several expletives in German as he progressed. He rode to see Schurz, then Howard, bombarding them with his invective, and then assembled his staff and proceeded to defame the northern press, Howard, Hooker, and their staff officers. "It was an astonishingly good oratorical effort," von Fritsch wrote. Schimmelfennig then followed up his speech with a scathing official report on 10 May to his immediate superior, Schurz, which more than any other extant letter or report clearly explained the Germans' sense of betrayal.[18]

> General, the officers and men of this brigade of your division, filled with indignation, come to me, with newspapers in their hands, and ask if such be the rewards they may expect for the sufferings they have endured and the bravery they have displayed. . . . It would seem a nest of vipers had but waited for an auspicious moment to spit out their poisonous slanders upon this heretofore honored corps.

Schimmelfennig continued, stating that the accusations in the northern press were bad enough, but could be singly dealt with, as they were "but emanations from the prurient imaginations of those who would live by dipping their pens in the blood of the slain." However, the official dispatches and letters leaked to the public "dated 'headquarters of General Hooker,' and signed by responsible names," compounded the problem immensely. A detailed account of his brigade's performance at Chancellorsville followed, and then Schimmelfennig added a concluding paragraph:

> General, I am an old soldier. To this hour I have been proud to command the brave men of this brigade; but I am sure that unless these infamous falsehoods be retracted and reparations made, their good-will and soldierly spirit will be broken, and I shall no longer be at the head of the same brave men whom I have had heretofore the honor to lead. In the name of truth and

common honesty; in the name of the good cause of our country, I ask, therefore, for satisfaction. If our superior officers be not sufficiently in possession
of the facts, I demand an investigation; if they are, I demand that the miserable penny-a-liners who have slandered the division be excluded, by a public
order, from our lines, and that the names of the originators of these slanders
be made known to me and my brigade, that they may be held responsible
for their acts.[19]

Schimmelfennig felt a lot more than depression as he wrote these lines. His
language reveals a sense of betrayal, and it certainly mirrored the mood of his
troops. Like Schurz, he cried out for justice for his men. Although he filed his
report early and the mood of at least some of the German rank and file of the
Eleventh Corps would recover in the weeks ahead, Schimmelfennig probably
represented the overall feeling throughout the Eleventh Corps during May 1863.
It was not one that boded good things for the future. There was only one possible way to help heal the pain until another battle came along: turn inward,
internalize, and seek solace and vindication among other Germans. The German-language press would prove helpful in this regard, even though it did little
to change the attitudes of Anglo Americans by virtue of its foreign language.

"For the Idiocy of the Commanding Generals the Poor Corps Must Now Take the Fall"

The German American press, normally bitterly divided by partisan and
regional differences, united on the subject of Chancellorsville. Newspapers in
both the eastern and western theaters of operation expressed outrage at the
depictions of the Eleventh Corps and its German soldiers in the Anglo American press and quickly attempted to disprove the allegations, defend the courage
of the soldiers, and place the blame for the defeat where it supposedly belonged.
What was reported, the tone of the editorials, and the breadth of coverage varied somewhat from paper to paper, due in part to the political and geographic
diversity of the German American communities from which they hailed. Still,
an unmistakable sense of ethnic solidarity shone forth in the months after the
battle. The German immigrants of the Civil War era would never unify, and
the editors of the major newspapers were partially responsible for that, but the
outrage over Chancellorsville and the resulting nativistic attacks brought them
closer together than they had ever been before.

As the Eleventh Corps retreated northward with the rest of the Army of the
Potomac and reoccupied its old camps, the officers of the German regiments

found time to dispatch lists of the dead, wounded, and missing to the major German-language papers. These lists appeared side by side with the early editorials reporting the first nativist attacks lodged against the Germans. The irony was not lost on the German editors. One of the first themes they argued, and one that was ignored by the Anglo American sheets, was the fact that the numbers of dead and wounded throughout the German regiments indicated that some of them, at the very least, had held their ground and fought. There was no way they all could have run or they would not have suffered such casualties. As the Pittsburgh *Freiheitsfreund* maintained, "the dead and wounded of the late battle show they [the German regiments] did not fall back without a fight." Of course, the Germans lost hundreds as prisoners, and some of the regiments, notably those in Von Gilsa's brigade, had broken and fled, but the sacrifice in blood evidenced by the published casualty lists made allegations of German cowardice appear blind, untruthful, and disrespectful to the German dead.[20]

It struck many German Americans as especially ungrateful that the English-language papers would so quickly and enthusiastically blame the Germans for the Chancellorsville defeat when they had more than proved their mettle earlier and elsewhere in the war. One editorial in the Philadelphia *Freie Presse* recounted the martial deeds of German soldiers up to Chancellorsville, observing that "the German names which appear in the 'dead and wounded' lists of every major battle of this war show how bravely their namesakes fought. . . . Have we not sent able generals and a hundred thousand German soldiers into the field?" Sarcastically asking whether the "cowardly Germans" created the Union defeats of First Manassas, the first day at Shiloh, the assaults upon Vicksburg, and other battles, the editorial then warned its "readers of American birth" not to be persuaded by the slander of the English press. The Germans had fought well on numerous fields before and including Chancellorsville, and their spilled blood alone should have silenced any rumors of cowardice. The *Louisville Anzeiger, Milwaukee Seebote*, and Highland, Illinois *Highland Bote* even printed a translation from the "copperhead" *Milwaukee News* that defended the Germans' fighting spirit: "These people sallied forth with fervor into the field; with patience, fortitude, and bravery they endured the hardships of the camp; with unbending courage they held back the assault in every important battle." "Bravely spoken!" shouted the editor of the *Highland Bote.* "The German adopted citizens and everyone whose sons belong to the shamefully criticized division have every reason to recognize and be thankful to the *News.*" He found it highly ironic that "it is exactly a shady and denounced 'Copperhead' paper that defends the brave German soldiers whereas it is exactly one of the most 'loyal' papers that has to be the one that brands them as 'cowardly Dutchmen.'" Regardless of partisan affiliation, it would take more than the recounting of past valor to refute the criticisms lodged against the Germans.[21]

Most editors tried to prove to their readers that the reports in the Anglo American press were false, that the accusations of cowardice were founded on pure fantasy, and that the German regiments had fought as well as could be expected under the circumstances. They used all manner of official reports, letters from soldiers in the field, and even concocted evidence in their editorials—anything that could be construed as excusing the Teutonic soldiers from the calumnies heaped upon them. A sense of hyperbole or desperation pervaded some of these stories, whereas others were straightforward and reported the facts as truthfully as possible. On 12 May the *Philadelphia Demokrat* reprinted in full a letter from Adolph von Steinwehr, who commanded the Eleventh Corps' Second Division. "It heartily pleases us that a brigade of the Eleventh Corps will be freed from these accusations," the editor crowed. Steinwehr's letter reported the dispositions of his division on 2 May, praised the stand of Buschbeck's brigade, and attempted to exonerate at least his portion of the corps from criticism. It was reprinted by many newspapers after the *Demokrat*'s initial publication. "Despite their limited strength, [the second brigade] most decisively resisted the enemy," Steinwehr wrote. "Colonel Buschbeck showed such an extraordinary bravery and prudence that he can rightfully claim the thanks of the government." The Cincinnati *Woechentlicher Volksfreund*, printing the general's letter on 20 May, expressed relief that some of the truth had finally come out, stating that the letter "fulfills our expectation, that our view will be substantiated through further news." In Illinois, the wounded Friedrich Hecker and his 82nd Illinois were singled out for praise by the *Belleviller-Zeitung* for displaying "great bravery" and suffering heavy losses, indicating that Illinois Germans had nothing to fear from nativist accusations.[22]

Lieutenant Colonel Louis Schirmer, Chief of Artillery for the Eleventh Corps, wrote a letter defending the role of the corps artillery on 2 May. The New York City German-language press picked up his report and extolled it as evidence that their soldiers had fought well at Chancellorsville. The batteries of Captains Wiedrich and Dilger retreated only at the last possible moments, Schirmer claimed, and conducted their retreats well. "These captains then repeatedly took position with their batteries and directed a fearful destruction on the ranks of the storming rebels." At one point in the battle, "18 guns fired uninterruptedly and attempted to halt the advancing masses of the enemy, which they partially did," but the deadly holes in the grey ranks were repeatedly filled, and the infantry defending the artillery was forced to retreat. The artillery then had to retreat, Schirmer explained. To counter the exaggerated artillery losses claimed by the English-language press, he continued, "The losses of the artillery in our 11th Corps is 8 cannon, 10 caissons or limbers, 3 officers and c. 80 men dead and wounded and 130 horses, and not, as some papers allege, 13 and 17 guns." In closing, the artillery chief hyperbolically observed that "the artillery comported itself bravely and damaged the enemy's ranks so severely that they are completely shattered. The battlefield was bedecked with dead and wounded rebels and this compensates our losses." In a final stab at those who belittled the Eleventh Corps, Schirmer added, "that the Eleventh Corps fell back is not due to the men, but instead to their deployment and the lack of decisiveness of certain officers of high rank."[23]

Letters from two German infantrymen made the rounds of the New York and Philadelphia German newspapers in mid-May and seemed to prove the lie to nativistic accusations. A soldier in the 29th New York wrote of his stand on the Buschbeck line, "what could a brigade counting 1500 muskets do against 10 to 12,000 men . . . ?" Yet "the first brigade held firm and withdrew only after they had already been flanked on both sides by the enemy." The writer wanted the papers to print his letter "because the 29th New-York Regiment will soon be mustered out of the federal service, and the members of the same are concerned if their entrance into New York is to be honorable or honor-less." A second letter, probably written by an officer in the 75th Pennsylvania, not only appeared in the eastern papers, but was also reprinted in some of the Midwestern sheets. The accounts appearing in the Anglo American press were "incorrect, or better put, a pack of lies," and the officer felt it his duty "to present the truth as clearly and closely as possible." Yet in this instance the truth probably took a backseat to defensive indignance and exaggeration. Of the disposition of the Eleventh Corps, the writer correctly noted, "we were practically hanging or resting in the air, and the Rebels would have been regular donkeys if they had not used this opportunity." But he continued with the specious claim that the Confederates appeared "drunk" and "fought with the courage of desperation," adding that "The [entire] Corps stood firm about 3 to 4 times, and I did not notice anything resembling a panic. About 2–3 hours after the battle, the whole Corps was reassembled again, and took its new position in the battle line. . . . It is a lie, too, that our people threw their guns away, but almost everyone did throw their heavy knapsacks away . . . since no one can fight with those knapsacks on their back." Who was responsible for the disaster? "The poor Corps now has to pay for the stupidity of the commanding generals. Hooker and especially Howard have to be blamed for this defeat." Providing ammunition for another major German American defensive argument, the officer lamented, "Our Corps missed Gen. F. Sigel."[24]

Franz Sigel's absence at Chancellorsville became one of the favorite whipping boys for the German-language press. Again, this theme was universal among the newspapers regardless of political affiliation and geographic location, and was continually offered as a reason for the German soldiers' less-than-stellar performance. Ironically, however, by so doing the editors unconsciously gave a sort of tacit acknowledgment that the Eleventh Corps could have fought better. And there was certainly no guarantee that an Eleventh Corps led by Sigel would have succeeded where Howard failed, although it is likely that Sigel would have paid more attention to reports from German scouts who discovered Jackson's flank march. At the time, German Americans focused on what could have been as a salve for what actually occurred.

Philadelphia Germans were told emphatically that Sigel's presence at Chancellorsville would have changed events for the better. The *Freie Presse* argued on 7 May that "had General Sigel not arrived at his unlucky decision to relinquish the command of the 11th Corps, had this seasoned and beloved leader still stood at the peak of the German division, the scenes which the Know-Nothingism is now using to resurrect the almost-dead hate against the Germans would certainly not have occurred. That is the conviction of the majority of the Germans."[25]

The *Highland Bote* agreed that Sigel's absence created the defeat, which in turn spawned the resurge of nativism. The "bigots, witch-burners, temperance men, and Know-Nothings that hate the German population from the bottom of their soul," wrote the editor, had been silenced up to this point in the war because the Germans "had sent equal, if not better officers and soldiers as the Americans" into the service. But now the Germans' enemies had "their much wished-for opportunity to attack the 'cowardly Dutchmen.'" The editor bemoaned the lost Sigel, but wondered "what kind of spectacle would have been made" if the Eleventh Corps had still retreated under his command. "The old German-haters are and remain still German-haters!" The Pittsburgh *Freiheitsfreund* claimed that "the nativist Halleck" was to blame for forcing Sigel to resign and had carried "undue influence with Lincoln" thus far in the war. "The Generalisimo" was doing all he could to hurt the cause of the Germans, the editor complained, and the "nativist perfidy of the correspondent of the New York Times" had given him his greatest victory yet. The end result of the disaster at Chancellorsville should be the reinstatement of Sigel—"The Stonewall Jackson of the North"—at the head of his German troops. Under the leadership of Sigel once again, the Eleventh Corps might soon avenge the attacks against its honor. More ominously, the New York *Criminalzeitung und Belletristiches Journal* remarked that "it is still in question" whether "the old [German] regiments will quickly reorganize" without Sigel in charge of the corps. "The situation will probably be strongly helped if Sigel once again takes over the 11th Corps."[26]

German troops in the field agreed with the editors of the major newspapers regarding Sigel's absence and its effect on the late campaign. Corporal Friedrich Kappelman of the 82nd Illinois wrote from "Camp Schurtz" on 10 May: "I still want to say that if Sigel had been in command the 11th Corps would not have been so badly defeated." Several men of the 74th Pennsylvania agreed. Lieutenant Friedrich Knöbel asserted: "it was bad luck that Sigel was not there. Under Sigel what happened would not have come to pass, since he would not have allowed himself to be surprised." Martin Seel was certain that "if Sigel would have been commanding, this defeat would not have been suffered and this disgraceful retreat would not have occurred." Louis Schleiter, also of the 74th and attached to Howard's staff, wrote that "the mood among the troops is such, that only their unconditional trust in Sigel—and hope that he will lead them in the next battle—prevents them from sinking further. 'If only Sigel were here, this would not have happened to us!' is the cry from all of them."[27]

Soldiers in the 26th Wisconsin especially lamented Sigel's absence. Adam Muenzenberger predicted a severe consequence if Sigel did not get his command back: "the rumor goes round that General Sigel has resigned. If it is true then Scherz [sic], Steinwehr, Stehel [sic], Cryzynowski [sic] and all generals under Sigel will retire—in fact the whole staff will quit. What will become of the German Division then?" Private Ernst Damkoehler went one step further. He combined both the "numbers of casualties" argument with the yearning for Sigel, and added elements of another major German American defensive argument when he wrote his wife about the battle: "The number of dead and wounded are sure evidence how the Regiment stood up and even though the whole Corps which had covered the retreat last summer at Bull Run under Sigel and saved the whole army from being imprisoned, and lost its good name through the stupidity of a General, Howard, the regiment is well respected." Whether Damkoehler really checked to find out others' opinions of the 26th is unknown, but it is probable he was being optimistic in his assessment of his regiment's post-Chancellorsville reputation among non-Germans. He did nonetheless speak for the vast majority of northern Germans in his criticism of Howard. That criticism would become one of the keystones of the German-language press's response to Chancellorsville.[28]

At first, not all Germans on the home front thought Howard was to blame. Friedrich Brautigam of the 82nd Illinois, receiving word about the disaster while at home recovering from an earlier wound, initially believed the reports first disseminated by the Anglo American press, and primarily condemned Schurz and his division in his diary entry of 6 May. "I am completely astounded by this crushing news; I would never, never have expected this from the bearers of our German honor. . . . They should have never, never brought this disgrace on the German fighting honor," he wrote, adding, however, "I want to hear more unbiased details about this matter before I judge too harshly." None other than the editors of the prominent *New-Yorker Staatszeitung* also found fault with Schurz, falsely accusing him of conspiring to remove Sigel and having himself made head of the Eleventh Corps before the battle. But then they proceeded to blame just about everyone else in their early editorials: all of the officers in general, because they were "responsible for preventing demoralization"; the men of Schurz's division, because they reportedly ran at the first shot; "President Lincoln and especially the German radicals, who have removed capable generals and replaced them with charlatans"; and finally Howard and Hooker, who must have been outgeneraled. It did not take long, however, for Howard and the Anglo American generals to become the exclusive villains.[29]

The Philadelphia *Freie Presse* printed a letter from an indignant soldier of the 74th Pennsylvania on 18 May that solidly put the blame of the disaster on the non-Geman commanders of the Eleventh Corps. "Whoever had the bad luck to blame the 11th Corps the newspapers will make blush with shame and compare with our point of view. We soldiers know that it is the fault of Corps commander Howard and then First Division commander Devens. The first division was poorly deployed, therefore completely misaligned [for the coming attack] and broke up our division [Third] in its flight." Forty-eighter Friedrich Kapp, visiting the camps of the German regiments in the week after Chancellorsville, wrote in his diary that the men told him, "'We will again be sacrificed in the next battle because of the incompetence of the native generals,'" and complained that Howard believed in winning battles "with prayers and bible-reading." Louis Schleiter joined in the attack on the corps commander, claiming he not only failed to heed warnings from his staff about the impending Confederate attack, refused Carl Schurz's request to realign his division in expectation of it, and generally "proved utterly incompetent in his duties," but also displayed notable cowardice. Witnessing the disorder of Schimmelfennig's brigade as fleeing elements from the First Division slammed into it, Howard reportedly yelled, "Stand, boys, and do not disgrace me entirely!" and then wheeled his horse and galloped to the rear. The *Milwaukee Herold*, operating on reports from its field correspondent, stated the issue quite plainly: "The main person to blame is the commander of the 11th Corps, General Howard."[30]

Even Anglo American veterans of Devens's division wrote poorly of Devens, Howard, and Hooker. Lieutenant Colonel E. C. Culp of the 25th Ohio remembered that at least Hooker had written to Howard before Jackson's attack, ordering him to investigate the alleged movement of Confederate troops to the west and take adequate precautions. Yet "no precautions were taken," argued Culp, even after numerous reports flooded Devens's and Howard's headquar-

ters about the imminent attack, many emanating from German officers who
had spotted the mass of Confederates. "The subsequent rout of the division
was possible only from the grossest neglect of all military precautions, and there
is no doubt but that the disaster resulted from Howard's and Devens's absolute
disregard of the repeated warnings received by them." Captain Osborn of the
55th Ohio agreed with Culp that Devens had been negligent in not acting upon
the intelligence of the scouts, declaring that "he received the information
coldly," and after three visits from concerned officers under his command,
"grew impatient" and called them "frightened." Private Hurst of the 73rd Ohio
likewise blamed Devens, maintaining that the general "was not in a condition
to appreciate the situation," and "rebuked and insulted his informants for
bringing such reports."[31]

On 16 May the *Pittsburger Demokrat* published a very similar version of
events, but particularly targeted Howard: "For the idiocy of the commanding
generals the poor Corps must now take the fall. Hooker and especially General
Howard are at fault. Both received several reports that the enemy had marched
to our right flank and concentrated there great masses of troops, but nothing
was done, we stayed where we were, even our reserve artillery was not once
brought into position. It remains just like the old song, 'What matters the lion's
courage of the soldier, with Generals that are not worth a shot of gunpowder—
and yet they would have been worth that.'" Jacob Smith of the 107th Ohio
echoed this theme years later, claiming that those who brought warnings to
Howard's headquarters were "laughed at and insulted" and "taxed with cowardice." The responsibility for the disaster that befell the corps "rest[ed] with
those in command of the Corps, who alone seemed to be so blind and incredu-
lous" he said. Sergeant Karl Wickesberg of the 26th Wisconsin spared even
fewer words condemning the corps commander. "In time the truth will come
out," he wrote bitterly, "It was all General Howard's fault. General Schurz was
going to give us reinforcements and give us some cannons to help us. But that
coward, I cannot call him by another name, said he was going to try it first with
what we have here. He is a Yankee, and that is why he wanted to have us slaughtered, because most of us are Germans. He better not come into the thick of
battle a second time, then he won't escape."[32]

The German Americans of the North were outraged at being made the
scapegoats of the Chancellorsville campaign. They and their friends, sons,
brothers, and relatives had spilled ample blood in defense of the Union, and
instead of receiving sympathy for their sacrifices, got back the equivalent of a
slap in the face. Their favorite leader, Franz Sigel, had not been permitted to be
with them, and Germans maintained that had he been in command of the Eleventh Corps the battle would have ended differently. The editorials that

appeared in the German-language newspapers, as well as the contents of private letters, argued that the Germans had indeed fought as well as possible and that not all had run. Most importantly, northern Germans united in condemning the resurgence of nativism that the Anglo American press unleashed, and roundly blamed Hooker and the non-German leadership of the Eleventh Corps for the debacle. The Germans were defending themselves from the prejudice and hostility they perceived had been resurrected by the Chancellorsville defeat. As they continued to do so, they grew increasingly indignant and more affronted. By the time of the Gettysburg campaign, the North's German American citizens were so affected by this perception that they strongly questioned their place as an ethnic group within greater American society. Friedrich Hecker declared to Schurz on 21 May, "if the [Union] fails it will be considered the 'Dutch's' fault, if we win the Germans will be considered to have no share in this victory, if compromise is made they will be the scapegoats of North and South alike. If this spirit prevails among this mongrel race of all tribes in the world—and if we are still alive—they will get double payback in the election of 1864."[33]

"Let Us Organize in Defence of Our Common Honor"

From the second week of May to the middle of June 1863, the opinions of the German-language press mirrored the emotions of German soldiers in the Army of the Potomac. Shock, anger, betrayal, and finally the bitter recognition of the need to unify crept into newspapers' editorials. Sometimes just one, or a few of these emotions were present, but occasionally all of them were evident. The result, however, was the same: the Germans of the North, at least in the east, temporarily halted on the road to Americanization, more aware than ever of their own ethnicity and girded by an irrepressible resolve to defend it. The war would drag on, Germans from around the country would continue to support the Union in the field and at home, and would ultimately amalgamate with the greater American population. But they would do so on their own terms and in their own time, because to rashly assimilate meant to accept all the negative qualities of Anglo Americans that had been made so apparent by the aftermath of Chancellorsville. Many began to ask themselves what, exactly, becoming an American would garner them if Americans were themselves so bigoted. Germans' enthusiasm for the war—and consequently for Americanization—was irrevocably altered.

The Chicago *Illinois Staatszeitung* was unabashed in expounding the issue of ethnic prejudice at hand. Its 7 May issue clearly blamed *New York Times* correspondent L. L. Crounse for slandering the Germans and instigating ethnic tensions out of Republican zeal. "The correspondent of the N.Y. Times looks to create the impression in his nativistic, abolitionistic perfidy and rage as if the German sections of the Corps performed especially bad, and the American ones rather well." Another Democratic German paper, the Cincinnati *Woechentlicher Volksfreund*, attacked the Know-Nothing rhetoric of both the *Times* and the *New-York Tribune*, claiming that "the Republican Party is transforming with amazing alacrity into a pure Know-Nothing Party." Yet the fact that these New York papers and their correspondents were Republican was only a small part of the problem.[34]

Since the Anglo American journalists had made such a stark and negative distinction between Americans and Germans, the editors of the Chicago *Illinois Staatszeitung* and Pittsburgh *Demokrat* followed their lead, specifically referring to the "American parts" of the Eleventh Corps, the "American officers and men" of the Army of the Potomac, and the "American newspapers" that attacked the Germans. They unequivocally intended their readers to see the clear-cut difference between Americans and Germans. They also did not classify German-speakers as German Americans, or, as Theodore Roosevelt would later put it, "hyphenated Americans"; rather, the editors of these two important newspapers considered them Germans and those who spoke English as Americans. These certainly were not the words of men who wanted their readers to become any more American than they already were. If the Americans so despised us now, the editorials insinuated, why bother becoming more like them? Additionally, the Americans, by sinking so low as to falsely accuse German soldiers of single-handedly losing the battle of Chancellorsville, and by flinging ethnic epithets, had proven just how vulgar they really were. The American journalists had even changed the spelling of Adolphus Buschbeck's name—the only German mentioned in a positive light—to the more anglicized "Bushbeck." The Germans, editor Georg Ripper of the *Demokrat* claimed, would not follow such a base example, even though he and other German editors had, "with mathematical certainty," concluded that American regiments and leaders were "really to blame" for the tragedy: "Yet we will not imitate the evil example of the Times correspondent, we make no malicious differences between the nationalities; the above parallels clearly show how groundless overall and stupid it is to make the Germans especially responsible for the sorry shame of the Eleventh Corps of the Army of the Potomac."[35]

Other German papers agreed with the *Staatszeitung* and the *Demokrat*. The Republican Cleveland *Wächter am Erie* called the preoccupation of the Anglo American press with purported German cowardice "stinking nativism." The Republican Pittsburgh *Freiheitsfreund*, arch-rival of Ripper's organ, echoed his

words in its 9 May editorial, attacking the "stupidity of the N.Y. Times correspondent for reactivating nativism" and blaming the other English-language
newspapers for reprinting the *Times* version of the battle verbatim. Lamenting
the anglicization of Buschbeck's name, the editor emphasized "how groundless
and stupid it is to single out the Germans especially for the tragedy" when it
was predominantly the American regiments under Devens that caused the rout.
The Allentown *Friedensbote* printed the *New York Times* version of Chancellorsville, but interspersed most paragraphs with several sentences of edited commentary. For example, at the conclusion of the *Times*'s account of "cowardly
Dutchmen" running straight back to Hooker's headquarters and the U.S. Ford,
the editor of the *Friedensbote* inserted, "The above reports appear to be not
without animosity when one considers that the troops that they describe have
until now developed the highest sense of courage under other commanders."
The editor agreed with his German colleagues in other cities that the "overwhelming power" facing the Eleventh Corps made ultimate retreat necessary,
but to condemn the Germans alone for that retreat was both prejudicial and
ignorant of the facts at hand. The Philadelphia *Freie Presse* reprinted Carl
Schurz's official complaints and requests for a court of inquiry on 12 May, in
order to clear his name and take a stab "at the insidious traitor's band in the
North," who were "overjoyed at the opportunity to blame Gen. Schurz for
incompetence and even cowardliness." Thus the newspaper portrayed the Germans' accusers not only as prejudiced liars, but also deadly enemies to the
country.[36]

Perhaps to back up his German comrades' complaints, a non-German member of the 119th New York wrote in to the Philadelphia *Evening Bulletin* to help
clear the name of Schurz and the other Germans. He was present when "three
times notice was sent to General Hooker that the enemy was turning our right
flank," and once the attack commenced, claimed "Schurz's division did not
throw down their arms and retire without firing a shot." Instead, the First Division had been the first attacked and the first to retreat, "it was they who broke
our line," and after forming a makeshift line behind the then disorganized
Third Division, "*began to fire into us.* Thus we were not only exposed to fire
from the enemy on our front and left flank, but from our own men in the rear.
Who *could* stand under such circumstances?" The First Division, which most
Germans knew was half-composed of American regiments, hence appeared to
be as bad as the Confederate enemy in this report. It would not be long until
northern Germans adopted a corresponding attitude to non-Germans, especially those who continued to berate Teutonic soldiers. Lieutenant Knödel of
the 74th Pennsylvania wrote again to the *Pittsburger Volksblatt* claiming "that I
don't doubt the entire blame will ultimately be thrown on us [by the general

public]." After explaining why Sigel's presence would have changed the outcome of the battle, he added, "I was efficient in the line of fire, but have no desire to offer my life again, as if in a game, to the idiocies which occurred in the 'upper levels.' Schimmelfennig has had enough of this type of military leadership and will probably resign." Schimmelfennig did not resign in the end, but did request to be transferred out of the Army of the Potomac when anti-German rhetoric surfaced again after Gettysburg.[37]

Speaking for all northern Germans, the *Philadelphia Freie Presse* issued a warning to its readers and German Americans in general on 29 May. The anti-German attacks in the Anglo American press had not abated, the morale of German soldiers in the Eleventh Corps had bottomed-out, and "what did it all mean?" editor Friedrich Thomas asked. "Is it stupidity or cunning calculation? Why now are only the Germans singled out?" Waxing sarcastic, he continued, "Are people angry in certain circles that the Germans and their leaders at Camp Jackson, Carthage, Pea Ridge, Bull Run, Shiloh, etc. did not act cowardly, but took on the war with a good attitude and boldly beat the 'southern brothers' of our northern cowards? Or do they wish that the Germans in our armies are forced home, in order to weaken the courage of our arms? What is it then?"[38]

The editor then suggested what he believed was the true motivation behind American nativist attacks: the German language. Emphasizing, like Georg Ripper of the *Pittsburger Demokrat*, the differences between Germans and Americans by clearly terming those who read German papers as German and those who did not as American, the editor claimed the actual "separateness" of the German-language press made Germans everywhere appear completely unlike "Americans" as well as incomprehensible to them. So long as the German press existed, Americans would never understand the Germans, because "the Americans don't understand German; moreover, they also don't know what the Germans want, and it really doesn't matter what is said, whether we remain quiet or whether we continue in a language that they cannot read. The German newspapers are for the Americans so many empty sheets of paper." Rhetorically asking what could be done to help the situation, the editor threw up his hands in despair. The German press would continue to print in German, and "hence the result is the same: because one doesn't understand us, he mistrusts, despises, and encroaches upon us. And that will last as long as the Germans neglect to make themselves understandable to Americans through the press." Thomas clearly believed the Germans were caught in a vicious circle, one which spawned nativist hate and misunderstanding. Just as important, they were unable, or unwilling, to leave the circle (i.e., the German language) behind because it was integral to their ethnic identity.[39]

In some German-language newspapers, warnings began to appear in the editorial sections about the nativist threat. Reports circulated that wounded Eleventh Corps soldiers had been struck down in the streets of Washington simply because they were Germans and therefore "cowards." Fear that the temperance movement would gain momentum from the recent Anglo American criticism grew rife. Indeed, the old nativists of the 1850s were frequently enmeshed with the temperance cause, so it was easy in this atmosphere of anxiety and despair to link the two together. After reporting an account of an anti-German editorial in a local American paper that accused Schurz's soldiers of being drunk at Chancellorsville, the *Highland Bote* of 22 May announced:

GERMANS WATCH OUT!

The Know-Nothings and Temperance men left us alone for a while because they needed us Germans for voting and fighting. Now the humbug is back again. . . . We must pay attention when [the local towns of] Lebanon and Greenville already belong to the Temperance men; it is high time the local German element unifies a little. Otherwise we will be spied upon, criticized, and labeled "traitors" right and left, during which time the enemy of our race (the Know-Nothings and Temperance men) will wait for an opportunity to grind us under foot.[40]

Less than a week later, on 4 June, the Philadelphia *Freie Presse* reported yet another slander against Germans. Word leaked out that the officers of the 25th, 55th, and 75th Ohio of McLean's brigade wished their regiments to be formally separated from the rest of the Eleventh Corps and had put that request in writing. This action was not motivated from "mistrust of our commanding general, but instead the unsoldierly character of the German troops with which we have been forced to serve, and with whom we must undeservedly share the blame." Under the headline, "New Nativistic Attacks Against the German Volunteers," the editor responded, "We can scarcely hold this news to be true." He recounted the "hundreds of knowledgeable witnesses" who had exonerated the German soldiers of the Eleventh Corps, placing the blame for the defeat instead on faulty deployment and the poor judgment of Howard, Devens, and Hooker before the battle. What editor Thomas failed to remember was that most of these witnesses had their reports published in German newspapers, and hence the American public did not read them. Still, how could the truth be so easily ignored? "Despite the energetic protest" of the 107th Ohio, a predominantly German regiment which refused to sign the petition of the other Ohio regiments, "it appears the will of nativism got its way. From Washington it is reported the German regiments will be detached from the 11th Army Corps and attached to Heintzelmann's Corps." If this exchange takes place as a "punishment," "without a military investigation" of the performance of the Germans in the last campaign, it would be seen by them as "a new, indeed egregious insult, which a tenacious nativism can hurl in the face of German honor." The proposed transfer never occurred, but the readers of Thomas's paper had probably reached the limit of their tolerance. The latest news was more than a betrayal of trust—it was an outright attack. It was time to quit refuting each new ethnic barb individually in each newspaper, clinging to a forlorn hope that the nativism would simply go away. The time had come to organize formally against the American assault.[41]

In late June, leading Germans from around the North, representing various local German American political societies, held a forum in Washington, D.C. to create a blanket organization to coordinate and unify the efforts of the local groups. Many of the delegates were minor forty-eighters and more than a few were federal bureaucrats working in the capital. They believed that in order to address the virulent rebirth of nativism, Germans needed to be nationally unified to meet the threat head-on. Only through political unity could the Germans then exercise the necessary strength, as one distinct voting bloc, that would force the hand of any major political party espousing anti-German philosophies. In this way, nativism could be contained and ultimately defeated. The delegates unanimously voted to form a pan–North American German National Committee, which would be based in Washington, coordinate the political activities of the local "chapters," represent the national interests of Germans across the North, and agitate to stifle the anti-German prejudice sweeping the country. "The need for a German American Organization is unquestionably before us," declared chairman Dr. C. F. Schmidt. "The ignominy, which was recently piled with lies and perfidy upon the German regiments and their leaders in the 11th Army Corps, is a new stimulus for an organization which alone promises us protection and power." The official address of the convention, signed by over thirty delegates, was reprinted in German newspapers throughout the North, and included strong words of indignation toward the federal government, the two political parties, the Union leagues, and especially the American press. Yet the delegates claimed "we are far from the thought of wanting to build a German-nativistic party. We wish as Germans to organize only on the grounds of equality and brotherhood as American citizens." They even went so far as to extend the olive branch to Anglo Americans but insisted that all Germans must persevere to achieve the goals of the national organization. Espousing a political philosophy described as "the radical middle," the German leaders proclaimed "through a pan-German organization we will raise ourselves at least to a balance of power in the decision-making process of all important political questions."[42]

On 2 June a great German American rally was held in the Cooper Institute in New York City specifically to denounce the charges made against the Germans in the Eleventh Corps and to demand satisfaction from the Anglo American press. It was the largest assembly of Germans yet witnessed in the United States. Thousands, primarily from the eastern states, attended, and the audience reflected the diversity of the German American population: old forty-eighters, filled with fiery indignance at the stain on German honor, crippled German veterans who demanded justice for their dead comrades, widows who had lost their husbands in the war. Presided over by the noted forty-eighter Friedrich Kapp, the rally was chaired by noted insurance mogul Hugo Wesendonck and included speeches by Brigadier General von Gilsa, Charles Goepp, and Kapp himself. Those present adopted nine resolutions that defended the Germans of the Eleventh Corps, explained the rout, thanked Germans soldiers for their prior service, blamed Howard, Hooker, and Halleck for the disaster, asked for Sigel's reinstatement, and lamented the resurgence of nativism.

Wesendonck opened the meeting by saying "this meeting is no political demonstration. . . . It has been called and is supported by men of all parties, and is emphatically a German demonstration." He then recounted the attacks made by the American press and compared them to what really happened at Chancellorsville, conclusively reiterating the major German American defensive arguments, especially the need to reinstate Franz Sigel. The criticism from the English-language newspapers especially rankled him. "Never in my life have I felt so indignant," Wesendonck continued, "as when I read these reports. Never has such a flood of insult been poured upon brave soldiers. Never have any reports contained more falsehoods and baser calumnies." Why did they continue, even "to this day," he asked? "They are not meant to disparage the German soldier only, they are aimed at the German population of the United States generally, nay, they are flung at the German nationality everywhere. It is our duty to rebuke these columniators, and to hurl these slanders back into the teeth of their fabricators."

Pennsylvanian Charles Goepp then rose to accentuate the "national blunder" that was made in accusing the Germans. The North needed the Germans now more than ever, he asserted. "From the inception of this war we have stood shoulder to shoulder with the loyal natives of every clime; and never dreamed of asking that our patriotism, which is a patriotism of choice, should be otherwise rewarded." Germans had loyally fought on every battlefield in every southern state, and now that a scapegoat was needed to explain the latest Federal defeat, the Germans were singled out. "It is for us to demand" that this wrong be corrected, he argued. "After the unprovoked and unrebuked assault which has been made, it is right, it is proper, it is a duty, to set forth our estimate of the value of our active adhesion to the Union cause."[43]

Goepp then listed all the achievements of the Germans up to Chancellorsville, exclaiming that the bitterest Union defeats were caused by mediocre and naive American generals. Somewhat disingenuously, he continued, "Without one word of invidious comparison, we do insist that the American people stand in need of the military knowledge of the German immigrants. Without a tinge of bitterness we say, that they have not, by their actions, manifested a sense of the full extent of that necessity." Were this oversight "simply a wrong," it would not receive such attention by the Germans. "But it is worse than a wrong," he insisted, "it is a blunder." Goepp then ended on an ominous note:

> So hasty has been the cry of slander against the German rank and file, that the criminal shortcomings of the high officers have passed unnoticed, and are likely to be repeated and repeated, until the command ceases to be useful to the country. . . . Soldiers cannot fight under the conviction that they are predestined to be the scapegoat of the imbecility of their commanders. If the Eleventh Corps is left under this ban, it will be betrayed, and slaughtered, and broken in engagement after engagement, until not a man of it will be left to bear the designation of the "cowardly Dutchman."[44]

Following Goepp, Friedrich Kapp took the stand to thunderous applause. "All we ask is justice," he proclaimed. "We desire to be no more, but we will be no less, than Americans; we mean to be weighed in the scale of our actions and our merits." He mentioned the slanders of the American press again, agreeing with his fellow speakers that Germans would no longer stand such insults. "I am free to confess myself deeply pained, by the ill-conceived hatred of the Americans which is so ready to burst forth, at the first semblance of an occasion." Reiterating Goepp's argument that the Americans were blind to the martial attributes of the Germans, he continued, "But it pains me still more to see, even at this late day, the Americans are so entirely unaware of the momentous sacrifices yet to be made" and still "are carried away by a paltry national conceit" aimed at Germans. "If this ebullition of ill feeling were a crime only, it would be of little use to protest against it. But it is worse, it is a blunder. It must inevitably chill the enthusiasm of the German population, and retard, if not prevent the reenlistment of the soldiers whose terms are just expiring." Kapp recalled that German volunteers "enlisted readily" before Chancellorsville, but now, "of those regiments which have just returned, not fifty men have reenlisted, in spite of liberal bounties and promises." Why was that? "I never knew a soldier who was willing to fight the enemy in front, when his comrades, or the people for whom he fights, stand ready to stab him from behind." Raising his voice for a climactic ending, Kapp issued a universal appeal to all Germans: "Let us organize in defence of our common honor." The cheers and applause following his speech reverberated out into the New York evening.[45]

The rally at the Cooper Institute in New York was duplicated on a smaller scale in several other northern cities with sizeable German American populations. Philadelphia, for instance, witnessed its own version on 13 June in the Turnerhalle "to answer the infamous calumnies that have been spread about the German regiments of the Eleventh Corps." Two Philadelphia officers in the 29th New York gave speeches, as did the editors of both the major German American daily newspapers and other respected dignitaries from the German community. Many of the primary arguments emphasized in New York were repeated, but the issue of a resurgent nativism took center stage. "Nativism, which was believed dead, only hid itself, and jumped at the first opportunity to air its hate through slanders," one delegate declared, and "the government owes the Germans a restoration of their honor through the publication of official reports." The well-attended rally closed with the adoption of resolutions demanding these reports, thanking German soldiers for their efforts thus far in the war, calling for the sacking of incompetent generals, and praising the bravery of the German soldiers at Chancellorsville. The meeting ended "with three hurrahs for the 11th Army Corps."[46]

Some of the Anglo American newspapers realized after the Cooper Institute rally, especially, that they had strongly offended the German speakers of the North. While the rally received no coverage from the *New York Herald* or Chicago *Tribune*, the 3 June *New York Times* included a long report of "the German Indignation Meeting." It reprinted almost all of Wesendonck's speech and excerpts from Kapp's. The report was decidedly objective, neither ridiculing the meeting nor praising it, but did specifically mention that the "mass of German citizens" assembled at the Cooper institute included "many names of weight and moment" in the German community and a not "inconsiderable contingent" of women. The next day the *Times* made small attempts at reconciliation, admitting that it had been too hasty in blaming the Germans for the defeat at Chancellorsville. The editor claimed to "regret to see a disposition in certain quarters to make an invidious distinction against our German soldiers," adding that "the miserable differences between the foreign and native inhabitants have outlived their day. One of the greatest results of this war will be the assimilation of all American blood." The Philadelphia *Freie Presse* reprinted this editorial without comment a week later, but it was clear the damage had already been done, and that the *Times*'s efforts were too little, too late. The major eastern

German papers, namely the *Freie Presse, Philadelphia Demokrat, New-Yorker Staatszeitung,* and New York *Criminalzeitung und Bellestrisches Journal,* all covered the rally in New York in great detail and with strong enthusiasm. Moreover, only a week after reprinting the *Times* article, one-half of the "current news" section of the *Freie Presse* was taken up by the report from the national German meeting in Washington, and the *Criminalzeitung* reported on 5 June that "a great weariness of America is showing itself among the German immigrants who fled here as political refugees after 1848."[47]

The German Americans of the North were strongly affected by the battle of Chancellorsville and the Anglo American response to it. Nativist attacks in the English-language newspapers, especially, wreaked havoc with German trust and morale. Soldiers and newspaper editors alike rallied to the defense of the German troops accused of cowardice, carefully refuting the outspoken criticism in the American press. Yet the shock and outrage at these accusations changed into a bitter sense of betrayal, and later into a realization that the best defense against nativism lay in unity. Germans throughout the northern states joined together for the first time in a real attempt to present a common defense against American prejudice. There was no doubt in the minds of the German immigrants at this time who was a German and who an American. Articles appeared in German-language newspapers starkly distinguishing the difference between Germans and Americans in the Chancellorsville affair, and several national meetings occurred in which German patriotism and virtue were held up against American slander and military failure. The German Americans of the North had clearly experienced a severe jolt on the road to Americanization. Chancellorsville forced them first to defend themselves, and then look to one another for solace and support. They would continue looking inward after Gettysburg.

A recruitment poster for the 40th Pennsylvania, later known as the 75th Pennsylvania Volunteers, 1861. Such posters were commonplace throughout the North's German American communities in the early months of the war. The Library Company of Philadelphia.

One of many handbooks translated into German during the war, *Lieder für Soldaten* (Songs for soldiers) contained verses for pro-Union patriotic aires. Other publications were more overtly ethnic, containing old German ballads and war songs. Below: two pages from the *Lieder*. The Library Company of Philadelphia.

16   Vom Kampf mit den Waffen.

Ob Jedem, der zum Kampfe geht,
Und Jedem, der Gefahr besteht!
Bald kehrt der Friede wieder;
Dann schallen Dankeslieder.

7.

Zuruf an Krieger.

Mel. Erhalt' uns, Herr, bei deinem Wort.

1. Bewaffnete! Der Kriegerstand
Bewacht, beschützt das Vaterland
Und stehet dem Gesetze bei,
Damit sein Ausspruch wirksam sey.

2. Gehorsam, Muth und Tapferkeit
Seyd stets zu zeigen gern bereit,
Doch auch im Krieg vergesset nicht,
Daß Fried' der Endzweck eurer Pflicht!

3. Ehrt Recht und Sitte, fürchtet Gott,
Nie sey die Wahrheit euer Spott!
Auch Kriegern soll sie heilig seyn,
Auch Krieger sollen Sünde scheun.

Vom Kampf mit den Waffen.   17

4. Zieht ihr in's Feld, so störet nie
Die Rechte Andrer—schützet sie!
Gewalt übt ungeheißen nicht,
Stets leit' euch Lieb' und Christenpflicht!

5. Seht zu, daß Keiner Frevel treib'
Daß Jeder schöne Greis und Weib
Und Kind, dazu den ruh'gen Mann,
Der widerstehn nicht mag noch kann.

6. Wer vor euch niederfällt, den hebt
Mit Bruderarmen auf! Wer bebt,
Den tröstet! Brüder, nie vergießt
Blut, wenn der Feind entwaffnet ist!

7. Dann seyd ihr wahre Helden, seyd
Vertheidiger der Menschlichkeit,
Dem Volk im ganzen Lande werth,
Von Gott und Vaterland geehrt.

8. Gott sey mit euch in Fried' und Krieg,
Mit euch in Niederlag' und Sieg,
Mit euch im Leben und im Tod —
Hier segne, dort beglück' euch Gott!

Colonel Henry Bohlen and staff, 1862. Bohlen was supposedly shot by his own men at Freeman's Ford. Robert Diem Collection, US Army Military History Institute.

Cross Keys battlefield, Virginia, c. 1912. Massachusetts Commandery, Military Order of the Loyal Legion and the US Army Military History Institute.

John C. Frémont's bungling at Cross Keys cost the Union a victory but provided the German Division its first taste of combat. Pennsylvania State Archives.

Augustus C. Hamlin served in the Eleventh Corps at Chancellorsville and later wrote a history of the battle exonerating his corps' performance. Pennsylvania State Archives.

Colonel William H. Jacobs of the 26th Wisconsin wanted to resign his commission after Chancellorsville but was rebuked by Carl Schurz, who wrote, "Whoever fights for a great cause has to consider that one's steadfastness will be crucially tested." Pennsylvania State Archives.

Colonel John A. Koltes of the 73rd Pennsylvania fell leading his German brigade at Second Manassas, buying time for Pope's army to retreat. Pennsylvania State Archives.

Colonel Wladimir Krzyzanowski was one of the most tactically gifted officers in the Eleventh Corps and fought effectively throughout the war. He was never promoted, reportedly because certain congressmen could not pronounce his name. Pennsylvania State Archives.

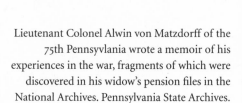

Lieutenant Colonel Alwin von Matzdorff of the 75th Pennsyvlania wrote a memoir of his experiences in the war, fragments of which were discovered in his widow's pension files in the National Archives. Pennsylvania State Archives.

T. A. Meysenberg, O. O. Howard's assistant adjutant general, probably protected his superior's reputation by withholding the famous "9:30 order" from the Eleventh Corps files until after the Gettysburg campaign. Pennsylvania State Archives.

Elias Peissner, beloved colonel of the 119th New York, alleged illegitimate son of the king of Bavaria, and friend of Carl Schurz, killed at Chancellorsville. Pennyslvania State Archives.

Major General Franz Sigel, darling of German Americans, had a sensitive ego and questionable military ability. His absence at Chancellorsville was strongly lamented by the German-language press. Pennsylvania State Archives.

Major General Carl Schurz. His fate and that of German America were intertwined during the war. Massachusetts Commandery, Military Order of the Loyal Legion and the US Army Military History Institute.

Brigadier General Louis Blenker, commander of the German division, 1861–62. Massachusetts Commandery, Military Order of the Loyal Legion and the US Army Military History Institute.

Colonel Adolph von Hartung, 74th Pennsylvania. US Army Military History Institute.

Brigadier General Francis C. Barlow. The detachment of his brigade from the rest of the Eleventh Corps proved a costly mistake. Massachusetts Commandery, Military Order of the Loyal Legion and the US Army Military History Institute.

Brigadier General Alexander Schimmelfennig, vitriolic defender of German American honor. Military Order of the Loyal Legion and the US Army Military History Institute.

Major General Howard striving to rally his troops on 2 May 1863. *Battles and Leaders of the Civil War*, ed. Robert Underwood Johnson and Clarence Clough Buel (New York: Thomas Yoseloff, 1956), 3:185.

Drawing on tan paper of Dowdall's Tavern and the 11th Corps line in front of it. Caption: "Dowdall's Tavern, about 6:30 PM on 2 May 1863, sketched by artist A. R. Waud." This remarkable pencil drawing clearly shows the Buschbeck line forming up in front of the tavern (Howard's Headquarters) as refugees from the shattered First and Third Divisions stream toward its temporary safety. Note the intact regiment in the foreground retreating in an orderly manner. Library of Congress, Prints and Photographs Division.

Below: The Wilderness Church appeared much like this wartime Matthew Brady photo when fighting swirled around it on 2 May 1863. Courtesy of Library of Congress, Prints and Photographs Division. Above: The Wilderness Church today.

National Union Ticket

ONE FLAG, ONE COUNTRY.

Für Präsident:

Abraham Lincoln
Von Illinois.

Für Vice-Präsident:

Andrew Johnson
von Tennessee.

Man untersuche vorsichtig das nachstehende Ticket.

Wähler.–Electors.

Morton McMichael,	Robert Parke,	John Wister,
Thomas Cunningham,	William Taylor,	David M'Conaughy,
Robert P. King,	John A. Hiestand,	David W. Woods,
G. Morrison Coates,	Richard H. Coryell,	Isaac Benson,
Henry Bumm,	Edward Halidah,	John Patton,
William H. Kern,	Charles F. Read,	Samuel B. Dick,
Barton H. Jenks,	Elias W. Hale,	Everard Bierer,
Charles M. Runk,	Charles H. Shriner,	John P. Penney,
Ebenezer M'Junkin,		John W. Blanchard.

Gedruckt bei King und Baird, No. 607 Sansomstraße, Philadelphia.

German American pro-Republican election poster, 1864. The Library Company of Philadelphia.

74th Pennsylvania Infantry monument at Gettysburg, in an 1888 photograph taken by W. H. Tipton. Note the boldly inscribed words, "German Regiment." Veterans of the regiment were proud of their regiment's ethnicity years after the war ended. Courtesy: Ken and Sue Boardman Collection.

„Das Ganze umschließt ein Rahmen mit sie mit unerschütterlicher Ruhe auf die sich Eichenblättern, oben in einem weiblichen vor ihr abspielenden Ereignisse herab-Kopf endend, die Geschichte darstellend, wie schaut.

German American monument in honor of Revolutionary and Civil War veterans, unveiled in Dayton, Ohio, in 1910. *Deutsch-Amerikanische Geschichtsblätter.*

6

Nativism and German Ethnicity after Chancellorsville

The aftermath of Chancellorsville confirmed for most northern Germans that the hated nativism of the 1850s had returned. In the last two years of the war, the residue of the battle lingered long, especially among German soldiers and civilians from the eastern states. The Eleventh Corps was split up in the fall of 1863, one division headed for the sea islands of South Carolina and the other two, along with the Twelfth Corps, sent west to relieve the Confederate siege of Chattanooga. Despite a good fighting record and participation in some of the bloodiest battles of the war, the legacy of Chancellorsville haunted the German regiments of the now shrunken corps. Open, public prejudice against the Germans from Anglo Americans never reoccurred to the extent it had after the battle, but the Germans, their ethnic consciousness now on high alert, were sensitive to even the slightest insult. The German-language press, its indignance somewhat assuaged by the victory at Gettysburg and subsequent triumphs, nonetheless quickly condemned any instances of nativism that cropped up, persisted in defending Franz Sigel as the champion of German America, and interpreted political events, such as the election of 1864, through ethnically tinted lenses. The mass meetings following Chancellorsville gave birth to the idea of a pan–German American political organization and a new political party, and Carl Schurz, who had failed in his earlier attempts to vindicate himself and his men, continued in his quest to subdue those who would criticize him and his soldiers.

Even among German American troops in the western theater, who were not directly affected by the events of 2 May 1863 and had known only victory, instances of nativism reminded them how Anglo Americans perceived them and made them question their role in the war. Perhaps as a result of the prejudice they experienced and the raised ethnic awareness that ensued, officers in the German regiments made certain that their commands remained in the hands of Germans, at the expense of Anglo Americans. If Americanization occurred during the last years of the war, its progress among the northern Germans was limited.

"I Did Not Forget About What Was Done to Us Last Spring after the Battle at Chancellorsville"

The campaign and battle of Gettysburg ended better for the Germans of the Eleventh Corps than Chancellorsville had. There were, however, some uncanny similarities between the two battles: once again, the men of the corps found themselves poorly deployed, outnumbered, and facing Jackson's veterans (without Jackson himself). Again, after most regiments had fought as long as humanly possible, they retreated, some of them in disorder, and casualties were high. A few German regiments, such as the 75th Pennsylvania, were so badly cut up by their stand north of the town on 1 July that they were reduced to the size of prewar companies. Nonetheless, just like after Chancellorsville two months before, cries of "flying Dutchmen" and "cowardly Germans" still rose from the lips of Anglo American soldiers, especially those of the First Corps, which also fought hard on the first day. They blamed the overlapping of their right flank, and subsequent retreat, on the premature giving way of the Eleventh Corps. The withdrawal of the two corps through the town of Gettysburg was disorganized and rapid, the Confederates hot on their heels, but in the end both corps rallied on Cemetery Hill and beat back several attacks by the enemy on 2 July. The big difference between the aftermaths of Chancellorsville and Gettysburg involved the Anglo American press. Because the Army of the Potomac prevailed in the latter battle, the correspondents and editors extolled the Federal victory and were not as interested in finding scapegoats. A few minor papers focused in on the Germans, castigating them for "running again," but these accusations were drowned out by the greater number and influence of papers that either praised the Germans or dwelled on the overall northern triumph.[1]

Gettysburg, however, still raised the ethnic consciousness of the North's German Americans. This time they were not fighting off nativist attacks in the English-language press, but rather basking in the achievements of their soldiers in the Eleventh Corps. Pennsylvania's German-language press, in particular, was so preoccupied with reporting the deeds of the German regiments that it seemed to disregard the significance of the greater Union victory. The editors, ecstatic in their conviction that the Germans had unilaterally fought well this time, believed Teutonic honor had been somewhat restored, Chancellorsville redeemed. The nativism of May and June, certainly not forgotten, had been superseded, at least for now.[2]

The rank and file of the German regiments of the Eleventh Corps did not feel the same way. Certainly the victory at Gettysburg was gratifying, but their immense blood sacrifice there, followed by either little notice in the American press or even further accusations of cowardice, made the triumph bittersweet. A visitor to the hospitals of the Eleventh Corps directly after the battle noticed that the German soldiers somehow seemed to be the last to receive medical attention, the last to receive their suppers, and "the government [did] almost nothing at all" to alleviate their plight. Although the corps "suffered fearfully in the late battle," its reputation was "still smeared by other corps and accused of cowardice, probably because it is mainly composed of Germans." The sheer number of wounded "contradicts this lowly accusation." The major of the 26th Wisconsin, wounded at Gettysburg, wrote a bitter letter of resignation condemning the lack of official repudiation of the false accusations, and First Lieutenant Peter Boffinger, also of the 26th, wrote from his hospital bed, "a friend is worth something here, because the Americans are very inclined to hold back the Germans. They view the immigrants as only good for work, and cheat the same where they can."[3]

As they were shipped away from the familiar fields of Virginia to their new assignments in Tennessee and South Carolina—or, rather, banished from the Army of the Potomac, as some of them maintained—the German soldiers of the old Eleventh Corps retained negative memories of Chancellorsville, the Army of the Potomac, and nativism. Even after several months in their new locations, some soldiers still rankled. Carl Schurz, right before departing for Tennessee with his division, confided to his sister-in-law, "I count the past six months as among the hardest of my life. The unlucky battle at Chancellorsville, unlucky especially for me and my command, brought me many bitter hours. To sit out slanders, which one is barely permitted to answer, because every defense would have been a complaint against higher commanders, to see enemies succeed who you despise and whom you can't answer without lowering one's self, and to hold quite still until the truth finally finds its own way—these were severe tests for a person of temperament." One of Schurz's soldiers, Martin Seel of the 74th Pennsylvania, agreed that Chancellorsville had been a turning point for him. Writing his brother from his new camp at Folly Island, South Carolina, Seel noted, "I have gathered from your writing that many people who are able to do military duty and are drafted, like to present themselves as impaired and incompetent in order to be set free. Well, I do not blame any German for that. I did not forget about what was done to us last spring after the battle at Chancellorsville and will not forget it in the future." If his brother were drafted, Seel recommended "to do your utmost to get off."[4]

German American soldiers from the Eleventh Corps were not alone in confronting the nativistic legacy of Chancellorsville. Whether by choice or not, Germans serving in other theaters of war also felt its sting, and became more aware of their German identity vis-à-vis their Anglo American comrades. Captain Wilhelm Vocke of the German 24th Illinois, serving in Major General William S. Rosecrans's Army of the Cumberland, wrote a telling letter in English to the editors of the *Nashville Union* on 10 June 1863, complaining about a recent account published in that newspaper that called the men of the predominantly German 37th Ohio "Dutch cowards":

It appears as if accusations of cowardice against the Germans after the late battles at Fredericksburg and Chancellorsville have spread almost like an epidemic among all Americans, and because of their apparent validity can scarcely be repeated enough. Correspondents of influential newspapers lead the dance, editors work mightily to fill their columns with the harshest condemnations of this apparent cowardice, obscure letter writers follow who don't know any better than to smear across the land the lowly cowardice of the corrupted "Dutch," and American newspapers print these stories. . . . In all American circles the accusation is repeated with the strongest calumnies. Let us discover how well this accusation against the Germans stands up.

Vocke began his defense by exploring the deeds of German soldiery up to Chancellorsville: the saving of St. Louis, the covering of the Federal retreat from First Manassas, the fighting done "by German regiments of Missouri, Illinois, and other western states" at Springfield, Pea Ridge, Fort Donelson, and Shiloh. He then proceeded to explore why the Eleventh Corps had been surprised at Chancellorsville, blaming Howard, and exculpating the German regiments' performance in the battle. Why, then, did Americans suddenly blame all German Americans for the defeat? The answer lay in their ignorance and complacency. Because less educated Americans "hardly knew their own history," they could easily be duped into believing exaggerated lies, and the "better educated," who knew better, did nothing to defend the Germans, and thus were guilty for their silence. Vocke rhetorically asked if Germans blamed "all Americans" for defeats caused by American soldiers, and concluded that a rout like that of the Eleventh Corps could have been suffered—and had previously been suffered—by troops of other nationalities. "If that is possible with French and American troops, why not also with Germans?" Concluding that the accusations of German cowardice springing up all over the country were completely unfounded, Vocke warned the American readers,

> Through such invective you only estrange . . . the masses of Germans from the cause of the nation and extinguish in them the fire of patriotism, which up to now has burned brighter in them than in the Americans themselves. Such treatment will simultaneously turn the Germans against this country, and could bring them so far as to leave it in the lurch at the critical moment when everything depends on them, regardless of the consequences.
>
> I implore you, Americans, whose desire for the nation's welfare is at heart, and for your own well-being, cease these slanders that have been directed at the Germans for over a month. It is in their best interests as well as yours. . . .

Vocke followed up this letter with several more over the coming months, making a name for himself as a western defender of German ethnicity and German rights.[5]

Gottfried Rentschler of the 6th Kentucky Infantry, a half-German regiment from Louisville, did not raise his voice in defense of his countrymen at Chancellorsville, but clearly expressed his opinion of nativistic practices extant in his predominantly Anglo American brigade. In a letter to the *Tägliche Louisville Anzeiger* on 10 March 1864 he wrote, "If a full company is needed for some easy service, e.g., Provost Guard, a German company is never taken. If an entire company is required for rough service, e.g., several days or several weeks as Train-Guard, a German company will be ordered whenever possible. As this happens on a company basis, so it happens to individuals in the mixed companies. As a rule, the German has to wade through the mud, while the American walks on the dry road." Rentschler added, "The German is a 'Dutch soldier' and as a 'Dutchman' he is, if not despised, disrespected, and not regarded or treated as an equal." In a later letter the Louisville German said that others may think "the mixing of Germans and Americans in the Army may be beneficial to both parties, but such a conclusion is in error." These were strong words about anti-German prejudice as exhibited on a daily basis in the western Union armies and evidence belying the Americanization impulse that supposedly characterized German soldiers' experiences in the war.[6]

Another episode in the fall of 1863 illustrated just how true Rentschler's words were, and how the stigma of cowardice still haunted the Germans. Brigadier General Leslie Combs, a Kentucky-born political general, wrote an incendiary letter to the *Louisville Journal* repeating the old line that the Germans of the Eleventh Corps had fled before the enemy, singling out Carl Schurz: "Our children have fought in every battle-field, and never one fled as Carl Schurz and his gang of freedom-shriekers did at Chancellorsville." Schurz, in camp near Chattanooga, found out immediately about the letter and replied quickly. Already supersensitive to the allegations of cowardice and frustrated in his earlier attempts to officially exonerate himself and his division, it is not surprising that the self-appointed champion of the Eleventh Corps' Germans would respond to this latest public attack. What is noteworthy, however, is the restraint Schurz displayed in his tactful answer to Combs, which was published and republished throughout the northern press. Schurz declared Combs a liar, and "avail[ed] himself of this opportunity to stop a slander which political enemies seem bent upon sustaining by frequent repetition." He admitted that publicly defaming Combs might be equated as a challenge, but did not shy away from it. "I do not, however, mean to fight a duel with Mr. Leslie Combs. Being a good pistol shot, I might perhaps easily kill him, which I should not like to do; or, if he is equally skillful, he might kill me—and I should be sorry to die on so trifling an occasion; or we might not hurt each other, and then it would be a farce." Instead of a violent encounter, Schurz invited Combs to "a different kind of contest," in which the Kentuckian would visit the German at his head-quarters, enjoy its hospitality, and then accompany him into the next battle. "There Mr. Leslie Combs may determine whether he will have the heart to repeat that calumny, or whether it would not be better for him and more hon-orable to retract it."[7]

Schurz's clever answer delighted the German American press. Most of the major papers reprinted his reply to Combs in full and added commentary that criticized this latest expression of nativism. A friend of Schurz's in Washington, equally gleeful at the general's public retort, exclaimed to him, "your friends here read it with great satisfaction," and praised the "tone and cut of it." Yet, he asked sarcastically, what could explain the recent exploits of the Eleventh Corps around Chattanooga? "From the reports it appears that some time since, a party of the 'cowardly Dutch,' belonging to the 11th Corps, ran into the woods and marched up a mountain, in the very fore of an entrenched enemy, and never as much as fired a gun, but charged right into the enemy's works to the great discomfiture of the rebels—this conduct is so reprehensible that the 'cow-ardly rascals' and 'clannish officers' ought at once to be sent to the rear in dis-grace. Now how in the name of the 'immaculate,' did this happen? And how is friend Joe [Hooker]?" Returning to a normal voice, the writer added, "We watch your cause and conduct of the Corps with great interest and believe that some great thing is in store for the abused and belittled soldiers who deserve better of the country."[8]

Schurz's friend referred to the night battle of Wauhatchie in his letter, a fight in which the German regiments under Schurz and especially von Steinwehr indeed distinguished themselves, but for which they again received only mini-mal credit in the northern press. A little less than half of the Eleventh Corps was composed of German soldiery at this point in the war, but the German American press persisted in viewing it as "our corps," and so, when reports trickled in that the Eleventh Corps had helped in opening up the so-called Cracker Line and saved General John W. Geary and his Twelfth Corps division from capture, the editors crowed it as a peculiarly German victory. In a few months, however, they would be complaining again about Anglo American prejudice.

Joseph Hooker had been put in charge of the Eleventh and Twelfth Corps when they were sent to Tennessee to relieve the siege of Chattanooga, with Howard retaining direct command of the Eleventh. Arriving in the area in early October 1863, the two corps played an instrumental role in breaking the siege, which had trapped William S. Rosecrans and the Army of the Cumberland. One of the first priorities was enlarging the Union supply line into the city, which the Confederates had not been able to cut, but had effectively strangled. The beleaguered Federals were down to half rations by mid-October and thus the new Federal commander, Major General George H. Thomas, ordered the Eleventh and Twelfth Corps into action. On the night of 28 October they engaged the Confederates. Buschbeck's brigade of von Steinwehr's division fixed bayonets and charged up a 200-foot-high, heavily wooded hill directly into the teeth of one of John Bell Hood's rebel brigades. Under heavy fire, the 73rd Pennsylvania "stormed up the heights with a thunderous hurrah," and, along with its sister regiments, pushed the Confederates out of their entrenched positions. Von Steinwehr's second brigade, composed of Anglo American regiments, also fought their way up a heavily defended hill, capturing six artillery pieces. Geary and his division of the Twelfth Corps, however, received the brunt of the inevitable Confederate counterattack, and Hooker dispatched Carl Schurz's division to Geary's aid.[9]

Here the trouble for Schurz and his subordinate, Friedrich Hecker, began. The history of that night is complicated, and the utter darkness of midnight only made the participants less certain of what exactly happened. Apparently, Schurz went forward to Geary's aid with one brigade, then came back and ordered up another, and successfully relieved Geary's embattled troops. He had purposefully left behind Hecker's third brigade but expected it to follow, and Hecker, understanding the gist of his superior's plan, had begun doing just that, when he received two orders contradicting Schurz's plan. First a dispatcher from Howard arrived, ordering him to halt, and then Joseph Hooker himself rode up, spoke briefly with the old forty-eighter, and reiterated the order to halt. Because the battle of Wauhatchie ended in a Union victory, opened up the Cracker Line, and led the way for the spectacular Federal victories at Lookout Mountain and Missionary Ridge a few weeks later, everyone quickly forgot the incident involving Hecker's brigade.[10]

Everyone, that is, except Joe Hooker, who published his official report of the Wauhatchie battle in early January 1864. Hooker still chafed from Chancellorsville, blaming the Eleventh Corps for his defeat there, and was disdainful of Schurz who had continually harassed him with requests to publish his report of the battle. First praising the overall performance of his troops at Wauhatchie, Hooker then stated, "I regret that my duty constrains me to exempt any portion of my command in my commendation of their courage and valor. The brigade dispatched to the relief of General Geary, by orders delivered in person to its division commander, never reached him until long after the fight had ended. It is alleged that it lost its way, when it had a terrific infantry fire to guide it all the way, and also that it became involved in a swamp. . . ." Hecker and Schurz easily identified themselves as the target of Hooker's allegation, and, determined to avenge themselves on him, demanded a court of inquiry to clear up their records. So did the German American press. The Rochester *Beobachter* declared, "The so-called 'Fighting Joe,' whose natural predilections made him into a gambler, rowdy, and drinker," had "fallen into a wasps nest" with this latest "false representation." These "lies implicate not only the Germans in general, but also especially their leaders, Schurz and Hecker." The Pittsburgh *Freiheitsfreund* was not surprised at Hooker's poor behavior, because he had been looking for "the earliest opportunity, since the battle of Chancellorsville where [he] accused the 11th Corps and especially General Schurz of negligence of duty," to attack them again. "We want to hope that this time the people will be presented with the straight goods, and that the press of the country will show that it will not permit superior officers to set up their subordinates unfairly and in a prejudiced manner."

Indeed, this time Schurz and the Germans prevailed over Hooker. The court of inquiry was granted, and as Schurz's biographer asserts, the German general easily proved to a court packed with Hooker's underlings that he and Hecker had simply been following orders and did nothing wrong at Wauhatchie; it had been the commanding general who held back Hecker's brigade. "Hooker, mercilessly cross-examined by Schurz, was unable to shake this testimony," and the court absolved Schurz and Hecker of any wrongdoing. Hooker, not surprisingly, was not charged with anything. Instead, the odium fell on Colonel Wladimir Krzyzanowski, who performed well at Wauhatchie, but who could not be present at the hearing and thus could not defend himself. Besides the damage done to his friend Krzyzanowski's career, the consequences of Schurz's victory for his own future were also high. By publicly forcing Hooker to swallow his words, the German ended his own military career. He knew he could never again serve under "Fighting Joe." When William Tecumseh Sherman consolidated the Eleventh Corps with the Twelfth in early April 1864 prior to the Atlanta Campaign, no place could be found for Schurz, and he was shelved, delegated as commandant of a training camp near Nashville. The German Americans of the North had lost their most ardent public defender in the field.[11]

Schurz's predicament did not go unnoticed by the German-language press. Several papers, including the *Illinois Staatszeitung*, Philadelphia *Freie Presse*, and the Rochester *Beobachter*, lamented the consolidation of the two corps and linked Schurz's professional problem to the status of German Americans in the army. "One of the main goals of General Hooker has been to leave Generals Schurz and Steinwehr without commands, thereby obligating them to resign after being shelved," the editor of the *Beobachter* complained, and "the German regiments, which have not been filled out by new recruits . . . have been consoli-dated, but not with each other; rather with American regiments, so that their special character is completely bleached out." It was not difficult to see the hand of "raw revenge" on the part of Hooker in this action, who wanted to pay back those "who in the name of the 11th Corps fought against his dishonest reports about the battle of Chancellorsville." The officers could resign and thus escape "the hate of Hooker," but not the soldiers. They were stuck where they were.[12]

"They Are Getting Their Foreign Dutch Comitioned over Us"

The editor's statement about the "bleaching out" of the German regiments bears further scrutiny. Other authors who have written on the ethnics in the Civil War, especially Ella Lonn and William Burton, have claimed that both Irish and German regiments tended to lose their ethnic identity in the later years of the war, and that this process was proof that the conflict hastened the Americanization of ethnic soldiers. A close analysis of the German American regiments from Pennsylvania in the last two years of the war, however, provides contrary evidence.

By 1864 each of the primary Pennsylvania German regiments had been numerically depleted to the point that their officers constantly worried about the viability of their commands. Calls for new recruits and requests to detach officers for recruiting duty flooded their superiors' desks. Writing the Provost Marshal at City Point, Virginia on 19 September 1864, Lieutenant Colonel Alex-ander von Mitzel of the 74th Pennsylvania insisted that eighty to one hundred men being retained there be forwarded immediately to his regiment. They had been duly enlisted in the 74th and "most of these men are reported to be Ger-man." The "final reorganization of the regiment depends to a great degree thus far on the speedy arrival of the said recruits," he claimed. Lieutenant Colonel Alwin von Matzdorff of the 75th Pennsylvania likewise went to great lengths to secure German recruits. As late as March 1865 he had the Pennsylvania Military Adjutant stationed in Nashville send an official notice to Harrisburg asking for more men. "The regiment was originally recruited at Philadelphia, and is com-posed principally of Germans," the adjutant wrote. Since the 75th "bears a very fine reputation in this Department," it deserved more German recruits.[13]

Analysis of original regimental papers suggests that the Pennsylvania Ger-man regiments continued to be led by Germans late into the war. When an officer was killed or discharged, strenuous efforts were made by those remain-ing to replace him with another German. Honorably discharged from the army as a result of his wound at Gettysburg, former Colonel Adolph von Hartung of the 74th Pennsylvania requested in July 1864 that Lieutenant Colonel Alexander von Mitzel be his permanent replacement, and suggested four other German officers for promotion, although a few officers with non-German names appeared on the rolls as equally qualified. Similarly, Captain Gottfried Bauer of the 98th Pennsylvania, temporarily in charge of the regiment, asked the state adjutant general in February 1865 whether First Sergeant William Fratz could be promoted to first lieutenant of Company H. No other candidate would do, Bauer argued, as "the company is composed of Germans and none of them is able to write or speak the English language." To some German officers' credit, they did realize occasionally that the English speakers under their command also required leaders who understood them, and accordingly in August 1863 Colonel Ballier of the 98th requested Andrew Curtin to appoint Arthur Beamish captain of Company A: "No other, than the English language is spoken in Comp. A, and A. Beamish being of Irish descent, his appointment to the Captaincy in Comp. A would be agreeable and satisfactory."[14]

Despite William Burton's and Ella Lonn's arguments to the contrary, the five immigrant German regiments from Pennsylvania retained a strong German flavor to the very end of the war. No evidence of rampant "Americanization" exists, for example, among the muster rolls and rosters of the two most solidly German units, the 74th and 75th Pennsylvania. Certainly, English-speaking recruits and draftees reduced the regiments' overall German ethnicity as original members of the two regiments were killed, wounded, or discharged, but the officer corps remained decidedly German. These officers, in turn, did not want to command non-German enlisted men. In March 1864 the 74th had twenty-nine officers, all but one of whom were born in Germany, from Colonel Adolph von Hartung down to the lowliest second lieutenant. Importantly, all the first lieutenants, such as Cornelius Knoebel and Carl Veitenheimer, had signed up in 1861 as enlisted men. The fact they had been promoted may well have been due to bravery in battle, administrative skills, or other merits, but considering the solid list of German-born officers this late in the war, ethnic favoritism no doubt played a role as well.[15]

The example of the 75th Pennsylvania is equally compelling. A "Roster of Commissioned Officers" dated 31 March 1865 reveals only eighteen officers total. Of that number, only one name is decidedly non-German—William J. Briggs, commanding Company C. While the place of birth was not given on this report, the other officers' names are so German-sounding as to leave no doubt: Koerper, Emleben, Gerke, Saalman, Ehrlich, Weigand, Haserodt, and Steiger to name a few. Fully one-half of the captainships and first lieutenancies were vacant, and only two second lieutenants were listed. All of the captains and lieutenants listed were promoted from the ranks. Certainly there were qualified enlisted men in March 1865 who could have filled some of the empty positions. The fact they were not promoted indicates three possible situations: in the opinion of the current officers, there were indeed no qualified men to fill the empty slots, either German or Anglo American; the regiment was too small to warrant any more officers; or there were qualified non-Germans available but the current officers refused to promote them. The actual reasons for the empty positions probably were rooted in all three possibilities, but it appears something other than merit was behind promotions in the 75th.[16]

The argument that the ethnic regiments ultimately became Americanized through the experience of the war cannot be substantiated by the records of the Pennsylvania German regiments. Burton states, "long before the war ended the German regiments were reorganized out of existence." This is false, as proven by the documents presented here. He also claims in his conclusion that ethnic regiments "suffered a gradual loss of ethnic identity and composition. The pull of neighborhood, state, personal friendship, occupation, and even alternative myth proved stronger than ethnicity." Although the Pennsylvania German regiments certainly enlisted non-Germans late in the war, the fact that their leadership remained solidly German challenges the notion that they lost their ethnic identity. As for the factors Burton lists as stronger than the pull of ethnicity, in the case of the Pennsylvania Germans such factors were clearly part and parcel of their identity as Germans. The "pull of neighborhood" and friends, for instance, reinforced German consciousness rather than detracted from it, as most of the soldiers had lived and worked in ethnic neighborhoods in Pittsburgh and Philadelphia before the war and enlisted with their German friends and coworkers from those neighborhoods. Americanization, simply put, was not a major influence in the Pennsylvania German regiments. The regiments were so ethnically German, in fact, that non-Germans attached to them actually experienced anti-American prejudice.[17]

On the receiving end outside of their regiments, especially after the battle of Chancellorsville, Pennsylvania's German soldiers displayed pro-German favoritism and actually dispensed much prejudice against non-Germans within their regiments. That they did so may have been a subconscious reaction to the nativism they had earlier experienced, but such actions also became a tool to ensure that their regiments remained German. Especially later in the war, when ethnically German men of military age became increasingly hard to find, and when an influx of non-German recruits and draftees threatened the ethnic homogeneity of their regiments, German officers resorted to prejudicial means to resist Americanization. Removing non-German officers from command or blocking the promotions of Anglo American enlisted men was a common occurrence. It was also a delicate matter, and frequently the victims of these plots wrote directly to Governor Curtin expressing their grievances. In some cases they clearly claimed the Germans were prejudiced against them. These letters support the inference that throughout the war the German regiments of the North remained predominantly German. "Americans," apparently, were not very welcome.[18]

Lewis Miller of Selinsgrove was instrumental in raising recruits late in the war among farmers from the central counties of the state. German recruits in the urban areas were drying up, and the leadership of the 74th Pennsylvania was forced to accept several new companies composed of non-Germans to ensure the viability of the regiment. Miller's company, which became Company D, was one of the newcomers. He was unanimously elected captain of his company of English-speaking soldiers, and it was hoped that he might be quickly promoted to the Majority. The Germans in the 74th, particularly the officers still clinging to control of the regiment in the spring of 1865, resented Miller and the threat he posed. A German who had assisted Miller in the recruitment of the company, First Sergeant E. P. Rohrbach, attempted to prevent Miller's promotion. As Charles Power of Selinsgrove (a friend of Miller's) wrote to the Honorable Eli Slifer on 25 May 1865, "by some trickery of this Rohrback and foreigners in the Reg't. Capt. Lewis Miller was wronged out of the Majorship of this Reg't." Rohrbach, interestingly, ultimately became major of the 74th.[19]

Miller's situation was typical in that he suffered the results of behind-the-scenes pro-German favoritism, but not outright anti-American prejudice. Sergeant Ezra W. Merrill of the 75th Pennsylvania also believed he had been wronged in favor of other, German officers for promotion, but did not mention prejudice. Recovering in a hospital from wounds received at Second Manassas, Merrill told Governor Andrew Curtin, "my regiment being German and myself being the only American sargent I may have been overlooked." Irving W. Combs of Company K, 74th Pennsylvania, expressed similar sentiments in August 1864. "This regiment being all germans has made it very uncomfortable for me," he claimed. Combs requested Curtin to "grant me a position" elsewhere, as "I have been ill treated in a great many cases, which is all passed by hoping that it might be for the best." Combs's pleas fell on deaf ears, however, and he ultimately resigned from the 74th.[20]

Perhaps the most obvious example of prejudicial conflict (regarding promotions) between German- and English-speakers within the Pennsylvania German regiments comes from the 74th Pennsylvania in the closing days of the war. The controversy over Lewis Miller's promotion was only a footnote to the larger and far more serious battle waged between several recently arrived Anglo American companies and their outnumbered, but veteran German adversaries.

Almost immediately upon arriving at the 74th's camp in Beverly, West Virginia, in April 1865, the new, one-year companies demanded an election for field officers since the 74th was currently being commanded by a captain, Gottlieb Hoburg. The election was held, and the colonel, lieutenant colonel, and major elected by a majority vote among all the officers. Hoburg was edged out by one vote (12 to 11), but the German candidates for lieutenant colonel and major were soundly defeated. Suddenly, the remaining Germans of the 74th found themselves under the command of Colonel John G. Wilson, Lieutenant Colonel Gavin A. McLain, and Major Samuel J. Pealer, all Anglo Americans, and all new officers with little or no previous military experience.[21] Hoburg wrote to Brevet Major General James McMillan, in charge of his brigade:

It appears that the new officers of this Regt. prefered to serve under such Officers who do not attempt to enforce discipline and as the old Officers (numbering six) who have served 3 1/2 years and lately passed a satisfactory and creditable examination, are most dissatisfied with the above result, I would respectfully recommend, that all the new Officers of this Reg't. be summoned before a board of examination as speedy as possible.[22]

McMillan sympathized with Hoburg, endorsing a letter Hoburg wrote to Governor Curtin requesting he override the election, and claiming that none of the new officers could pass the examination. Along with his personal petition, Hoburg also included recommendations from colonels of other regiments. He was determined to retain command. Predicting what was about to happen, Colonel-elect John Wilson also sought Curtin's help in legitimizing his election and had a powerful friend, probably a state senator, write the governor on his behalf. A. C. White of Jefferson County claimed, "Hoburg . . . will if he can defeat the commissioning of Capt. Wilson as Colonel. . . . Governor, Capt. Wilson has received the election. Will you not see that he is commissioned. I know you will."[23]

White's appeals to Curtin failed. Not only was the election overturned and Wilson denied the colonelcy, but he, Pealer, McLain, and three lieutenants from the new companies were also summarily dismissed from the service through special War Department orders. A few more Anglo American officers also resigned in the aftermath. Hoburg ascended to the colonelcy, Captain Carl Veitenheimer became lieutenant colonel, and Elias P. Rohrbach—the same first sergeant who conspired against Lewis Miller and had subsequently been promoted captain—became major. Anglo Americans had been completely swept out of the field officerships of the 74th and had vacated most of the captaincies, leaving them open for German non-commissioned officers.[24]

Wilson, Pealer, McLain, and the other officers who had been forced out attempted to have their former positions reinstated, but to no avail. The war had ended and the northern regiments were being mustered out one by one. There was little interest in official circles in recommissioning any officer at this late date. Nonetheless, the disaffected officers wrote Curtin again, on 30 June 1865, and asked him to help out their former comrades if he could not achieve anything for them: "We would ask your Excellency to have the men let home for the common reason that they are nearly all farmers and have crops to attend to and labor is very scarce in the country." If the governor did not release them, "they will loose heavily."[25] Again, Curtin failed to act in their favor. The enlisted men were still in the ranks by the end of July, and were heartily displeased by the fact. They took matters into their own hands on 20 July, writing Curtin an angry letter explaining their feelings throughout the last several months and clearly stating that they were the victims of prejudice:

> We would inform you that we as american soldiers and as men that have come out to put down the rebellion, to considder our selves in a grate measure imposed upon; In the first place by haveing foregners put over us for officers in the regt; our colonel and lieut colonel is both foreign dutch, and of what is termed the low class according to the history of them so far as we can learn; the one was a soap pedler and the other was a rag gatherer until they came to the army; and we know they are drunkards now; and as tiranical as any slave driver in the South. There was seven companys of us came to this regt last spring and they have dismissed three captains and have one under arrest and they are getting their foreign dutch comitioned over us; and even a man that served two years in the rebble ranks will be adgutant of the regt . . . we think hard of being kept here under such government robbers when the war is over, we have to drill 4 hours per day and in the morning from 5 to 7.[26]

The men continued with a description of the "drudgery" imposed on them by the German officers, such as requiring drill in "wet grass" and "saluting them as they pass." They closed their letter with appeals to the superfluity of their continued service, for compassion to their families at home "looking anxiously for our return," and a final jab at the Germans: "We wouldn't think so hard staying to the last if we had good kind field officers, but we as americans do not like to have our inferiors from another nation to rule and usurp athority over us." Some of these men refused to endure their plight any longer—forty-one of them deserted in June and July 1865. The one-year men of the 74th Pennsylvania, almost all Anglo Americans, clearly resented both the Germans themselves and the prejudice they brought to bear against them. Gottlieb Hoburg probably cared little what they thought, however; he and his countrymen had succeeded in keeping the 74th a German regiment. They did so not as a direct result of the nativism after Chancellorsville, but like German American reactions to the aftermath of that battle, the officers of the 74th were motivated by an intrinsic desire to maintain and defend their ethnicity against unwelcome Anglo American encroachments.[27]

"It Will and Must Bear Sweet Fruits"

In the political arena in the last two years of the war German American leaders also strove to preserve what they perceived were the rights of their ethnic group, although it is debatable whether the leaders in most instances spoke for the average German immigrant. It is certain that the ethnic self-consciousness of the North's Germans had been substantially raised by the nativism unleashed after Chancellorsville, and that that heightened self-awareness contributed strongly to efforts to politically unify German speakers throughout the Union from 1863–1864.

The public reaction of German Americans to the nativistic backlash after Chancellorsville, as exhibited in their newspapers and by the mass meetings called in Washington, Philadelphia, and New York, brought them together in a loosely knit solidarity against the common threat of Anglo American prejudice. Perhaps this threat was not great enough for Germans in all states and in all communities to join together formally in common cause, but seeds were definitely sown for a more permanent kind of political unity. That unity would manifest itself in the form of the "German Organization," created in Cleveland, Ohio, in October 1863. Seventy leading German-speaking editors, businessmen, academics, and politicians from all around the Union, representing dozens of local German political and public interest groups, met from the 18th to the 21st of that month to hammer out the framework of a new national organization and adopt a platform representative of their views. Forty-eighters dominated the meeting, with such notables as Carl Heinzen, Friedrich Kapp, Ludwig Greiner, Karl Roeser, and Friedrich Sorge present, and the tone of the proceedings was definitely radical. That most of the delegates hailed from the left wing of the Republican Party, and some, such as Sorge, were outright Marxists, contributed to this notion, and it also dissuaded some of German America's most prominent spokesmen and champions from attending. Schurz refused to attend, and Sigel, originally designated a delegate from Philadelphia, decided at the last minute not to come to the meeting, even though he was speaking in Cleveland at the time.[28]

The radical political nature of the German Organization handicapped it from the start. Originally called, much like the earlier Washington Conference, as a means to form a pan-German American blanket organization that would represent and lobby for the rights of all German immigrants, the meeting quickly became a clearinghouse for the radicals' political views. Indeed, many of the attendees from the June Washington assembly were present, hoping to accomplish the more idealistic goal of creating a bona fide organization that would defend the rights of Germans on the national level, and they were joined by many representatives from the eastern states, such as Kapp. But the Missouri and Boston delegates, led by Heinzen, set the tone of the meeting. Eleven planks formed the basis of the organization's new platform, and several of them—like the one demanding unification with "European revolutionaries to eject foreign intervention"—were so strongly contested by the more moderate delegates that they were ultimately dropped. Yet the platform that was eventually adopted left no doubt in what direction the German Organization was headed: the unconditional surrender of the Confederacy, complete and uncompensated abolition, a harsh reconstruction policy for the conquered South, a renewed enforcement of the Monroe Doctrine, the introduction of compulsory military service based on the Swiss model, and, most critically, "the support of any candidates for public office who come the closest to these views." As if reflecting the perception of stronger German radicalism in the Midwest, the headquarters of the central committee of the organization would be moved west to Cleveland, out of the orbit of the more conservative eastern Germans. That decision upset many in the New York and Pennsylvania delegations like Kapp, who had hoped to assert an eastern, more conservative dominance over the new organization.[29]

Sigel had wisely predicted how the wind would blow at the meeting, and sent a letter outlining his opinions of how the German Organization should politically align: "as a citizen and soldier of the American republic" he had to remain steadfast to the "Party of the Union." Only "within the Union-Party" could the "suggested principles and resolutions be brought to reality," and any sort of exclusive German political movement would be doomed to failure. According to one delegate, "this letter was met with great coolness, even with indignation, and the proposal to add the letter to the protocol was rejected with great majority." But Sigel had anticipated that the Midwestern radicals, led by their erstwhile leader Carl Heinzen, would assert their dominance in the new organization and agitate for an entirely new political direction, one that not only misrepresented the opinions of the majority of the North's German Americans, but also one that could potentially create a dangerous rift in the Republican Party. He wanted nothing to do with any of it.[30]

Sigel's concerns as expressed in his letter struck at the heart of the problems plaguing the German Organization. Although a majority present at the foundational meeting were enthusiastic about its future, believing, "it is a now a fact that cannot be denied, and it will and must bear sweet fruits," a vocal minority argued strenuously against some of the platform's political planks, and most of these men, like Kapp, were already ardent Republicans. What about German Democrats? The radical forty-eighters who gathered at Cleveland simply did not represent the views of the German American population, a slight majority of whom nationwide were Democrats, and even among Republicans their principles were considered too far left by most of their countrymen. Another major difficulty involved geographic differences, which were themselves connected to the political distance between the delegates and their constituents. If this organization would indeed represent the concerns of German America on a national level, pressuring the two major parties to adopt legislation friendlier to immigrants, it needed to reflect the hopes, fears, and realities of Germans *both in the East and the West*. Although they had temporarily if loosely unified in outrage to the nativism displayed after Chancellorsville, Germans in the great cities of the East and those living either on the farms of the Midwest or in that entrepôt of German radicalism, St. Louis, were not usually of the same political bent. About the only points they could ever agree upon in the prewar period—and again, during the Civil War itself—were that nativism needed to be repudiated and German Americans better represented in politics. There was no indication that the German Organization, as it was conceived in Cleveland, would even address these primary considerations, let alone provide a unified base from which to affect national change. On a basic level, the germ for the organization was born in the aftershocks of Chancellorsville, but ironically, when the delegates convened, nativism was supplanted by political radicalism as the primary focus. And the majority of German Americans could never agree to that. Editors of most of the major German American newspapers ultimately condemned the German Organization, and even its official organ, the Cleveland *Wächter am Erie*, finally abandoned it. As the editor of the Rochester *Beobachter* put it, the "stillborn" Cleveland Convention accomplished nothing for the unity of German Americans but instead "appeared clearly to work for the best interests of a certain presidential candidate."[31]

That candidate was "the Pathfinder" John C. Frémont, who had been shelved after his misadventure in the Shenandoah Valley at Cross Keys in 1862. His early abolitionistic actions against slavery in Missouri, well before Lincoln issued the Emancipation Proclamation, his undying hatred of rebels, and his strident criticism of the administration gave him a pedigree highly attractive to the German radical Republicans, especially in Missouri. They had grown tired of Lincoln's waffling on the slavery question, and when he did emancipate the slaves, they believed it long overdue and not revolutionary enough, especially since it allowed slavery to continue in the border states. The radicals also condemned what they perceived as the administration's lenient philosophy toward Confederates, and agreed with Frémont that the rebels should be harshly punished.

As Joerg Nagler explains, a strong undercurrent of support for a Frémont-like candidate lay at the heart of the radical resolves at the Cleveland Convention. Although he had not yet decided to run for the presidency in 1864, many dissatisfied Republicans hoped Frémont would, and the radical Germans wanted to ensure that he could count on them for their support. They had already tried to win Lincoln over to their concerns not long after Chancellorsville. After a mass meeting in St. Louis on 10 May, that, ironically, only tangentially addressed the nativistic backlash, the Missouri Germans sent James Taussig as their personal representative to speak with the president in Washington. But Lincoln politely rebutted the demands Taussig carried with him, which included giving Sigel and Frémont active military commands and inaugurating immediate emancipation in Missouri. Dissatisfied and indignant, Taussig reported to his colleagues that the president believed "there was evidently a serious misunderstanding springing up between him and the Germans of St. Louis which he would like to see removed." Although it would take some time for the radicals to completely abandon Lincoln, most had begun to take those fateful steps by the time the German Organization met in Cleveland in October. The future Frémont supporters hailed not only from Missouri, but also from Iowa, New England, Ohio, Indiana, and Illinois.[32]

Abraham Lincoln had a lot of troubles related to German American politics in the twelve months following Chancellorsville. The Frémont movement expanded by the day in the fall of 1863, thereby stripping away some of his heretofore staunchest Republican supporters, and the German Democrats grew bolder and more incendiary in their criticisms as the presidential election neared. Accusations of "Know-Nothingism" in the current policies of the government became one of their favorite rallying cries after Chancellorsville, and they seized upon and maximized any opportunity that provided an excuse to remind Germans of the nativistic background of the Republicans. On top of that, German Americans of both parties still harbored significant—and legitimate—concerns about Anglo American prejudice, and thus Franz Sigel's reinstatement to military command became a hypersensitive litmus test for the administration regarding its intentions toward German-born citizens. In February 1864, the *St. Louis Neuen Zeit* probably spoke for other papers when it claimed that the government "will have won back much in the hearts of the

Germans" when Sigel returned to active field command. "Give them back their old leader and you will find unbroken the old enthusiasm." He did not have to return to the Eleventh Corps, but "the Germans want him back in the field in an important command." The Cincinnati *Volksblatt* argued in March, "the Germans highly value Sigel as one of the proven, competent military talents of the land and are quite convinced that had he, rather than McClellan or Halleck, been at the head of the war's prosecution, the rebellion would have long ago shot its last bolt." Sigel himself lobbied extensively for his own reinstatement, asking, among others, powerful Indiana Congressman Schuyler Colfax to intercede on his behalf with Lincoln. On "leap day" 1864 Lincoln relented and assigned Sigel to the Department of West Virginia. Colonel David Hunter Strother, serving in that department, correctly identified why the president finally gave in: "The Dutch vote must be secured at all hazards for the Government and the sacrifice of West Virginia is a small matter."[33]

The magnitude of Strother's doom-croaking did not exactly come to pass, but he was right in questioning Sigel's military abilities. Delegated a secondary role in Ulysses S. Grant's grand strategy to press the Confederacy on all fronts that spring, Sigel led his small army steadfastly down the Shenandoah Valley in the first two weeks of May 1864, only to meet defeat at the hands of an even smaller Confederate force at New Market, Virginia, on 15 May. Most of his troops were not German this time around, and hence could not be ethnically stereotyped, but as symbol of German America, what happened to Sigel in the aftermath would be important to his countrymen. General-in-Chief Henry W. Halleck, Sigel's old nemesis, was not surprised by the defeat at New Market and told Grant, "[Sigel] is already in full retreat . . . if you expected anything from him you will be mistaken. He will do nothing but run. He never did anything else." A few local and national Anglo American newspapers, such as the Wheeling *Daily Intelligencer*, berated Sigel's abilities as a commander but said little about his ethnicity. Nonetheless, his removal from field command and placement in control of a reserve division frustrated many German Americans, who once again internalized his plight and saw in it yet more evidence of the resurgence of nativism. The *Pittsburgher Volksblatt* exclaimed, "General Sigel is a witness to the recovery of American nativism." Although he had held his "outnumbered force" for eight days at Winchester, "the nativists whisper around that he failed in his duty." The editor, of course, failed to mention that Sigel had to retreat to Winchester because of his defeat at New Market, but still thought he knew why the general was under fire: "Sigel is a 'Dutch' General. He offers Nativism all it could ever want." The Democratic Columbus *Westbote* wrote of Sigel's sacking, "in such a manner 'German loyalty' is repaid by the backstabbing, nativistic, Abolitionpack. The 'Dutch General' had done his duty—the 'Dutch General" can now go." In a prediction about how all of this would play out politically, the editor spouted:

> The despicable German abolition-press will call forth a storm of indigna-tions and the 'intelligentsia' will moan and curse, but the German Republi-can press does not matter to Lincoln anymore and they receive from the government in return for their vote one kick in the face after the other. That's what you get—Sigel sacked . . . and Schurz, who once cried, 'we will be recognized, we will be respected,' so it appears, a zero.

The editor's despair about the division and weakness within German American political ranks was quite telling. Split among Democrats, Republicans, and Fré-mont radicals, the Germans had lost much of their previous clout with the administration and could do little to protest, let alone redress any lingering post-Chancellorsville nativism. But they were obviously still worried about it. What happened to Sigel was perceived as proof that anti-German prejudice was definitely still afoot, and in the presidential election of 1864, that issue would be an important one for the Germans.[34]

The election of 1864 has been well documented by previous authors, so a detailed analysis of the campaign is not necessary here. Just how each of the three parties—later two, as Frémont bowed out on 22 September—attempted to court German American voters is not as well understood. Each candidate marshaled several different arguments to attract ethnic votes, and these natu-rally varied depending on the locale, but one of the most convincing had to do with nativism and the recognition of German contributions to the war effort. It was important to make Germans feel comfortable if one wanted their political support, or at least, make them feel uncomfortable with the other parties.

The Republican Rochester *Beobachter* tried to assure its readers that its party of choice "will absolutely not allow the specter of nativism to influence its elec-tion." There was nothing to fear from the "Ghost of Know-Nothingism," because Republicans "know that the United States needs immigration more than immigration needs the United States, and that a restriction of immigrants' rights would depress even further the already poor reputation of this land in Europe." But a "purely German party," which the editor alleged the Frémont supporters desired, could only hurt the aspirations of German Americans by stirring up suspicions and even hatred among Anglo Americans, especially if splitting the Republican vote resulted in a Democratic victory. None other than Francis Lieber, the old Dreissiger and former South Carolinian, echoed these arguments in a highly influential pamphlet published by the Loyal Publication Society in New York, entitled "Lincoln or McClellan: Appeal to the Germans in America." Lieber's emphasis, however, struck at two other salient points: first, a Democratic victory would result in an independent Confederacy and the subsequent balkanization of America, akin to the "petty state domination and provincial pomposity" German immigrants had left behind; and second, the old nativists were now Democrats! Referring to the Democratic National Convention in Chicago that had nominated George McClellan, Lieber rhetorically asked, "and of what sort of people was this mixed-up convention composed? In the first place, a great proportion consisted of old 'Know-nothings.' They openly proclaimed themselves such. Can you Germans, vote on the same side with these men, whose only principle has been to shut in your faces the gates of this wide continent . . . or else, as you are here already, to take from you the right of citizenship?" Clinching his point, Lieber added, "Will you vote with those who, like their friends, the rebels, would load you with infamy, and who speak of you as the offscouring of the earth?"[35]

Lieber massively overestimated the nativist influence in the Democratic Party, which in 1864 was higher than in 1860, but still amounted to a tiny fraction of the party's membership. Regardless of the hyperbole, his appeal apparently failed to sway most German Americans in New York, who voted resoundingly for the Democrats in November. No doubt strongly responsible for that was the powerful *New Yorker Staatszeitung*, which argued that the draft had been specifically aimed at Germans and Irish, and that the re-election of Lincoln would not only guarantee more years of bloodshed, but also mean a victory for nativists who would rather see immigrants die in battle than their own kin. In an ingenious reference to a bloody period of German history, editor Georg Ripper of the Pittsburgh *Abendzeitung* warned that a vote for Lincoln equaled a vote for "a thirty-years war" because the South would never give up, and the result of such an endless conflict would be "the retrenchment of radicalism and Puritanism in their rule over the land." Should that occur, "the triumph of still unborn fanatical and intolerant projects" was a certainty. One of them would surely be prohibition, he argued. "Puritanism—or its political representative, the Republican party," with "all of its excrescences of corruption, prohibition, nativism, and abolitionism" had set its sights on lager beer. For the Germans, the potential loss of their beer halls was tantamount to a major blow at their ethnic identity. The Know Nothings had been strong supporters of temperance in the 1850s, and hence it was natural to equate nativism with temperance. Indeed, in the postwar period, German Americans' battles against the forces of temperance were frequently depicted in anti-nativistic terms.[36]

As former Republicans themselves, Frémont's German supporters were not likely to dwell on temperance-related issues. Instead, in their short-lived campaign, they pilloried the head of the Republican Party, Abraham Lincoln. They, too, however, frequently played the nativism card, blaming the president for doing little in regards to German Americans. Forty-eighter Caspar Butz, in his *Deutsch-Amerikanische Monatshefte*, a half-political, half-literary journal that uncannily began publication in 1864, asked his readers,

> And what has Lincoln done to deserve the love and affection of the Germans, whom he purports to value so highly? Has he, perhaps, so highly recommended and rewarded our brave German soldiers and officers that he deserves our special thanks? Is his acceptance of Sigel's treatment by his Halleck already forgotten? Do Osterhaus and Willich have their long-deserved second star? Have Mersy and Hecker received generalships? As far as we are concerned, we must publicly acknowledge that we fail to find any particular gratefulness in our breasts.

After their candidate withdrew from the race, Frémont's supporters reluctantly returned to the Republican camp. Only about a dozen, primarily radical German-language daily newspapers had enthusiastically supported the "Pathfinder" to begin with, so his elimination from the contest did not exactly shake German America to its foundation, but his candidacy had symbolized a strong impulse among some of the North's Germans to politically unify. They desired this unity because of a raised ethnic consciousness that their experiences in the war up to then had created, and the seminal event in that creation had undoubtedly been the battle of Chancellorsville.[37]

Lincoln's re-election in November 1864 all but ensured the triumph of the Union and signaled impending victory for the cause that so many German American soldiers had paid the ultimate price for. Most of those dusty, hardened veterans who still remembered the events of 2 May 1863 continued serving to the very last, marching to the sea and through the Carolinas with Sherman as part of the Twentieth Corps. The survivors of the 26th Wisconsin, 82nd Illinois, and 27th Pennsylvania, for instance, witnessed the final death throes of the rebellion in the flames of Columbia and in a rural North Carolina hamlet called Durham Station. Others, such as the men of the 74th and 75th Pennsylvania, waited out the end of the war on garrison duty in Tennessee, Georgia, or Western Virginia. Their regiments shrunken to the size of prewar companies or flooded with new Anglo American draftees, the officers of the German regiments nonetheless preserved an ethnic flavor in their commands that persisted to the final mustering out. As they returned home to their neighborhoods in New York and Philadelphia, Chicago and Milwaukee, these men must have taken great pride in having faithfully served their adopted Fatherland. They and their fallen comrades had surely proven the nativists wrong through their innumerable sacrifices and had preserved the right of law and the Constitution. But their memories were long, and their joy in the final victory and homecoming was no doubt tempered by a gnawing concern that not every issue ignited in the fiery furnace of war had been fully extinguished.

Chancellorsville and the Civil War in German American Memory

I n the November 1883 issue of the *Deutsche Pionier*, a Cincinnati-based historical, news, and literary journal for German Americans, an article appeared entitled, "The Assimilation of the Germans." Its main theme questioned the need for Germans to quickly Americanize. About half-way through, the author, "J. G.," included these thoughts:

> We fought in the war of the rebellion on your side; our part of the population sent a full delegation to the ranks of the Union army, and we fought bravely together. We mourn together and take pride together when we honor the dead, who fell in defense of us both, and our combined means have erected soldiers homes for the crippled heroes of the war. . . .
>
> But must we all go the same way? Just as the individual has certain personal characteristics that make him unique, so it goes with peoples and nations. So it is with the Anglo Americans and so it is with the Germans. Must everyone live exactly like everyone else, and is the existence of our nation threatened when we do not spend our days in the same manner? Must we citizens of German background go to "Camp Meetings," "Women's Crusades," "Prize Boxing Matches," "Sit-Down [Temperance] Tourneys," "Minstrel Shows," or listen to the religious-political babble of a preacher in the joyless and dusty halls of a Presbyterian church?
>
> You do not need to participate in our excursions, picnics, and theatre shows on Sundays. You do not need to drink our beer and our wine, or to sing our songs. It is not necessary that you learn the beautiful German language, so that we can understand each other. But do not force men, who are proud of their American citizenship and their sincerity and honesty, to become hypocrites.[1]

In this small article, the author struck at two important issues that occupied the thoughts of German Americans in the postwar decades, especially those who had lived through the Civil War. Indeed, he intertwined them. The first was the memory of the war. The second was Americanization.

For the veterans of the Eleventh Corps, their comrades from the western armies, and German American intellectuals, these two themes were inextricably related. Try as they might, it proved impossible to extract the memory of the war from the idea of assimilation. At monument dedications, and in histories, newspapers, literary journals, and personal correspondence, German Americans often depicted their experiences in the war with an eye towards how they had proven their national loyalty. The blood of those who fell in the war and the deeds of their arms proved their Americanism, they argued. But at the same time they did not view the war itself as an assimilative force. Rather, it had served to heighten their ethnic consciousness, either by making them proud of their ethnic contributions to victory or retrenching their ethnicity in self-defense against nativism. The specter of Chancellorsville haunted their celebrations of the war, and even among veterans who had never served in the East, they believed they still had to prove their value as soldiers and citizens. Their personal *sacrifice* for the Union during the Civil War made unassailable their patent as American citizens, but it did not Americanize them. What they had endured at the hands of nativism made them naturally reluctant to jump into the melting pot. Events such as the German unification in 1871 and the increasing numbers of immigrants from eastern and southern Europe also affected their thinking. In the postwar period the German-born wanted all other Americans to respect what they had done for the country and view them as equal citizens, but most did not want to relinquish their Germanness. Their ethnic consciousness remained high, and because of that they would become more American only on their own terms and in their own good time.

The study of Civil War memory has recently become a popular topic among historians, but very few have examined the memory of immigrant soldiers and civilians. Of that limited number, even fewer have contributed to our understanding of the German American veteran. Stephen Engle examines Franz Sigel's postwar career in some detail, and indicates the reverence German Americans had for their wartime leader in later years, but does not venture much beyond his biographical subject. David Blight and Stuart McConnell briefly reference scattered German veterans' celebrations and organizations in the context of their overall studies of Civil War memory, but spend little time developing the idea of a separate ethnic (let alone German) interpretation of the war (which was certainly not the purpose of their studies). Margaret Creighton, in her analysis of German Americans, women, and blacks during the Gettysburg campaign, devotes considerably more space to the idea of immigrant memory, correctly noting that veterans of the Eleventh Corps returned to Gettysburg in the postwar decades to dedicate their monuments, that Carl Schurz continued to rankle under the wartime criticisms of his conduct at Chancellorsville, and that Augustus Hamlin and Wilhelm Kaufmann did much to counter the popular memory of Germans in the war in their histories. But she focuses mainly on how Anglo Americans perceived the Germans and how that perception changed over time—or not—rather than analyzing the complexities of German American memory itself. And, like Martin Oefele, who in his study of German-born officers in the U.S.C.T. also traces the impact of Kaufmann and tackles the problem of postwar German American "myth-making," Creighton believes the war pretty well assimilated the German veterans and their families. Oefele does an excellent job chronicling the creation of the "Myth of 1860"—the belief among Germans that they were primarily responsible for Lincoln's nomination and election—and accurately notes that "the majority of German Americans developed a selective public memory that fitted both the American understanding of a war to save the Union and their own needs for ethnic distinction." But his evidence for this claim is unfortunately scant, and in the end, he, too, subscribes to the general assimilation model.[2]

Although they do not devote much ink to postwar memory, Wolfgang Helbich and Walter Kamphoefner, in their recent anthology of German American letters from the Civil War era, do question the assumption that the war ultimately Americanized the German veterans who survived it. Based on the letters in their book, they argue that "one should fundamentally mistrust" this assertion. Stephen Engle also admits that many German Americans "became more sensitive about their ethnicity" after the war. These two viewpoints seem quite reasonable and are supported by the historical record.[3]

"An Injury Once Done Can but Rarely Be Repaired"

Years after the last accusations of "cowardly Dutchmen" disappeared from the English-language newspapers, the memory of Chancellorsville and its resultant nativism remained strong among German Americans, especially veterans of the battle. In postwar histories written in German, German-language literary and historical journals, private letters, and even in English-language veterans' publications, the sting of prejudice was quite evident even past the turn of the century. Certain Anglo American histories and accounts of the battle enhanced the perception among Germans that nativism still lingered. The ghost of 2 May 1863 would not die and kept reminding Germans that they had a stigma attached to themselves, one that constantly needed countering. In so doing they kept revisiting and strengthening their own ethnic identity. Even after the guns fell silent, the Civil War continued to retard the Americanization of the Germans.

As early as 1864 German Americans began to chronicle their participation in the war. Small biographical articles on leading Teutonic officers and short histories of some of the more prominent (especially western) German regiments appeared in the various German-language historical and literary journals. Poems and short stories were written that eulogized fallen German soldiers or recounted their martial deeds, and eventually several German American histories of the war became available that covered all aspects of the conflict but tended to focus on the uniquely German contributions to Union victory. Some of these publications mentioned nothing about nativism or Chancellorsville, but several of them contained strong insinuations about anti-German prejudice, the neglect of German American sacrifices, and the diminution of German American achievements. A few openly criticized or lamented the nativistic aftermath of Chancellorsville, defended German valor in the battle, and attacked Anglo Americans.[4]

In 1866 Rudolph Lexow, the new editor of the prominent New York–based *Deutsch-Amerikanische Monatshefte*, wrote an introductory article "In Remembrance" that reflected on the results and meaning of the recently concluded war. His tone was one of somber reminiscence mixed with admiration for the renewed vitality of an America freed from the shackles of slavery and the destruction of war. But at the end of his piece he warned his readers not to forget recent events. "Is it really so long ago?" he rhetorically and cynically asked. "Allow us the admonition also to remember the German men, who offered so much valuable service to the land of their adoption. Is Bohlen forgotten, even though he died a hero's death for the cause of freedom? Has the memory of Blenker been buried with his corpse, although he was the first to save a Union army? Does the name of Schimmelfennig live no more among us, even though it was his now-cold hand that carried the national banner into Charleston? Does one no more remember the deeds of Sigel because greater deeds have since occurred and his were met with ingratitude?" Lexow then proceeded to list several other prominent German-born officers who fought for the North, and asked if they, too were forgotten because the war was over. He answered his own rhetorical question with a touch of sarcasm: "It may have been long, long ago since you served your country, but you are not forgotten."[5]

A year later, the first history of the Civil War written by a German American, the radical forty-eighter Ernst Reinhold Schmidt, was published in both the United States and Germany. At first glance, it was a fairly innocuous tome, tracing the history of the conflict in an unbiased and lively narrative. Starting with the campaign of Second Manassas, however, Schmidt began to laud the German regiments and condemn the wartime nativism in lengthy footnotes. At Chancellorsville, Schimmelfennig's and Krzyzanowski's brigades of Schurz's division, along with Buschbeck's brigade of von Steinwehr's division, were the only ones that apparently fought in the Eleventh Corps, and "when the first excited reports about the battle flew throughout the land, one was altogether ready to blame the unhappy outcome on the 'cowardice' of the Eleventh Corps, and the heretofore humbled nativistic pride found a sinister satisfaction in the fact that that Corps was composed of German troops." The commanding generals of the army did little to correct the misconceptions, Schmidt argued, and although much about the affair still "remains in the dark," "at least what the Germans realize" is that the men of the Eleventh Corps "did not besmirch their honor." Again, after Gettysburg, "the condemnations and infamies of individual military critics and newspaper editors were vented against the Eleventh Corps, and especially against the German regiments," but the foresight of von Steinwehr in consolidating the defensive position of Cemetery Hill and the hard fighting done by the Eleventh Corps north of town on 1 July secured the Union victory. "This is the honorable truth and befitting monument to the slandered, misunderstood, or forgotten German regiments of the Eleventh Army Corps." The first history of the Civil War written by a German American, then, defended the German regiments with strong language, passively downgraded the value and roles of Anglo American units, and rebuked the wartime nativism in no uncertain terms. This was not language or argumentation that supported an assimilative vision for America's German citizens.[6]

Subsequent histories followed in Schmidt's vein. For instance, E. Schlaeger's *The Social and Political Situation of the Germans in the United States*, published in Berlin in 1874, did not attack Americans or nativism, but hyperbolically asserted that "the German regiments distinguished themselves on all battlefields in the most glorious manner, and it is no exaggeration if one claims no other nationality in the Union sent so strong a contingent to the millions of the Army than the Germans." Martin Luecke's 1892 work, *The Civil War of the United States*, fairly even-handed for the most part, nonetheless purported that "only a part of the German brigades under Steinwehr and Schurz did anything to resist the onrushing enemy or hold him up" on 2 May 1863. Again, Anglo American efforts went unrecognized on the first day at Chancellorsville.[7]

The most blatantly pro-German history of the war was unquestionably Wilhelm Kaufmann's *The Germans in the American Civil War*. Published in Germany in 1911, Kaufmann wrote in a distinctly nationalist style that reflected the ethnocentric hubris of the German empire. Like the earlier chroniclers before him, his work was plagued with filiopietism, exaggerations, and myriad historical errors, but Kaufmann nonetheless provided much valuable data on German Americans in the war that otherwise would have been lost. In great detail, he illustrated the uniquely German "saving of Missouri" for the Union cause in 1861, the early exploits of Franz Sigel and his German regiments in the West, and the misery of Blenker's march over the Virginia mountains. Probably to make up for the fact that "slanders and hateful attacks are often made" by Anglo American historians and veterans, Kaufmann overpraised the Germans. It was as if Teutonic numbers, foresight, and generalship alone had kept the Union cause alive in the first two years of the war. Turning his attention to the Chancellorsville campaign, for which he drew extensively from Hamlin, he also spared no invective in denouncing the nativism that resulted from the Federal defeat. Although "the defensive fight Buschbeck and Schurz led . . . was the finest single deed at Chancellorsville and one of the best in the entire Civil War," the northern people "sought some balsam to overcome the burning sense of humiliation, and they fell on the extenuation that *the cowardly Germans lost the battle for them*! The entire Anglo American press, with the notable exception of the *Chicago Tribune*, eagerly reached for this excuse to cover up the defeat, and the lies which were spread on the conduct of German soldiers were even more disgraceful than the leadership in that battle." According to Kaufmann, the extent of the calumnies spread about the Germans "by West Pointers" would be "almost comic if [they] had not been preserved through the years," and he spent considerable ink refuting them in detail and blaming the defeat, not unfairly, on Hooker and Howard. Even Lincoln came under fire for not defending his "just, intimate friend," Carl Schurz. "There [was] no statement from Lincoln at any later time to soften the humiliation of the Germans or to shift it onto those genuinely guilty." Kaufmann put the Anglo American leadership on trial in his book, made his judgments, and passed a verdict: guilty of nativism.[8]

For his part, Carl Schurz never really got over Chancellorsville. In various postwar articles as well as his famous *Reminiscences* he made a point of carefully describing the actions of his division and of the German troops in general, demonstrating that they had been the victims of circumstance and poor deployment. He also continued to lash out at his superiors, whom he clearly believed responsible for the disaster, obviously stifling what might have been even more vituperative language. Unquestionably, the memory of the slanders he and his command suffered burned brightly in his prose. He admitted that he had fought the prejudice as much as possible during the war, but a tone of indignance—and regret—still pervaded his discussion of the Virginia battle and its aftermath. It was as if he recognized the negative stereotype of the Germans in the war could not be fully eradicated. "Public opinion," he noted, "is generally swayed by first impressions, and an injury once done can but rarely be repaired." Schurz became famous as a champion of German acculturation in the decades after the war, but to him becoming American was necessary for his countrymen because the "Anglo-Saxon race," which included all those descended from British *and* German stock, needed to consolidate its birthright on the American continent. According to one theorist, "Schurz ma[de] his claim to stay in the United States not a privilege but a right, a right accorded him by virtue of his German heritage." To secure that right, the enemies of "true Americanism," slavery and nativism, needed to be destroyed. The war had killed slavery, but not nativism. Hence, in a sort of reverse logic, Schurz believed German Americans could only attain their racial inheritance as Germans in the United States if they assimilated and thus silenced the nativists. Was this truly a man who wanted to acculturate for acculturation's sake? Or was he instead "forced" into it? Regardless of his true motives for urging assimilation, Schurz's experiences in the war and at Chancellorsville in particular affected him until he died in 1906. As his biographer put it, "For the rest of his life he sought vindication."[9]

Other German officers present at Chancellorsville wrote in the postwar era about their experiences and left the impression that they still rankled over the public image of the German component of the Eleventh Corps. Major T. A. Meysenberg, Howard's adjutant at Chancellorsville, read a paper before a group of Missouri veterans in 1892 that failed to give much credit to the stands made by Schurz's and Steinwehr's commands, but nonetheless clearly absolved the corps of ignominy: "Scattered over a long distance, with the enemy presumably to the east and south, no soldiers in the world could have done much better than the Eleventh corps." Regarding the allegation that the Germans were responsible for the panic, Meysenberg trotted out the old German defense that claimed the majority of the corps was Anglo American. Then he took a stab at Hooker, adding "the defeat became inevitable after the first of May, when it was apparent that the original, beautifully-conceived movement had been abandoned." Hooker, interestingly, also still lost sleep over Chancellorsville, claiming in 1872 that the Eleventh Corps, and especially its Germans, "ran like a herd of buffaloes." Like Schurz, and no doubt partially because of Schurz's post-Chancellorsville agitation against him, Hooker never seemed to get over the battle and held a deep grudge against the Germans that he kept until he died. Most of them returned the favor.[10]

Hubert Dilger, in his correspondence with Augustus Hamlin in the early 1890s, praised the latter's efforts to bring to light the "truth" about 2 May 1863 in his history. To Hamlin he wrote, "Your work will raise quite a disturbance amongst the 'Heroes,'" meaning the old-line Army of the Potomac officer clique. He especially disliked Sickles for his prejudicial and deceitful remarks published in the Joint Committee investigations, and believed that the unlucky Eleventh Corps "had been cursed from its organization." Citing "petit jealousies of the different German cliques combined with Howard's unfitness" as the reasons behind the corps' problems, he believed "the old soldiers owe to you

[Hamlin] an everlasting debt of gratitude for your fearless and energetic defense of their honor. . . ." But Dilger thought it unfair to exclusively blame Howard for the defeat. Former First Lieutenant Karl Doerflinger of the 26th Wisconsin agreed. "Erring is human," he wrote in his postwar reminiscences, and "the patriotic, loyal, and courageous commanding officers, whose errors in judgment alone were responsible for the disaster of the Army of the Potomac at Chancellorsville, deserve our compassion." Yet he reserved only scorn "for those contemptible criminals who conspired in the fabrication of the lies and calumnies heaped upon the Eleventh Corps as a whole and especially its contingent of men and officers of German birth or descent." These "narrow-minded representatives of prejudiced chauvinism" created the image of the "Flying Dutchmen," although the Germans' "patriotism, their love of liberty, their military spirit and discipline, their culture, their proportion of enlistment and their fighting quality compared favorably with any other element of our American people." Doerflinger could hardly have added any more clichés to his list of German attributes, but then proceeded to argue, in true Prussian style, that the strict schooling and upbringing of German children "had taught these German American boys and their ancestors not only knowledge, but obedience to the requirements of duty and the commands of their superiors." Hence they had made good soldiers, he exclaimed, and any criticism against them was the result of Anglo American jealousy. To hammer home his now badly stretched nationalistic argument, he added, "in contrast I will state that I frequently heard American-born ex-soldiers boast of having disobeyed and insulted their officers in the field, prolonging our war and increasing our losses." These were not exactly words that radiated Americanization.[11]

Also strongly pro-German were the editors of the *Deutsche Pionier* in a two-segment biography of General Adolph von Steinwehr published in 1877. Amounting to a mini-history of German American involvement in the Civil War, the von Steinwehr biography vociferously defended not only the general's actions during the Chancellorsville campaign and beyond, but also attacked Anglo Americans for their prejudicial inclinations both during the war and afterward. The German regiments in Blenker's brigade had supposedly saved the routed Union army from annihilation after First Manassas but then received as a reward for their bravery "the jealousy of the Americans," which was only satiated by ordering the German division on the "wild goose chase" march over the Virginia mountains. Suffering terribly in that ordeal, the division was prevented from achieving victory at Cross Keys because of Frémont, another Anglo American, who prematurely ordered the retreat. Skipping any real discussion of Second Manassas, the editors proceeded to Chancellorsville. "With a true relish the American reporters and historians of the late war pitched into the German division under Schurz. They still grasp after distortions and lies in order to find fault with the hated 'Dutchmen.'" In order to convince their readers that they told the truth about American feelings, the editors cynically offered an example "of the impartiality (!!!) of the anglo-american reporters." A reprint of the infamous *New York Times* account of 5 May 1863 followed. It was obvious "with what shameful lies one has to deal with." But these clearly did not end with the cessation of hostilities. The publication of early histories of the war, such as Horace Greeley's *The American Conflict* (1867), compounded the problem. Greeley was a known German hater, the biographers insinuated, and believed "that the Germans were cowards 'as a matter of course.'" His chronicle not only omitted von Steinwehr's role at Chancellorsville, but also attributed no valor to the German troops in general. Defeat meant that Anglo Americans then in the high command and even today needed to blame someone else to shroud their own shortcomings. The choice was easy: "Yes, yes, when it is recognized that someone's incompetency or errors must be covered up, there one can make an easy and comfortable scapegoat, and the Germans possess the special quality to be the designated scapegoats."[12]

A biography of Carl Schurz appeared three decades later that incorporated the same kind of language. Published in the widely read *Deutsch-Amerikanische Geschichtsblätter*, a historical journal, in celebration of the statesman's death, the article included a lengthy passage on his involvement in the war. Regarding Chancellorsville, Schurz became "the target of fantastic defamations," and "almost the entire English-american press placed the blame for the defeat on the Germans and their leaders." Explaining that the German regiments could not fight well because of their poor deployment and the surprising nature of the enemy attack, the author noted that the "cries of 'dutch cowards' continued uninterrupted for weeks" and were "supported with groundless accusations in any case." Yet the Eleventh Corps had still done the best it could in the battle, and "it is unquestionable that it was precisely the brave German commanders who strove the hardest to stave off the catastrophe created by Howard." Schurz was preeminent in this list, but alongside him the biographer placed von Steinwehr, Schimmelfennig, Buschbeck, von Gilsa, Hecker, and Dilger. Moreover, Schurz's defense of his ethnic comrades against "the piled up infamies wanted for nothing," and his subsequent battlefield performances made him "a proud model . . . among his German American countrymen." Nothing flattering at all was mentioned about American commanders.[13]

William Vocke, the former officer in the German 24th Illinois Infantry who had demanded redress about prejudicial anti-German comments appearing in the western newspapers in 1863, had toned down his defensive invective only a little by 1896, when he delivered a speech to Illinois veterans. The indignance and outrage at the post-Chancellorsville nativism remained strong in him thirty years after the battle ended. Even though his regiment was hundreds of miles away from the Virginia wilderness at the time, Vocke still smarted under the obloquy cast upon his countrymen. Providing the popular name "Schneider" to represent German-America, Vocke said that "the cowardly slander of Schneider's men occasioned by the disaster at Chancellorsville seems to have created at the time a perfect 'Schneiderphobia,' not only in the press of the country, but also in the Army of the Potomac." He then offered an example of a prejudiced report, citing Brigadier General John C. Robinson of the First Corps, highlighting the biased comments and lampooning them. Vocke turned the tables on the nativists, calling them "cowards" for being so base as to criticize the Germans and then poked fun at their inaccurate recollections and accusations. The investigation of the Committee on the Conduct of the War was little more than a "farce," and only recently was the truth coming out thanks to the efforts of authors such as Theodore Dodge and Abner Doubleday. But "the prejudice which was created against Schneider's great army on account of the unmerited abuse and the base charge that his men were to blame for the defeat at Chancellorsville is deep-seated and far-reaching." Unfortunately, anti-German nativism was still not dead, because "we experience it among Grand Army men even at this date." These men were and are "prompted by blind race-prejudice," and amounted to nothing more than "the most unpatriotic wretches."[14]

"Our Dead Heroes Have Furnished Us the Criterion of the True American"

That sort of prejudice was one reason the German veterans from the eastern ethnic regiments were not scattered throughout "mixed" Grand Army of the Republic posts (GAR), but were instead concentrated in a few entirely ethnic ones. Much like African American veterans of the Union army, who had also experienced extreme prejudice during the war and formed their own posts composed exclusively of former black soldiers, German American veterans throughout the postwar North created all-German posts. Not all German veterans belonged to such organizations, but it appears that those who served in ethnic regiments tended to cluster together just like they did in the war. The John Koltes Post 228 in Philadelphia, for example, was composed almost entirely of German veterans from the 27th, 73rd, 74th, 75th, and 98th Pennsylvania and the 29th New York. Five of those regiments served in the Eleventh Corps and each was present at Chancellorsville. The 75th Pennsylvania had a thriving veterans' organization that was determined to disseminate the story of the regiment to the greater public, and had "a reputation of being the best organized regtl. Vet. Ass. In the state of Penna.," according to former Sergeant Hermann Nachtigall, secretary of the association. In a private letter to Augustus Hamlin, he wrote, "the episode of Chancellorsville very frequently forms the topic of conversation among [the men]. . . . Although numerous essays have since been written about that terrible conflict and disaster . . . yet the stigma still remains, and very frequently the phrase is heard, 'I fights mit Sigel and runs mit Howard' and I am sorry to say that one frequently has to hear slurs thrown even by men who call themselves Comrades—and Comrades, too, of the G.A.R. It seems to me that the government should take measures to set matters right before the whole country."[15]

The federal government never did anything to officially exonerate the Germans, but the German veterans themselves made it a matter of public record to exculpate themselves and their comrades in postwar celebrations. Their speeches and memorials given on the occasions of monument unveilings, in particular, demonstrate, just like their private letters, speeches, and articles published in German-language journals, that the nativism of the Civil War was not forgotten and German achievements needed to be trumpeted in order to be remembered. Unfortunately, most of the people listening were not Anglo Americans.

At Orchard Knob, Tennessee, on 14 November 1897, survivors of the 75th Pennsylvania met to dedicate the regimental monument honoring their service in the Chattanooga campaign. Several members of the regimental veterans' association rose to speak, tracing the history of the regiment in both theaters of war, its ethnic composition, and its most shining moments. One of those moments was Gettysburg, according to Lieutenant Albert Steiger, who asserted, "This German regiment, although thrice ordered to withdraw, was the last to retire from the field, and was, in action, still performing yeoman service on the battle line while some of the distinctively American troops were actively engaged in beating a precipitate retreat." This retreat, he stated, "caused our regiment exceptionable loss; and yet, strange to say, there are those among our English speaking companions who are want to speak in terms of derision and ofttimes find themselves inclined to stigmatize the 'Dutch' as lacking in the staying qualities of good soldiers." What originally caused this prejudicial stereotyping? "Much of this adverse criticism of the conduct of the German soldier, in action, is due to the incidental retirement of the troops comprising the Eleventh army corps, mostly composed of Germans . . . at Chancellorsville."[16]

Steiger then enumerated some of the traditional German defenses of their performance during the battle: unheeded warnings of the flanking movement, overwhelming enemy numbers, poor deployment by Union commanders. The

Confederates apparently also "fought like Trojans . . . imbued with the spirit of desperation fomented through alcoholic inspiration." All of these reasons premeditated against a successful defense by the Eleventh Corps, but still criticism rained down upon the heads of the German veterans of the organization. "It may not be amiss to remind our English speaking companions, who are so readily inclined to deride the soldierly qualities of their German associates, that . . . it is perhaps well to remember that the English regiments of the Corps were among the first to give way under the ever pressing dare devil onslaught, while it was left to the exclusively German commands to stem the tide of the ferocious assault." Faced with such facts, Steiger wondered why not "a more consistent consideration should be accorded these sorely pressed soldiers by their English speaking comrades." The "odium" cast upon the Germans for Chancellorsville "by many of our extreme selfishly disposed American compatriots" needed to finally end. It was painful enough to remember the losses of friends and relatives who fell in the war, but coupled with the nativistic persecution that yet persisted, the memory of the war was almost too much to bear. Echoing the sentiments of North-South reconciliationists, who wished to put aside former wartime differences to speed the healing of the nation, Steiger thought it would be far better if veterans of all nationalities could simply unite in supporting "our common country." "Her glory should be our pride; her welfare, our first care; her honor, our sacred trust."[17]

Other German veterans were not as outspoken as Steiger in condemning the lingering nativism, but were still quick to point with pride at instances of German valor. On 3 July 1893 the 41st New York unveiled its monument at Gettysburg. One speaker recounted the history of the regiment and claimed it and the Eleventh Corps "made a sturdy fight" at Chancellorsville. Even though Jackson's "first attack" fell on the 41st, the men "fired three well-directed volleys, and then retreated, stopping from time to time to rally with other regiments at various points and deliver their fire." Although the clouds of memory probably got in the way of historical accuracy here, the speaker admitted that "some of the men joined in the stampede, usual under such circumstances," but made it clear that "the body of the regiment moved steadily . . . and formed again" to fight another day. Christian Boehm of the 45th New York gave an oration in German at his regiment's monument dedication in 1888. Understandably concentrating on the battle at Gettysburg, Boehm concluded by exclaiming, "Now may this handsome monument eternally stand and show posterity that sons of the German nation fell here as heroes and good patriots, and that the foreign-born also truly fulfill their duties to their adopted Fatherland, and, when necessary, bravely sacrifice their lives." Speakers at the Gettysburg monument unveilings of the 58th and 68th New York similarly related with pride the roles of their regiments at Chancellorsville and Gettysburg. In the former battle, one veteran recounted that "Schurz's regiments held their ground for a half hour or more," and "made a gallant effort to stem the tide of defeat, and did not abandon their position until one-fourth of their number had fallen." Although not dripping with bitterness like Steiger's speech at Orchard Knob, the New Yorkers' addresses at Gettysburg indicated that the veterans of these German regiments also believed they had nobly done their duty and deserved public recognition.[18]

"To have been a member of the Seventy-fourth Pennsylvania is a prouder distinction than any patent of nobility that king or potentate might confer. And, as Germans, we are all proud of their record." Former Captain Paul Rohrbacker must have glowed as he spoke of his regiment's service and its ethnicity at the dedication of its monument at Gettysburg on the twenty-fifth anniversary of the battle. "It has become fashionable for Anglomaniacs to belittle everything that does not come from England, and call England the mother country," he continued. "Nothing is further from the truth. It was disputed a century ago. It is less true now. The whole world is the mother country of this land. We Germans are not here since yesterday." He then recounted the favorite German American story about the saving of St. Louis and Missouri in 1861, Blenker's covering of the retreat at First Manassas, and the names of just about every German general and prominent officer in the war. "Loyally and faithfully they served their country in the winter's cold and during the summer's heat you find them inhaling the poisoned breath of the swamp," he asserted, and on the march and in camp "you might have heard them singing German songs— songs from the Rhine, the Danube, the Weser, and the Main." These men and thousands who followed them enlisted "as free men, not as hirelings," and "offere[d] their life for the preservation of this land." Rohrbacker never mentioned Chancellorsville or nativism, but was obviously referring to the latter as his rhetoric tried to "prove" the Americanism of his comrades from the 74th. To him, being a loyal American meant being true to his German ethnicity, celebrating it and the deeds of his comrades, and *not* accepting prejudice:

> Were these soldiers less patriotic because they spoke German and sang German songs? . . . Were the blows dealt by them less vigorous because they were given by German arms? . . . I tell you, my friends, twenty-five or fifty years hence the descendants of those men who fell or fought at Gettysburg will be as proud of the deeds of his ancestor and of his Americanism, as are to-day the children of those who fought at Bunker Hill, or Lexington, and looking back at the history of our time, these Americans will wonder that there ever could be any jealousy or Knownothingism, because the ancestor

of one landed at Castle Garden or East Boston. We should measure the worth of the American citizen by his honesty, his capacity, his patriotism and his sympathies, independent of whether he or his father entered the family of the republic yesterday or a few decades before; *our dead heroes have furnished us the criterion of the true American*, for he cannot be called an American, who, though he came down from the signers of the Declaration of Independence itself, stirs up ill feelings among his fellow citizens.[19]

Rohrbacker then argued that powerful nations could only achieve their power through unity of national feeling. Citing Germany as an example, he claimed that "we, as German Americans, familiar with the history of the past, glory in a united Germany." With that last statement, he not only betrayed some nationalistic pride in the old country—pride which several authors have argued motivated renewed German American attempts at unity after 1870—but also pitted the United States against Germany and found America wanting. What the United States lacked was a nationalistic spirit, its growth hampered, apparently, by continued Anglo American nativism. Such prejudice forcibly separated ethnic Americans from the rest of the citizenry and obliged them to retain, or even enlarge their ethnic consciousness. Germans had fought honorably for the flag and Union as ethnic Germans; nativism was foolish and, importantly, un-American; the German war dead bought with their blood their countrymen's rights as Americans—these were Rohrbacker's primary points (echoing in several ways Steiger's comments), and without even mentioning Chancellorsville, he struck at the core of German Americans' feelings about the battle, its lingering aftermath, and the war as a whole. There was no need for Anglo Americans to continually harass German immigrants for being "cowardly Dutchmen" because the war was over, the Union preserved, and the rights of Germans as citizens secured through blood sacrifice. It was downright unpatriotic to preserve nativism. But as long as the descendants of "the signers of the Declaration of Independence" persisted in casting aspersions on German Americans, stirring up "ill feeling," as Rohrbacker put it, then the Germans would still be loyal, but would also continue being German.[20]

"Treu Dem Neuen Vaterland": The Pluralistic Postwar Vision

Several scholars have pointed out that German America from the 1870s to 1914 increasingly assumed a "culturally pluralistic" appearance, one that is in accordance with Rohrbacker's verbiage. This belief structure, evident throughout the German-language press, German American academic writings, and in

German American artistic endeavors, stressed at once the desirability and benefits of assimilation *and* the defense of German ethnicity. Leading proponents of
this vision argued that American society owed many of its finer qualities to
Teutonic immigrants and that the country would continue benefiting only if
the Germans were permitted to continue being German. As increasing numbers
of southern and eastern European immigrants arrived in the last decades of
the nineteenth century, German leaders believed their ethnic group would only
become more valuable to the nation, and correctly noted that, in comparison
with the newcomers, the Germans did not appear as different from Anglo
Americans as they once did. The latter group supposedly *needed* the gifts the
Germans could offer, now more than ever, and therefore the argument went
that the German-born should preserve their ethnicity. In other words, what
made German Americans different also made them excellent, contributing citizens. Thus, the German cultural pluralists retained the use of the German language and, indeed, strictly defended it; fought desperate political battles against
the forces of temperance and Sunday laws; relished and supported German cultural folkways and institutions, such as the Biergarten, the Turnverein and
other ethnic societies; and essentially did everything they could to retard outright Americanization. There were opponents of this movement, the so-called
anti-Germanizers, who also made their presence felt, and the question of how
much the leaders spoke for the average German American is still being debated.
Historians and sociologists supporting the pluralistic image of post–Civil War
German America nonetheless hold the scholarly high ground at this point.[21]

In this effort to retain their ethnicity for the good of the country, German
American cultural pluralists made frequent references to the Civil War. Two
primary arguments emerged as early as 1865 that continued on past the turn of
the century. First, the bloodshed and sacrifices of their soldiers had fully earned
Germans' rights as American citizens. No one could dare challenge the patriotism and intent of the country's Teutonic immigrants anymore, regardless of
how German they wanted to remain. German American writers seemed to relish this point, repeatedly offering their readerships the exaggerated idea that
they had not only been the ones to tip the election to Lincoln in 1860—an old
myth that still perseveres—but also that their soldiers had been decisive in winning the final Union victory. The blood spilled in defense of the Union became
the Germans' entry card into the club of full American citizenship.

The second major point reminded Germans of the nativism that re-emerged
in the Civil War era. Because of that bitter memory, German Americans had
no business leaping into the melting pot. To do so would be hypocritical and
reward prejudiced Anglo Americans, their erstwhile detractors. It was important to look to the future and join with other Americans in building the nation,

but not at the expense of their German ethnicity. As they moved forward, German citizens needed to remember the past.

Friedrich Kapp had been quick to defend German honor directly after Chancellorsville and remained one of the most outspoken champions of German ethnicity directly after the war. He would become known as an assimilationist later on, but his early speeches and writings actually reveal a thought process more akin to cultural pluralism. Asked to give the final speech that would close the activities of the Ninth German Sängerfest in Jones Wood, New York City, in July 1865, Kapp reminded the audience that German "Sängers and Turners were first" to take up arms in defense of the flag, and "had displayed their devotion to the Republic on almost all battlefields of the colossal war." He mentioned this "not in the vain spirit of exaggeration," but simply to set the record straight. However, "The times are happily over when the German hurls from himself as quickly as possible his entire history and education so that he may fast become a practical American. The Knownothing movement has had the positive effect of negating the idea that there is no higher plane of existence than to sink to being the disciples of Americanism. The firmer we hold on to the spiritual treasures of our nationality, the more recognition and respect we will find from the natives." In a textbook declaration of pluralism, Kapp then exclaimed, "Let us settle down here as well as we can, naturalize so far as we wish to, but let us work towards the good and betterment of the United States in correspondence to the spirit of our past and our character." Another famous forty-eighter, Judge Johann B. Stallo of Cincinnati, spoke in very similar terms in a speech about nativism in the school system in 1866. To a large audience assembled in the Cincinnati Turner hall, he proclaimed, "We are ready to thankfully accept all that is good that is offered to us from [other peoples]; we will attempt to repay this value with a corresponding counter-gift. But we are not prepared to sacrifice our own nature, our inner freedom and moral sturdiness." Then he spoke in more ominous terms. If forced to choose, because of others' nativistic proclivities, between "civil liberty, which America offers me, and spiritual freedom that is readily available from the German spirit, I would with heavy heart but without vacillation take my children with me back to the old German earth." He ended by saying that he hoped German Americans would never have to make such an unfortunate decision, that "at the celebratory banquet of the American republic the tankard of German thought may also be passed around."[22]

The indomitable Friedrich Lexow, one of the most virulent early proponents of a pluralistic vision for his countrymen, published article after article in the *Deutsch-Amerikanische Monatshefte* in support of this philosophy. In a series of 1866 articles on the assimilation of the Germans, he argued that "what we enjoy here we have earned; the blood of our heroes has dearly bought for us this country as a homeland. We are not foreigners in America, in that we are fully equal with the natives. . . . Our nature, our individuality and customs have the same entitlements as all the others." He reiterated the argument, like Kapp, that Germans had much of value to bequeath their new home, and were willing to learn from Anglo Americans in areas where they were uniquely qualified and experienced. "The German is by nature an unmitigated lover of freedom, and he wants it not just for himself, but for all people. The upright enthusiasm for the good and beautiful is a beneficial German quality," as were countless others that Lexow listed in a fit of ethnocentric largesse. All of these could be given freely to improve the nation, he insisted, but Germans who too quickly received from the greater American public without retaining their ethnic identity found themselves in a "no man's land that no one cares for. They simply become bad Americans . . . and experience shows us that Germans who Americanized in this manner are not among the best citizens of the republic." Lexow explained why he thought these immigrants had done what they did: "Behind us lies a time that we do not fondly remember. The German word was not cherished and cultivated, the banner of German custom not held high in victory. The German in America disowned his heritage where he could, urged himself to forget that he was a German, and the goal of his ambition was the complete, quick, plunging into that which he understood as Americanism. So it was not by all, but by many, yes, by the majority. This time of humiliation has been overcome. A better recognition of what lies ahead for us in America is now leading the way, and what was once the rule has become the shameful exception."[23]

Nativism as the primary reason not to Americanize and to hold on to German ethnicity was the primary topic of one Dr. Welsch, who wrote a philosophical piece in an 1867 issue of the *Monatshefte*. Even bolder in his beliefs than editor Lexow, Welsch postulated that the few Americans who had "Germanized" had benefited greatly and that increasing German immigration would ultimately bring about a greater influence of Germans in the United States in the years to come. That could only be a good thing for the country, he argued, because Americans who had no contact with Germans exhibited "ignorance and narrow-mindedness, complacent peddling and active loafing, bloated pauperism and naked bestiality." Yet the "German immigration does not force the natives to Germanize . . . but it also rejects the demand to Americanize, because it possesses too much pride in its own worth, too much independent strength and too much confidence in its future" than to "make other concessions to cocky nativism."[24]

Similar ideas could be found in the pages of the major German American newspapers in the postwar era. The *Philadelphia Demokrat* urged "every German American" to "have pride in his heritage and knowledge of the worth and service of his people to the country." His "language and his way of life are fully within his rights" to exercise, as they were earned and "founded in two centuries worth of cultural work" in the nation. The *Pittsburgher Volksblatt* also told its readers to look back on the German American past with pride, arguing that lingering nativist feelings from the war were responsible for "the shrouding of the efforts of the German American element in the struggle for freedom in the new Fatherland." But that problem could be overcome if more German-born writers engaged in preserving the history of their element, thus informing their countrymen of their ethnic group's valuable services in the past. By placing German American history on an equal plane with Anglo American history, an effective counterattack could be mounted against the "impertinence" and "injustice" of the nativists.[25]

As we have seen, some German American historians answered this challenge, but few of them were even-handed in their efforts. Most espoused a very pro-German interpretation of the war and evinced little interest in a more pluralist vision. L. W. Habercom was an exception. His *Our Adopted Fatherland: a History of the United States*, published in Milwaukee in 1889, exemplified the cultural pluralist philosophy being propounded in the major German-language newspapers and journals of the day. Claiming that Germans had a special patent on "thoroughness" and "faithfulness" as character traits, their service in the Civil War proved their other great, ethnic characteristic: patriotism. "We have mentioned that the German Americans gave their all for the Union when it was in danger, that they were counted among the first patriots who rallied to the threatened starry banner in April 1861, that they bravely held out and fought. German troops created the core of the Union armies at the beginning of the war. German officers were counted among the best in the service of the Union." In sum, "German loyalty could be relied upon, and never more faithfully than in the Civil War." Habercom then clinched his major point: "May German thoroughness, faithfulness, and patriotism evermore remain the watchwords of the German element in the United States, and always sharply and precisely stamp themselves on the American national character." A better marriage of German Civil War memory and pluralistic philosophy would be hard to find.[26]

On 26 November 1910 the German American residents of Dayton, Ohio, assembled in the German American Memorial Building to dedicate a monument. It was the first of its kind in the United States, a monument honoring *all* German soldiers who had fought in America's wars. Dominating the structure was a Union soldier, rifle held at the ready, and a great patriotic shield that read, "Treu dem neuen Vaterland (loyalty to the new Fatherland). An inscription in English declared, "In memory of the men of German blood who aided in the War of the Revolution to establish the Union of the states and in the Civil War offered their lives to perpetuate that Union." For two days the citizenry celebrated the unveiling with speeches, parades, and, of course, eating and drinking. Finally, Reverend H. G. Eisenlohr from Cincinnati gave the primary speech. He told the assembled listeners that this celebration was a "celebration by American citizens to honor other Americans," and added that they were not there to extol the memory of Germans at the cost of other patriots. "We are all citizens of the same country here," he proclaimed, "but we all want to stand at the same level! Nothing more but nothing less. And because one from the other side sees fit to overlook German accomplishments, so we may safely emphasize them." Much of what was good in the United States originated with the Germans, he said, and he implored his audience "not to forget your German ancestry." Raising his voice for the conclusion, he exhorted, "Do not disclaim your Deutschtum! It is a dearly-bought inheritance, well worth treasuring." This monument "does honor not only to those who served, but is also a constant reminder for us. Throw away finally that false shame, be proud that you are a German, or thankful that you descend from Germans!"[27]

It had taken fifty years, but the German Americans had at last shaken off the legacy of Chancellorsville, evincing signs of cultural unity and ethnic strength unseen since the Civil War itself. How eerily unfortunate that within the decade Anglo Americans would again stigmatize German immigrants as undesirable citizens, this time because of World War I. And this time German America would not rally and recover from the sting of nativistic xenophobia, but instead crack irrevocably apart.

The memory of Chancellorsville and the Civil War remained very powerful among German Americans in the last decades of the nineteenth century. It is impossible to determine how much the barb of nativism still lingered among the veterans and predisposed them to certain actions—such as discouraging Americanizing trends among family members and friends—but it is not a gigantic leap of faith to postulate that their thoughts and memories must have somehow transferred to their loved ones, and indeed the greater German American population. These men had represented their ethnic group during the Civil War. They were its heroes, its models. The hopes and dreams of northern Germans marched with Blenker's division, fought at Cross Keys and Second Manassas, and retreated at Chancellorsville. The coverage of these events in the

German-language press proved the extent of public interest in the ethnic regiments and their fates during the war. If we cannot definitively connect the nativism unleashed during the Civil War to a slowed acculturation rate among German Americans in the postwar era, we *can* trace the uncanny chronology of events: increased ethnic consciousness in the first two years of the war, the battle of Chancellorsville and expanding nativism, followed by German indignance and attempts at unity in response, and then a pluralistic celebration of German ethnicity in the postwar decades that stressed the benefits of remaining German to immigrants. Certainly, as Paul Rohrbacker of the 74th Pennsylvania insinuated, the unification of Germany in 1871 played a major role in the renaissance of German ethnic pride in the United States. Public agitation for temperance and Sunday laws especially in the 1880s and 1890s also did little to endear teetotaling Anglo Americans to their German American neighbors, who felt their natural-born rights were under attack. But something unsettling, even sinister from the Civil War—the most prominent event in the lives of nineteenth-century Americans—haunted German immigrants in the postwar decades. They could not rid themselves of it until the eve of the Great War, an event that ultimately proved the undoing of most German American communities across the United States.

All these years after the decline of the little Germanies in our cities and the vanishing of the German tongue from urban neighborhoods, the history of German America during the Civil War can inform us about how we as a nation react during times of crisis, how many Americans still view ethnic and immigrant citizens, and how those citizens react to prejudice during periods of national stress. Although it would be unthinkable today for a nativistic political party to gain national prominence as the Know Nothings briefly did in the 1850s, it is not a great stretch to hypothesize that one of the major parties could seriously espouse nativist tendencies today. Whether or not these tendencies would manifest themselves as bills in Congress is debatable, as is the dubious proposition of such bills actually becoming laws. But all we have to do to find modern echoes of the prejudice suffered by the Germans in the Civil War era is to recall the almost knee-jerk reaction against Muslim Americans after 11 September 2001. Throughout the United States, American citizens with even Muslim-sounding last names were singled out for ridicule, harassed in public places, and otherwise made to feel uncomfortable. Even people whose ancestors had emigrated generations earlier but who had Middle Eastern surnames frequently came under suspicion not only by their fellow citizens, but also by the federal government itself. Although it is difficult to confirm, certain national agencies probably possess "blacklists" composed of names of persons whose only crime is, in most cases, having the wrong last name or ethnicity. The similarities between post–9/11 America and the North in the Civil War are not at all exact, but in both instances the country was outraged at an attack on its native soil, by the violation of its sovereignty, and by the shock of being plunged suddenly into violence. In both cases, sizeable populations of the foreign-born existed whose loyalties *seemed* questionable, yet in nearly all cases they were not. Both periods also witnessed a prewar uneasiness with immigrants in general, in which thousands of jobs traditionally earmarked for poorer, "native-born" whites and blacks began to be taken by increasing numbers of newcomers; in the 1840s and '50s it was the Irish and Germans, in the 1980s and '90s it was primarily Hispanic, East Asian, and Middle Eastern immigrants. Debates about whether or not to shut off immigration, build walls along the border with Mexico, and how, exactly, to "keep America American" proliferated at all levels of society in the 1990s, and although not as potentially threatening to the foreign-born as the Know Nothings of the 1850s, still set the stage for a backlash later when the crisis exploded.

After both 9/11 in 2001 and Chancellorsville in 1863 a scapegoat was needed to salve a wounded nation. A viable "foreign" enemy (Al-Qaeda may or may not be considered entirely "foreign" depending on one's sources; Confederates were perceived as foreigners by most northerners) clearly created the immediate disaster both times, but it could be argued that bungling at the top levels assisted the enemy in wreaking such havoc. To cover up this mismanagement, someone—or some group—had to take the blame. Clearly we have progressed a great deal as a society since 1863, and thankfully the majority of the American population did not automatically resort to ridiculing all Muslim Americans for the tragedy on 9/11. But alarmingly large elements of the population did, and still harbor such sentiments six years later. At the very least, a feeling of general distrust seems to exist between Muslim and non-Muslim Americans echoing that between German and Anglo Americans after 1863 (indeed, other historical examples could be inserted here, such as the treatment of Japanese Americans after Pearl Harbor). And like the German communities of the Civil War era, modern Muslim communities in the United States and Britain have turned inward, reinforced their religious and ethnic beliefs, and argued strenuously in defense of their civil liberties against what they perceive as encroachment from the majority population. Even more similar is the approach that some Muslim and Arab Americans have taken regarding military service, believing they must prove their Americanism by enlisting. Japanese Americans volunteered for the armed services in extremely high numbers after Pearl Harbor for the same reasons.

The great difference among these examples is, of course, that Germany was never the attacker of the Union, so the loyalties of German Americans could not be questioned in the 1860s in the same way as those of Japanese or Arab Americans in later periods. Instead, German Americans fought steadfastly throughout the Civil War to preserve the Union, all too often offering, as Lincoln eloquently said, "the last full measure of devotion." How ironically tragic it is, therefore, that this major ethnic group, which more than proved its patriotism, received the nativistic prejudice that it did during the war. The Germans' reactions to that intolerance is instructive today: in a multiethnic nation, a group unfairly singled out for blame for a national disaster will naturally retreat unto itself and reinforce its own separate identity. The America of the late nineteenth century was strong enough to withstand that sort of cultural pluralism; it remains to be seen if the United States of today is. In a modern nation of immigrants, in an age when multiculturalism is supposedly celebrated, the memory of German America and its reactions to Chancellorsville is especially salient. We ignore it at our own peril. Perhaps the tombstone of nativism has finally been carved, but its date of death is sadly not yet inscribed.

Notes

Notes to Introduction

1. *Report of the Joint Committee on the Conduct of the War* (reprint: Broadfoot Publishing Company, 1999) 4: 12, 66, 85, 30–31, 35–36, 45, 127, 141; Bruce Tap, *Over Lincoln's Shoulder: The Committee on the Conduct of the War* (Lawrence: University Press of Kansas, 1998), 179–80; Carl Schurz, "Reminiscences of a Long Life," *McClures Magazine*, June 1917, 175.

2. For the purposes of this study, the term "German American" or "German" indicates a person or persons either born in any of the nineteenth-century German states or their immediate offspring, i.e., sons and daughters, then living in the United States. The term "Anglo American" indicates a person or persons born in the United States and descended mainly from colonial-era English or Scots-Irish colonists.

3. For detailed discussions of the importance of courage, see Gerald F. Linderman, *Embattled Courage: The Experience of Combat in the American Civil War* (New York: The Free Press, 1987) and James M. McPherson, *For Cause and Comrades: Why Men Fought in the Civil War* (New York: Oxford University Press, 1997).

4. Horace Greeley, *The American Conflict: A History of the Great Rebellion in the United States of America, 1860–1865* (G. and C. W. Sherwood, 1866); William Swinton, *Campaigns of the Army of the Potomac* (1867 [reprint: New York: Smithmark Publishers, 1995]), 286–87; Abner Doubleday, *Chancellorsville and Gettysburg* (1882, reprint New York: De Capo Press, 1994), 29–30; *National Tribune*, 12 December 1892; Theodore A. Dodge, *The Campaign of Chancellorsville*, 2nd ed. (Boston: Ticknor and Fields, 1881); Samuel P. Bates, in *The Battle of Chancellorsville* (Meadville, Pa.: Edward T. Bates, 1882), 174.

5. Augustus Choate Hamlin, *The Battle of Chancellorsville* (Bangor, Maine, 1896), 34–47, 66–78, and especially 154–66, "Abuse of the Eleventh Corps" and "Examples of Calumny and Falsehood."

6. John Bigelow, *The Campaign of Chancellorsville: A Strategic and Tactical Study* (New Haven: Yale University Press, 1910), 479–80.

7. Edward J. Stackpole, *Chancellorsville: Lee's Greatest Battle* (Harrisburg, Pa.: Stackpole Books, 1958), 239–40; Ernest B. Furguson, *Chancellorsville: The Souls of the Brave* (New York: Alfred A. Knopf, 1993); Stephen W. Sears, *Chancellorsville* (Boston: Houghton Mifflin, 1996). Furgurson devotes 11 out of 350 pages of text to the actual fighting done by the Eleventh Corps and Sears allocates 9 out of 449 pages.

8. All translations from the original German are mine unless otherwise indicated.

9. Don Yoder quoted in David L. Valuska and Christian B. Keller, *Damn Dutch: Pennsylvania Germans at Gettysburg* (Mechanicsburg, Pa.: Stackpole Books, 2004), 2–3. My definition of nativism stems somewhat from the scholarship of Tyler Anbinder and his definition of the term. See Tyler Anbinder, *Nativism and Slavery: The Northern Know-Nothings and the Politics of the 1850s* (New York: Oxford University Press, 1992), xiv.

10. A growing body of recent historical literature is deepening our understanding of German Americans in the Civil War era. Most of this scholarship has been produced in the last twenty years. Wilhelm Kaufmann, *The Germans in the American Civil War* (1911;

reprint Carlisle, Pa.: John Kallmann Books, 1999), originally published in German, has been of limited use to American scholars until recently because of the language barrier, and is further plagued by nationalistic rhetoric, ethnocentrism, filiopietism, and errors in fact (see chapter 6). Ella Lonn, *Foreigners in the Union Army and Navy* (Baton Rouge: Louisiana State University Press, 1951), has long been the standard reference about ethnic Americans in the war, but is now dated and has always been plagued with stereotypes, errors in fact, and giant chronological omissions. Her commentary on the Germans tends to be anecdotal, not analytical. John Higham, in *Strangers in the Land: Patterns in American Nativism* (New Brunswick, N.J.: Rutgers University Press, 1955) and in various subsequent articles, has touched upon the subject of Germans and other ethnic minorities in the war, but his analysis is based on a very limited primary source pool, and comes down clearly in favor of the erroneous "melting pot" thesis; William L. Burton's *Melting Pot Soldiers: The Union's Ethnic Regiments*, 2nd ed. (New York: Fordham University Press, 1998), first published in 1987, greatly enhanced and expanded upon Lonn's work, but is similarly beset with problems, namely, overgeneralizations, a strong reliance on secondary sources, and almost no use of foreign-language sources. Burton also cites Lonn for much of his commentary on the Germans. A number of good journal articles, regimental histories, biographies, and translations of soldiers' letters and diaries have also been published over the past three decades; in the interest of space, I will list only some of the highlights: James S. Pula, *The Sigel Regiment: A History of the Twenty-Sixth Wisconsin Volunteer Infantry, 1862–1865* (Campbell, Calif.: Savas Publishing Company, 1998); Stephen D. Engle, *Yankee Dutchman: The Life of Franz Sigel* (Fayetteville, Ark.: University of Arkansas Press, 1993); also by Stephen Engle, "A Raised Consciousness: Franz Sigel and German Ethnic Identity in the Civil War," *Yearbook of German American Studies* 34 (1999): 1–13; Hans L. Trefousse, *Carl Schurz: A Biography* (1982; reprint New York: Fordham University Press, 1998); Walter D. Kamphoefner, "German Americans and Civil War Politics: A Reconsideration of the Ethnocultural Thesis," *Civil War History* 37, no. 3 (1991): 232–46; Earl J. Hess, ed., *A German in the Yankee Fatherland: The Civil War Letters of Henry A. Kircher* (Kent, Ohio: Kent State University Press, 1983); and Joseph R. Reinhart, ed. and trans., *Two Germans in the Civil War: The Diary of John Daeuble and the Letters of Gottfried Rentschler, 6th Kentucky Volunteer Infantry* (Knoxville: University of Tennessee Press, 2004). Reinhart currently has another letter collection in press on the German 32nd Indiana, which promises to be interesting. The recently published *Deutsche im Amerikanischen Bürgerkrieg: Briefe von Front und Farm* (Munich: Schöningh Verlag, 2002), ed. Wolfgang Helbich and Walter D. Kamphoefner, is a valuable addition to the literature (and is soon to be translated into English), but is analytically limited—it is primarily a collection of soldiers' letters. Works by two other German scholars, Jörg Nagler, *Frémont contra Lincoln: Die deutsch-amerikanische Opposition in der republikanischen Partei während des amerikanischen Bürgerkrieges* (New York: Peter Lang, 1984), and Martin W. Oefele, *German-Speaking Officers in the U.S. Colored Troops, 1863–1867* (Gainesville: University of Florida Press, 2004), although limited in scope, have been helpful in the preparation of this study and also represent important contributions to the literature. Dean B. Mahin, *The Blessed Place of Freedom: Europeans in Civil War America* (Washington, D.C.: Brasseys, 2002), which attempts to place German Americans in the context of the entire war and all the other ethnic groups' participation, provides a useful introduction to the subject of Germans in the war, but is based almost exclusively on published secondary sources and provides little new material on the actual reactions of German Americans to wartime events. A forthcoming work on German Americans in the Confederacy, by Andrea Mehrländer, promises to be a splendid analysis, and I might also recommend David L. Valuska and Christian B. Keller, *Damn Dutch: Pennsylvania Germans at Gettysburg* (Mechanicsburg, Pa.: Stackpole Books, 2004), and Christian B. Keller, "Pennsylvania and Virginia Germans in the

Civil War: A Brief History and Comparative Analysis," *Virginia Magazine of History and Biography* 109, no. 1 (Summer 2001): 37–86.

1. German Americans, Know Nothings, and the Outbreak of the War

1. Political, religious, class, and provincial differences aside, German immigrants in the antebellum cities quickly came to understand that they held in common the fact that they were German speakers in a predominantly English-speaking country and all hailed from that part of Europe where German was spoken. The prewar nativist movement certainly drew them together. Nadel contends that most German urban dwellers tended to owe allegiance to so many different clubs and groups within their communities that they could not devote their loyalty to just one or two—thus risking estrangement from the others they valued—and therefore directed their loyalty "to the whole expressed by a combination of all them—the German-American community of Kleindeutschland." See Stan Nadel, *Little Germany: Ethnicity, Religion, and Class in New York City, 1845–1880* (Chicago: University of Illinois Press, 1990), 8.

2. Nadel, ibid.; John A. Hawgood, *The Tragedy of German-America: The Germans in the United States of America during the Nineteenth Century—and After* (New York: G. P. Putnam's Sons, 1940; reprint 1970, Arno Press), 253. Hawgood has come under fire by modern historians for his sketchy attribution methods and radical (perhaps pro-German?) views, but his argumentation remains, in my opinion, both logical and thought-provoking.

3. *Eighth United States Census, 1860: The Statistics of the Population*, xxii–xxix. This percentage of foreign-born in the overall American population does not, of course, include their immediate offspring, who undoubtedly remained tied to the ethnic communities and cultures of their parents. Those numbers could not be conclusively calculated, but would probably add another ten to fifteen percent (at least), making the "immigrant" population of the country no less than twenty-five percent of the aggregate. The standard works on antebellum immigration and the Anglo American reactions to it include Ray Allen Billington, *The Protestant Crusade, 1800–1860: A Study of the Origins of American Nativism* (1938, reprint Gloucester, Mass.: Peter Smith, 1963); Dale T. Knobel, *"America for the Americans:" The Nativist Movement in the United States* (New York: Twayne Publishers, 1996); and Tyler Anbinder, *Nativism and Slavery: The Northern Know Nothings and the Politics of the 1850s* (New York: Oxford University Press, 1992).

4. Knobel, 99–100, and Knobel, *Paddy and the Republic: Ethnicity and Nationality in Antebellum America* (Middletown, Conn.: Wesleyan University Press, 1986), 167–68; Oscar Handlin, *Boston's Immigrants, 1790–1880: A Study in Acculturation* (1941, reprint New York: Atheneum, 1974), 203–6. The Know Nothings also tended to attack corruption in government and vowed to cleanse state and city governments of undemocratic influences, many of which they blamed on bosses who catered to immigrants in order to secure their votes.

5. Hawgood, *The Tragedy of German-America*, 250–53.

6. A high percentage of the forty-eighters had moved into the West by 1860, congregating in such cities as St. Louis and Chicago and giving them a more radical—more Republican—flavor. The forty-eighters, sometimes called "the Greens," were frequently opposed to the older generation of German leaders, often called "the Grays," who had emigrated to the United States in the 1830s, and tended to be more conservative. The forty-eighters quickly rallied to the Republican banner in 1860, whereas the Grays ("Dreissiger") were slower to do so, and sometimes supported the Democrats. A good discussion of the much-emphasized and, arguably, overplayed split between the two generations of German-born leaders may be found in Walter D. Kamphoefner, "Dreissiger and Forty-eighter: The Political Influence of Two Generations of German Political

Exiles," in Hans L. Trefousse, ed., *Germany and America: Essays on Problems of International Relations and Immigration* (New York: Brooklyn College Press, 1980), 89–99.

7. See Lesley Ann Kawaguchi, "Diverging Political Affiliations and Ethnic Perspectives: Philadelphia Germans and Antebellum Politics," *Journal of American Ethnic History* 13, no. 2 (Winter 1994): 3–29; James M. Bergquist, "German Communities in American Cities: An Interpretation of the Nineteenth-Century Experience," *Journal of American Ethnic History* 4, no. 1 (Fall 1984): 9–30; and Stan Nadel, *Little Germany*, for revisionist views on the thesis. More standard works include Frederick C. Luebke, *Germans in the New World: Essays in the History of Immigration* (Chicago: University of Illinois Press, 1990), 8–82; Kathleen Neils Conzen, *Immigrant Milwaukee, 1836–1860: Accommodation and Community in a Frontier City* (Cambridge, Mass.: Harvard University Press, 1976), particularly chapters 1 and 4; Bruce Levine, *The Spirit of 1848: German Immigrants, Labor Conflict, and the Coming of the Civil War* (Chicago: University of Illinois Press, 1992), particularly chapters 4, 5, 8, and 9; Michael Holt, *Forging a Majority: The Formation of the Republican Party in Pittsburgh, 1848–1860* (New Haven: Yale University Press, 1969); Paul J. Kleppner, "Lincoln and the Immigrant Vote: A Case of Religious Polarization," in Frederick C. Luebke, ed., *Ethnic Voters and the Election of Lincoln* (Lincoln: University of Nebraska Press, 1971); and Kleppner, *The Cross of Culture: A Social Analysis of Midwestern Politics, 1850–1900* (New York: The Free Press, 1970).

8. Kawaguchi, "Diverging Political Affiliations," 5–11; Anbinder, *Nativism and Slavery*, 266–67; Mahin, *The Blessed Place of Freedom*, 6–7; Valuska and Keller, *Damn Dutch*, 14–15.

9. Historians have disputed the actual numbers of German-born soldiers who enlisted in the Union armies. Estimates range from a low of 187,000 to a high of 216,000. This number clearly does not include the sons of original immigrants, who, I would argue, should also be included when computing the numbers of ethnically German troops. See Dean B. Mahin, *The Blessed Place of Freedom: Europeans in Civil War America* (Washington, D.C.: Brasseys, 2002), 15, for a decent discussion of the numbers issue. See Lonn, *Foreigners in the Union Army*, chapters 2 and 3, and Burton, *Melting Pot Soldiers*, 35–37 and chapter 4, for a discussion of early ethnic, especially German, support for the Union war effort.

10. Beyond civilian support for the formation of the various ethnic regiments, Burton barely treats the home front at all, but his book admittedly focuses on the regiments. Lonn's chapter 18 contains much useful information on German home front activities in the Midwest, but fails to link this ethnic war support to anything more than loyalty to the Union.

11. "Jahres-Bericht der deutschen Gesellschaft der Stadt New York, am 31. December 1861" (New York: Druck von M. W. Siebert, 1862), 15, 17.

12. Philadelphia *Freie Presse*, 22 and 29 April, 6 May 1861; *Philadelphia Demokrat*, 22 April, 13 and 20 May 1861; Kawaguchi, "The Making of Philadelphia's German-America," 296–97; Oswald Seidensticker, *Erster Teil der Geschichte der Deutschen Gesellschaft von Pennsylvanien* (Philadelphia: Neudruck von Graf & Breuninger, 1917), 244. Philadelphia had more numerous and well-endowed German organizations—which in turn provided much more care proportionately to the families of the soldiers—because the German immigrant community in Philadelphia was older, more numerous, and wealthier than its counterparts in other cities with larger German immigrant populations.

13. Philadelphia *Freie Presse*, 1 January and 12 August 1863; Mrs. Adolph Spaeth, ed., *Life of Adolph Spaeth, D.D., LL.D.* (Philadelphia: General Council Publication House, 1916), 79.

14. Egg Harbor City *Egg Harbor Pilot*, 21 March 1863.

15. Pittsburgh *Freiheitsfreund und Courier*, 22 and 23 April 1861. There were clearly two separate groups because the names of the officers in each organization were different.

16. Pittsburgh *Freiheitsfreund und Courier*, 30 May 1861.

17. Ibid., 9 May 1861. Interestingly, the issues of April and May were littered with patriotic poetry written by an H. P. Müller, extolling the virtues of the patriotic wife, mother, and sweetheart. See especially "The Patriotic Mother," 27 April 1861; "Maidens' Love," 6 May 1861; and "Cradle Song," 26 April 1861, in which a German mother tells her newborn infant about his father "down in the sunny South, fighting bravely for "Freiheit und Recht." "May his arm never tire, may he honor the German race!" (Möge er zieren das deutsche Geschlecht!).

18. Hirsch letter reprinted in ibid., 6 November 1861; for editorials lamenting the condition of the families, see 8, 16, and 21 December 1862 and 8 and 9 December 1863. It is unclear exactly when the German ladies' aid societies dissolved, but I discovered no references to their activities after December 1861. The *Freiheitsfreund* did contain several appeals in December 1863 editorials for the support of soldiers' families through the voluntary taxation of local residents—indicating earlier charitable organizations among the Pittsburgh Germans were no longer active.

19. For a fuller discussion of Deutschtum and its development among German Americans in the antebellum period, see Valuska and Keller, *Damn Dutch*, 13–15.

20. For instance, the Philadelphia *Freie Presse* for the months of April, May, June, and July 1861 contained no clear references in either editorials or the classifieds for German support of pan-northern soldiers' relief organizations, such as the United States Sanitary Commission. See Kawaguchi, "The Making of Philadelphia's German-America," 187–94, for the identification and demographic analysis of the major German wards of the city. According to her calculations, the 19th, 16th, 11th, 17th, and 12th wards were most populated with Germans. That Anglo Americans recognized certain city sections as "German" is supported by an advertisement in the *Freie Presse* of 1 Janaury 1863 announcing the opening of a "Military and Naval Branch Office" for the exclusive use of German-speaking patrons. Located at 458 North 3rd Street, the office was a new German branch of a business that assisted widows, mothers, and other relatives in filing claims for fallen soldiers' pensions.

21. The Philadelphia *Freie Presse*, *Philadelphia Demokrat*, *Pittsburgher Demokrat*, and Pittsburgh *Freiheitsfreund* were the major urban German papers examined in this case. Naturally, the Republican *Freie Presse* and *Freiheitsfreund* contained much more coverage of the forty-eighter colonels and generals than the Democratic papers, but regardless of political affiliation they all repeatedly featured news of special interest to their German readers first and in the most prominent locations.

22. Earl J. Hess, "Sigel's Resignation: A Study in German-Americanism and the Civil War," *Civil War History* 26 (1980): 5–17; Stephen Engle, "A Raised Consciousness: Franz Sigel and German Ethnic Identity in the Civil War," *Yearbook of German-American Studies* 34 (1999), 1–18; and, also by Engle, *Yankee Dutchman: The Life of Franz Sigel* (Baton Rouge: Louisiana State University Press, 1993), 90–100.

23. *Louisville Anzeiger*, 10 January 1862; Chicago *Illinois Staatszeitung* editorial reprinted in *Louisville Anzeiger*, 12 January 1862; Columbus *Westbote*, 16 January 1862; Philadelphia *Freie Presse*, 11 and 13 January 1862.

24. Particulars of the New York demonstration, including the resolutions, were printed in the *Louisville Anzeiger*, 22 January 1862. For the Wisconsin legislature's resolutions, see the Columbus *Westbote*, 23 January 1862.

25. *Louisville Anzeiger*, 19 March 1862. Another good example of the German-language press's preoccupation with things German involves Sigel's tour of Pennsylvania while campaigning for the Republicans in the fall of 1863. Every speech he made was

reprinted verbatim in the *Freie Presse*, and editor Thomas himself introduced the general at his 4 October rally in Philadelphia's Concert Hall, which was attended by "thousands," according to Thomas's editorial about the event. Reading the editorials and reprinted speeches that resulted from Sigel's visits in Philadelphia and Pittsburgh, an uninformed reader might mistake the German general as the presidential candidate. See especially the *Freie Presse*, 5 and 10 October 1863.

2. Before Chancellorsville: Sigel, Blenker, and the Reinforcement of German Ethnicity in the Union Army, 1861–1862

1. A review of some of the prominent works on the lives of Civil War soldiers reveals little mention, and in some cases acknowledgment, of ethnic soldiers in the Union army. Bell Irvin Wiley, in his landmark book, *The Life of Billy Yank: The Common Soldier of the Union* (New York: Bobbs-Merrill, 1951), includes two pages on the subject but derives most of his information from Ella Lonn; James McPherson's *For Cause and Comrades: Why Men Fought in the Civil War* (New York: Oxford University Press, 1997) has barely a paragraph on ethnic soldiers, though McPherson admits his survey of soldiers' letters contained few ethnic examples; and Reid Mitchell's *Civil War Soldiers: Their Expectations and Experiences* (New York: Viking Penguin, 1988) briefly describes Confederate reactions to German "hirelings" on p. 29 but neglects any further discussion of German soldiers. James I. Robertson's *Soldiers Blue and Gray* (Columbia: University of South Carolina Press, 1988) spends only two paragraphs on the Germans, but Robertson admits "Germans were the most numerous foreign nationality in the Union armies" (p. 27); and Gerald Linderman, *Embattled Courage: The Experience of Combat in the American Civil War* (New York: The Free Press, 1987), fails even to mention the Irish or Germans.

2. Calculating statistics drawn from all enlisted age groups, E. B. Long claimed that the average age of Union soldiers was 25.8 years (*The Civil War Day by Day*, 707), but James Robertson asserts in *Soldiers Blue and Gray*, "a typical Civil War soldier was a white, native-born farmer, Protestant, single, and in the 18–29 age bracket" (p. 25). His mentor, Bell Irvin Wiley, came to a similar conclusion, drawing strongly from Benjamin A. Gould's official statistics: "in the first year of the conflict the largest single age group among the men who wore the blue was the eighteen-year-olds" and the "next largest category was the twenty-one-year-olds." The most numerous professional group "[was] the farmers." See Wiley, *The Life of Billy Yank*, 303–4.

3. Company E, 27th Pennsylvania; Company A, 73rd Pennsylvania; Company H, 74th Pennsylvania; Company B, 75th Pennsylvania; and Company B, 98th Pennsylvania were the companies randomly surveyed, amounting to a total of 475 men. In ascending order by regimental number, the average age of men in each regiment was: 29.34, 33.16, 29.45, 29.27, and 28.26 years old. Among the German states, Württemberg was listed as the birthplace most frequently, with Baden, Hessen (including Kur-Hessen, und Hesse-Darmstadt), Prussia, and Bavaria claiming the largest number of soldiers in decreasing order. Pennsylvania was listed as the birthplace of over fifty soldiers, but most of the names listed were of unquestionable German ethnicity, and thus must represent men born in the United States of German-born parents. Company E of the 27th Pennsylvania was a "mixed" company, containing seventeen recruits born in Ireland and eleven born in other, non-German European countries. Comparison with the roster of the regiment contained in Bates's *History* confirms that the regiment was indeed ethnically German overall, but the presence of so many Irish in this particular company indicates that the regiment contained non-German elements, an inference that certain letters to Governor Andrew Curtin substantiates (see next section). See the descriptive books of each company contained in the regimental descriptive books, 27th, 73rd, 74th, 75th, and 98th

Pennsylvania, RG-94, National Archives and Records Administration, Washington, D.C. [hereafter NARA]).

4. He was also probably married, although this fact cannot be completely substantiated. A "List of Married Members of Co. A, 27th Pennsylvania. Vols Regiment" (27th Pennsylvania, unbound records filed with muster rolls, RG-94, NARA) indicates that fifty-three out of ninety-five men were married at the time of enlistment in 1861.

5. Lesley Ann Kawaguchi argues ("Diverging Political Affiliations and Ethnic Perspectives: Philadelphia Germans and Antebellum Politics," *Journal of American Ethnic History* 13, no. 2 [Winter 1994]: 3–29) that Germans in this city aligned themselves politically and socially based on a shared German ancestry from a particular German state, as well as on religious differences between Protestants and Catholics. Prussians sought the company of Prussians and favored the same in business, politics, and social organizations, and southern Germans organized clubs and political organizations with memberships strongly dominated by themselves. For many years prior to the war, even Philadelphia's German newspapers were printed in a provincially specific slant that targeted particular segments of the German population. This practice was dying out by the 1850s. For a good review of the failed 1848 revolutions in southern Germany and the animosities spawned between Prussians and southern Germans, see Theodore Hamerow, *Restoration, Revolution, Reaction: Economics and Politics in Germany, 1815–1871* (Princeton: Princeton University Press, 1957) and Jonathan Sperber, *Rhineland Radicals: The Democratic Movement and the Revolution of 1848–1849* (Princeton: Princeton University Press, 1991).

6. Jacob C. Kappler, 99th Pennsylvania, to "Dear Wife," 13 June 1861, letter contained in Jacob C. Kappler collection in the Society Collection of the Historical Society of Pennsylvania, Philadelphia (hereafter HSP); Alphons Richter to parents and sister, 30 October 1861, reprinted in Wolfgang Helbich and Walter D. Kamphoefner, *Deutsche im Amerikanischen Buergerkrieg: Briefe von Front und Farm, 1861–1865* (Paderborn, Germany: Schoeningh Verlag), 158.

7. *The Pennsylvania Fifth*, 17 June 1861, published at "Camp McDowell, Virginia" by the 5th Pennsylvania Infantry, hardcopy at the Pennsylvania State Library; also see the 10 June issue, preserved at the Virginia Historical Society, Richmond, VA; Joseph S. Johnson, 96th Pennsylvania to Jacob Johnson, 22 June 1862, reprinted in Skippackville *Neutralist und Allgemeine Neuigkeits-Bote*, 8 July 1862 (Johnson was a new recruit at the time of writing); see June–August issues of the *Neutralist*, particularly 8 and 23 July 1861, 6 August 1861 for letters from "C. B. A."

8. Earl J. Hess, ed., *A German in the Yankee Fatherland: The Civil War Letters of Henry A. Kircher* (Kent, Ohio: Kent State University Press, 1983), 92; Wilhelm Brecht's letter reprinted in the Allentown *Unabhängige Republikaner*, 15 April 1863; Pretz diary entry for 9 October 1863, reprinted in Amos A. Ettinger, "An Allentonian in Florida During the Civil War: The Diary and Letters of Alfred C. Pretz, 1861–1865," *Proceedings of the Lehigh County Historical Society* 12 (Dec. 1939): 50–80; Sebastian Mueller to parents and sister, 16 June 1862, transcribed in MMC Sebastian Mueller Letterbooks, Library of Congress, Washington, D.C. (hereafter LOC); Martin W. Oefele, *German-Speaking Officers in the U.S. Colored Troops, 1863–1867* (Gainesville: University Press of Florida, 2004), 31.

9. Franz Schwenzer, 47th Pennsylvania to "Dear Wife," 9 October 1861, Fort Ethan Allen, Virginia (Civil War Misc. Collection, Franz Henry Schwenzer letters, 1861–1862, United States Military History Institute, Carlisle Barracks, Pennsylvania (hereafter USAMHI). As a musician, Schwenzer was paid more than the average enlisted man.

10. Schneider quoted in Constantine Grebner, *We Were the Ninth: A History of the Ninth Regiment, Ohio Volunteer Infantry, April 17, 1861 to June 7, 1864* (Kent, Ohio: Kent State University Press, 1987), 195; Aldoph Frick to mother and siblings, 29 September

1862, reprinted in Helbich and Kamphoefner, *Deutsche im Amerikanischen Buergerkrieg*, 401; Albert Krause to parents and siblings, 11 September 1862, reprinted in ibid., 256.

11. Burton, *Melting Pot Soldiers*, 110; "Jahres-Bericht der Deutschen Gesellschaft der Stadt New York," 15; Stanley Nadel, *Little Germany: Ethnicity, Religion, and Class in New York City, 1845–80* (Urbana: University of Illinois Press, 1990), especially chapters 2–4; *Belleviller Zeitung*, 1 August 1861, reprinted in Hanno R. E. Hardt, "A German American Editor Supports the Union, 1860–62," *The Journalism Quarterly* 42, no. 3, 457–60. Nadel's book remains the best work documenting life in the North's nineteenth-century German neighborhoods.

12. R. B. Goodman, "Acting Lieut. of Compy B, 27th Pennsylvania, to 'His Excellency Andrew G. Curtin,'" 30 November 1861 (RG-19, Microfilm 3662, roll 15, 27th Regiment [part], Pennsylvania State Archives, Harrisburg, PA [hereafter PASA]). Goodman's letter was four pages long.

13. Charles Galagher to "Govener Curtin Honourable Sir," 23 August 1861, ibid. The "Irish and American Mixed Company" Galagher referred to was Co. F under the command of Captain Sperring, which served throughout much of the war as guards for an armory in Washington, D.C. They never rejoined the regiment. Not all Irishmen in the 27th were pushed out of the regiment, however. A notable exception is Peter A. McAloon, whose family emigrated from Ireland in the 1850s. Peter's father was handicapped by a work-related accident, and Peter became the chief breadwinner for his family. He worked as a bookkeeper and secretary of the all-Irish Montgomery Artillerists militia in prewar Philadelphia, and became friends with Max Einstein, the organizer of the 27th. When the war broke out, McAloon was instrumental in bringing the Montgomery Artillerists into the ranks of the 27th, and apparently became friendly with Adolphus Buschbeck, Einstein's replacement. Due to his highly placed friends and to bravery displayed on the battlefield, McAloon won the respect of his German fellow officers. He remained loyal to the regiment, ascending even to the Lieutenant Colonelcy, until he died leading it in a charge up the slopes of Missionary Ridge in November 1863. The fact that McAloon succeeded to the command of the predominantly German 27th suggests that the Germans made exceptions when purging their regiments of non-German officers. See Peter McAloon's mother's pension file, app. 47.905, certif. 31.440, NARA. I would like to especially thank Mrs. Patricia A. McAloon, of Watertown, WI, a direct descendant of Lt. Col. McAloon, for her generosity in sharing this information and answering questions.

14. See the citations for Lonn, Burton, and Kaufmann from the introduction, and Helbich and Kamphoefner, op. cit. Lonn actually has a chapter entitled "Life in Camp and Field," but it is mainly composed of scattered anecdotes about special occasions in camp, such as celebratory banquets, holidays, and parades. Additionally, Lonn mixes these stories from Irish, Scandinavian, Swiss, French, and German units, the result being an uncritical mélange of ethnic experiences in the camp. Kaufmann devotes almost no space to a discussion of the daily lives of German soldiers, but concentrates instead on chronicling the campaigns in which they fought. Burton's study, better organized than Lonn's or Kaufmann's, does an excellent job of analyzing the political influences behind the formation of German regiments in general, but provides very little analysis of the lives of the soldiers themselves. Helbich and Kamphoefner have made the best contribution so far in the introduction to their edited collection, but their work is not intended to be an analytical study, consisting instead of heretofore unpublished soldiers' and civilians' letters.

15. See any of the regimental order, letter, and endorsement books for the 27th, 73rd, 74th, 75th, and 98th Pennsylvania regiments in the National Archives. In 1862 and early 1863 some of the regiments were copying important brigade and divisional orders in both English and German. With few exceptions, the regimental books were written in

English after April 1863. The records of the three-month 21st Pennsylvania were incorporated with the 98th, and were completely in German. There is also some evidence that non-official communication between enlisted men and officers was written in German; as late as November 1864 two men of the 74th Pennsylvania illegally detained in Alexandria appealed to their commander in a letter written in German script. "As we are both German-born, we hope you will excuse us if we address you in our native tongue" (Als wir beide . . . Geburtsdeutsche sind so hoffen wir auch bei Entschuldigung zu finden, wann wir Sie in unsere Muttersprache anreden). For these soldiers, writing in German was preferable to writing in English, especially when they knew their commander was also German. See 74th Pennsylvania, Regimental Papers Filed with Muster Rolls, NARA.

16. Lt. Colonel A. Buschbeck to Governor Andrew Curtin, 29 November 1861 (RG-19, Microfilm 3662, roll 15, PASA); *Skippackville Neutralist und Allgemeine Neuigkeits-Bote*, 8 October 1861: "Die deutsche Sprache ist die vorherrschende"; Court-Martial of Private Joseph Roth, Company C, 27th Pennsylvania, Hunters Chapel, VA on 4 February 1862 (RG-94, 27th Pennsylvania Unbound Regimental Papers Filed with Muster Rolls, Box 4254, NARA); General Order 1, Brigadier General William S. Rosecrans to "Comrades of Blenker's Division," 17 April 1862 (RG-94, 75th Pennsylvania Regimental Order, Letter, and Endorsement Book, NARA); General Order, Major General John Frémont to his division, 13 June 1862 (RG-94, 74th Pennsylvania Regimental Order, Letter, and Endorsement Book, NARA). In October 1861, the Union high command authorized the consolidation of all ethnic regiments in the Army of the Potomac. All but a handful of the German units then serving in the Army were transferred to Ludwig Blenker's division and placed under his command. By February 1862, Blenker had three brigades containing the following German infantry regiments: Brigadier General Julius Stahel's (8th and 39th New York—a multiethnic regiment—45th New York, 27th Pennsylvania); Colonel Adolph von Steinwehr's (29th, 54th, and 68th New York, 73rd Pennsylvania); and Brigadier General Henry Bohlen's (58th New York, 74th and 75th Pennsylvania). The German 41st New York was unattached but assigned to the division. All together, the old forty-eighter commanded 10,117 soldiers, the vast majority of whom were Germans. The German division was the largest concentration of German American soldiery ever created in the war, and most of its regiments formed the core of the later Eleventh Corps when it fought at Chancellorsville.

17. Kaufmann, *The Germans in the American Civil War*, 101; Brigadier General Louis Blenker, special order, 26 September 1861 (RG-94, 73d Pennsylvania Letter, Order, and Endorsement Book, NARA). Before Blenker forced him to resign, Colonel Max Einstein of the 27th Pennsylvania was particularly known for ensuring sutlers stocked with beer visited his regiment.

18. Ibid. Admittedly, these ideas are conjecture, but are based on impressions gained while reading the regimental books of the Pennsylvania German regiments.

19. Colonel Max Einstein, 27th Pennsylvania to Major General McClellan, 19 August 1861 and A. P. Putic, Capt. commanding Subsistence, to Major H. F. Clarke, Chief Com. of Sub., Army of the Potomac, 10 September 1861 (both found in RG-94, 27th Pennsylvania Unbound Regimental Papers Filed with Muster Rolls, Box 4259, NARA).

20. Oswald Seidensticker, *Geschichte des Männerchors in Philadelphia, 1835–1885* (Philadelphia: Verlag des Männerchors, 1885), 54–55; Lieut. Colonel Lorenz Cantador, 27th Pennsylvania, circular to officers and men of the regiment, 21 December 1862 (RG 94, Unbound Regimental Papers Filed with Muster Rolls, Box 4259, NARA); Colonel Franz Mahler, 75th Pennsylvania to Brigadier General Henry Bohlen, 30 April 1862 and Mahler to M. O. Reichenbach, Philadelphia, 17 November 1862 (both in RG-94, 75th Pennsylvania Order, Letter, and Endorsement Book, NARA). It is unknown whether Buschbeck succeeded in forming his brigade band, as no further reference to it was discovered.

21. "Ein Besuch im Lager der deutschen Brigade Blenker," unknown author, Skippackville *Neutralist und Allgemeine Neuigkeits-Bote*, 8 October 1861. German Americans also celebrated special German-only holidays, such as Sylvester, with much singing, and, of course, drinking. A soldier of the 74th Pennsylvania wrote the Philadelphia *Freie Presse*, "we celebrated the Sylvester evening in undisturbed peace and in a joyful mood . . . the saloon, situated in the staff officer's quarters, suffered greatly; with champagne and punch, toasts and German songs punctuated the evening" (10 January 1862).

22. Lieutenant Colonel Alwin von Matzdorff to Annie von Matzdorff, 16 March 1862 (Annie von Matzdorff's Widow's Pension File, certif. 361.665, app. 549.875, NARA); Theodore Sander, 27th Pennsylvania, 16 May 1862 letter printed in Skippackville *Neutralist*, 10 June 1862; Frank J. Jacobs diary entry, 11 April 1862, transcription and translation of diary at LOC; Hugo E. Wolt, "Excerpts from the Diary of an 8th Man," *New-Yorker Criminalzeitung und Belletristisches Journal*, 2 May 1863; Kaufmann, *The Germans in the American Civil War*, 167–69.

23. Ibid.; Hermann Nachtigall, *History of the 75th Regiment, Pa. Vols.*, 1886, (reprint and translation by Heinz D. Schwinge and Karl E. Sundstrom [North Riverside, Illinois: W. P. Printers, 1987]), 14–15; Frank Jacobs diary entries, 16–23 May 1862, LOC; Otto Heusinger, *Amerikanische Kriegsbilder: Aufzeichnungen aus den Jahren 1861–1865*, 1869 (reprint: Wyk auf Foehr, Germany: Verlag für Amerikanistik, 1998), 42–46; David Delpech, "La longue marche de la division Blenker," *Le Courier de la Guerre d'Amerique* 52 (4th quarter 1999): 18–26; *Philadelphia Demokrat*, 24 April, 7 May, 3 June 1862. Colonel Henry Bohlen bombarded Blenker with letter after letter begging for more provisions for his brigade during the march, and Blenker, in turn, kept dispatching appeals for the same to Washington, but apparently only a few supply trains were ever dispatched during the German division's nine-week ordeal. See RG-393, pt. 2, Entry 5396, Letters Sent Dec. 1861–Nov. 1863, 11AC, contained in vol. 21/79 20 AC, NARA.

24. *Philadelphia Demokrat*, 21 and 28 April 1862; *New-Yorker Criminalzeitung und Belletristisches Journal*, 9 may 1862; Heusinger, 33; Leonhard Schlumpf diary entry for 12 April 1862, transcription and translation of diary in Civil War Times Misc. Coll, USAMHI; Colonel Henry Bohlen, 75th Pennsylvania, to Andrew Curtin, 21 April 1862 (RG-19, box 45, folder 13, PASA). Bohlen's letter contained an attachment listing all the men drowned, their rank, and their marital status. Of the 48 who drowned, 20 were married and 16 had children at home.

25. Urlich Helmcke, 27th Pennsylvania, 4 May 1862 letter printed in *Skippackville Neutralist*, 27 May 1862. Another veteran of the "crap trip," writing years later in the *National Tribune*, claimed that the sufferings of the march "gave to the soldiers an opportunity to test their inventive genius." Instead of burning any fence rails they found for firewood, many soldiers actually placed the rails side by side on the ground, about 4–6 inches apart, and then placed their gum blankets on top, creating a "bed" which kept their bodies from touching the cold, water-logged earth. See "Loyal Mountaineers," *National Tribune*, 3 September, 1891.

26. Burton, *Melting Pot Soldiers*, 87–88; Schlumpf diary entry, 7 April 1862; Heusinger, *Amerikanische Kriegsbilder*, 52–3, 65; Alfred E. Lee, "The Battle of Cross Keys," *Magazine of American History* 15 (1885): 488; OR, I, vols. 15, 8.

27. Robert K. Krick, *Conquering the Valley: Stonewall Jackson at Port Republic* (New York: William Morrow and Company, 1996), 170–80; Gustave Struve, *Diesseits und Jenseits des Oceans: Jahrbuch zur Vermittelung der Beziehungen zwischen Amerika und Deutschland* (Coburg, Germany: F. Streit's Verlagsbuchhandlung, 1864), 55.

28. *New York Times* quoted in Krick, 180; *New Yorker Belletristisches Journal und Criminalzeitung*, 18 July 1862, also see 20 June for a detailed report of the battle; Philadelphia *Freie Presse*, 12 June 1862; Cincinnati *Täglicher Volksfreund*, 19 June 1862; Paul quoted in *Philadelphia Demokrat*, 21 June 1862; Theodore Sander letter printed in the

Skippackville Neutralist, 1 July 1862; August Horstmann to parents, 16 June 1862, reprinted in Helbich and Kamphoefner, *Deutsche im Amerikanischen Buergerkrieg,* 184.

29. Struve, *Diesseits und Jenseits des Oceans,* 55; Burton, *Melting Pot Soldiers,* 88–89; Trefousse, *Carl Schurz,* 117–19. Schurz had practically no military experience at the time of his appointment, but had gained fame in the 1860 presidential election for allegedly bringing thousands of German votes to the Republican banner in the Midwest. That claim has been strongly disputed by scholars in the last several decades, but there is no doubt that Schurz was a major representative of the Germans, ranking only behind Sigel in significance.

30. *New-Yorker Criminalzeitung und Belletristisches Journal,* 8 August 1862. The reputation of the Germans for plundering civilians only grew worse during the Second Manassas campaign, but this time their actions were condoned by the commanding general. Pope wanted to make the rebels pay, and ordered the wholesale destruction and ravaging of the Virginia countryside through which his army marched. Members of the 27th Pennsylvania were more than willing to oblige. In a letter published in the *Egg Harbor Pilot* on 23 August, brothers Wilhelm and Emil Preiser boasted, "There in Creighesville we made 'reconnaissances' all day among the outlying farms up to an 8 mile circumference, and took away all the useful horses, all beef cattle, meal, salt, etc. The boys happily went on these plunderings because you can imagine that there were several milk buckets to empty and many a chicken to snatch. The farmers in this section will long remember the 27. Regiment. I had almost forgotten, that all negroes were also to be taken away, which the farmers feared the most." What happened to the newly freed slaves? "The blacks will now be turned into teamsters."

31. *Philadelphia Demokrat,* 13 September 1862; Otto Heusinger, *Amerikanische Kriegsbilder,* 77. Heusinger was not alone in his belief that members of the 75th Pennsylvania shot their own colonel. This report circulated—and kept reappearing—in German-language sources for years later.

32. 54th New York Infantry Regimental Letter and Order Book, synopsis of events in 1862, RG-94, NARA; Trefousse, *Carl Schurz,* 122; Hermann Nachtigall, *History of the 75th Regiment, Pa. Vols.* Trans. by Heinz D. Schwinge and Karl E. Sundstrom (North Riverside, Illinois, 1987), 18; Carl Schurz, *Reminiscences of Carl Schurz* (New York: McClure, 1907–8), II, 366; John J. Hennessy, *Return to Bull Run: the Campaign and Battle of Second Manassas* (New York: Simon and Schuster, 1993), 204–6, 214–18. The hard-fighting 75th Pennsylvania, which did not retreat with the 54th and 58th New York when the South Carolinians counterattacked, lost 30 dead and 103 wounded.

33. Hennessy, 222.

34. Ibid., 403–5; Heusinger, 86; *New-Yorker Criminalzeitung und Belletristisches Journal,* 5 September 1862.

35. Mark H. Dunkelman, "Hardtack and Sauerkraut Stew: Ethnic Tensions in the 154th New York Volunteers, Eleventh Corps, during the Civil War," *Yearbook of German American Studies* 36 (2001): 72, 75–76.

3. The Battle of Chancellorsville and the German Regiments of the Eleventh Corps

1. Eric Benjaminson, "A Regiment of Immigrants: The 82nd Illinois Volunteer Infantry and the Letters of Captain Rudolph Mueller," *Journal of the Illinois State Historical Society* 94, no. 2 (2001): 140–1; James S. Pula, *For Liberty and Justice: The Life and Times of Wladimir Krzyzanowski* (Chicago: The Polish-American Congress Charitable Foundation, 1978), 64–68; Kaufmann, *The Germans in the American Civil War,* 198–99.

2. Stephen D. Engle, *Yankee Dutchman: The Life of Franz Sigel* (Fayetteville: The University of Arkansas Press, 1993), 156–58. Engle believes the departure of Sigel the month before the advent of the 1863 spring campaign was a critical error: "Sigel left when his superior knowledge of tactics would have been extremely useful at Chan-

cellorsville and would have given him the opportunity to prove his worth as a commander." Had Sigel been in command on the afternoon of 2 May, it is conceivable he would not have summarily disregarded the myriad warnings of an imminent Confederate attack that numerous German officers and scouts reported. All of these warnings were dismissed out of hand by the officers to whom they were reported.

3. Capt. Theodore C. Howell, Co. D, 153rd Pennsylvania to his wife, 19 March 1863 (Lehigh County Historical Society, MPF502Hovell); William Charles to "Dear Ann," 6 March 1863, quoted in Mark H. Dunkelman, "Hardtack and Sauerkraut Stew: Ethnic Tensions in the 154th New York Volunteers, Eleventh Corps, during the Civil War," *Yearbook of German-American Studies* 36 (2001): 79; Otto Heusinger, *Amerikanische Kriegsbilder: Aufzeichnungen aus den Jahren 1861–1865* (Leipzig, 1869), reprint Wyk auf Foehr, Germany: Verlag für Amerikanistik, 1998, 110; Lt. Col. Alwin von Matzdorff, 75th Pennsylvania, to Annie von Matzdorff, 20 March 1863 (transcriptions of this and other letters by Annie von Matzdorff in her widow's pension file, NARA, certif. 361.665, app. 549.875, hereafter referred to as Matzdorff Pension File); Diary of Friedrich Otto Baron von Fritsch, unpublished manuscript written in 1903, Library of Congress, Manuscript Division, MMC416, 146–47 (hereafter referred to as "Fritsch"). Howell was not a German himself, but most of the men in his company were of German birth or direct German descent.

4. Fritsch, 147; Oliver Otis Howard, *The Autobiography of Oliver Otis Howard, Major General, United States Army* (New York: The Baker and Taylor Co., 1917), 1: 349. James Pula notes that "to the German free-thinkers [Howard's] demeanor exuded a much despised clericalism," and the regimental commanders "found it impossible to elicit from their men that 'spontaneous' cheer that traditionally greeted general officers as they rode before their troops" (Pula, *For Liberty and Justice*, 74).

5. RG-94, Unbound Regimental Papers Filed with Muster Rolls, Box 4259, 27th Pennsylvania, NARA; 75th Pennsylvania Regimental Letter, Order, and Endorsement Book, NARA; Alwin von Matzdorff to Annie von Matzdorff, 13 April 1863, Matzdorff Pension File; Adam Muenzenberger to wife, 12 April 1863, available at www.agro.agri.umn.edu/~lemedg/wis26/26pgam63.htm; and Pula, *For Liberty and Justice*, 74. Howard also appears to have begun warming up to his troops by the time of the review, remarking with delight in letters to his wife about how beautifully the Germans had decorated his headquarters for the president's visit. See O. O. Howard to Elizabeth Howard, 10 and 12 April 1863, Bowdoin College Library Special Collections.

6. William Simmers and Paul Bachschmid, "The Volunteer's Manual, or Ten Months with 153rd Penna Volunteers" (Easton, Pa.: D. H. Neiman, Printer, 1863), 18; Alwin Von Matzdorff to Annie von Matzdorff, 28 March 1863, Matzdorff Pension File; Adam Muenzenberger to wife, 20 April 1863. Carl Schurz had a mixed, but improving reputation among the Germans in the Eleventh Corps. Most of them knew he was a recent political appointee, some disliked his forty-eighter radicalism, and others resented the fact that someone with no military experience could succeed the likes of Blenker and Bohlen. But in the end, the fact that he was a German mattered most to the troops, as did his preoccupation with their care and well-being. In the latter area he was often compared with Sigel (see 15 November 1862 *Louisville Anzeiger* for an example). After Chancellorsville, where most German Americans believed Schurz had displayed both competence and bravery, his reputation was secure with his ethnic countrymen. Soldiers and civilians alike vigorously defended him against nativistic accusations stemming from the Anglo American press.

7. Sears, *Chancellorsville*, 146–47; Carl Schurz, "Reminiscences of a Long Life: The Eleventh Corps at Chancellorsville," *McClure's*, June 1907, 162; Otto Heusinger, *Amerikanische Kriegsbilder*, 115.

8. *Weekly Pittsburgh Gazette*, 5 May 1863, "An Incident of the Late Advance."

9. Sears, 164–65, 181; William H. Weaver diary entry, 29 May 1863, reprinted in Easton *Daily Free Press*, 3 May 1913; Doerflinger quoted in James S. Pula, *The Sigel Regiment: A History of the Twenty-sixth Wisconsin Volunteer Infantry, 1862–1865* (Campbell, CA: Savas Publishing Company, 1998), 115; Louise Winkler Hitz, ed., *Letters of Frederick C. Winkler, 1862–1865* (William K. Winkler, 1963), 46, 49–50; Bigelow, *Chancellorsville*, 259.

10. Hamlin, 37; Pfanz, "Negligence on the Right: The Eleventh Corps at Chancellorsville, May 2, 1863," available at http://www.morningsidebooks.com/notes/eleventh.htm, 1; Sears, 271.

11. Hamlin, 36–37; Schurz, "Reminiscences of a Long Life," 163.

12. Furgurson, *Chancellorsville*, 148.

13. Ibid., 148–49.

14. Schurz, "Reminiscences of a Long Life," 164–65; Bigelow, *Chancellorsville*, 279.

15. Kellogg quoted in A. H. Nelson, *The Battles of Chancellorsville and Gettysburg* (Minneapolis: Alansan, 1899), 37–38.

16. Nelson, 34; Furgurson, *Chancellorsville*, 149–54; OR, I, vol. 25, 386; Pfanz, "Negligence on the Right," 3. Nelson is forthright in his accusations of Howard, claiming that he "willfully disobey[ed]" Hooker's orders, thereby committing "one of the highest crimes known in military law. The penalty is death" (p. 40). If Kellogg's affidavit is true, and there is no reason to doubt it, then Howard and/or Meysenberg knew full well that ignoring Hooker's order was the immediate cause of the disaster that befell the Eleventh Corps at Chancellorsville, and afterward squirreled away the incriminating document until intervening events—such as Hooker's dismissal—made it safer to file it officially. In this light, Howard's postwar protest that he never received the order appears to be a lie designed to protect his reputation. Perhaps the actual order disappeared from the files of the War Department to erase the evidence that would incriminate Howard. Regardless of what happened to it originally, the actual order has somehow returned to the official Eleventh Corps files. I found it in NARA, RG-393, pt. 2, Entry 5319, Letters Received, January 1863–1864, 11th A.C.

17. Hartwell Osborn, *Trials and Triumphs: The Record of the Fifty-Fifth Ohio Volunteer Infantry* (Chicago: A. C. McClurg and Co., 1904), 68–71; A. B. Searles quoted in "On Picket at Chancellorsville," *Boston Journal*, n.d., copy in archives, Fredericksburg-Spotsylvania National Military Park, Fredericksburg, Va. (hereafter FSNMP); Edward C. Culp, *The 25th Ohio Vet. Vol. Infantry in the War for the Union* (Topeka, Kans: Geo. W. Crane and Co., 1885), 61–62; Owen Rice, *Afield With the Eleventh Army Corps at Chancellorsville* (Cincinnati: H. C. Sherrick and Co., 1885), 23.

18. Otto Heusinger, *Amerikanische Kriegsbilder*, 117.

19. Eugene Blackford memoir, Civil War Misc. Collection, 3rd series, USAMHI; Simmers and Bachschmid, "The Volunteer's Manual," 22–23; A. B. Searles, "On Picket at Chancellorsville"; Francis Stofflet quoted in Easton *Daily Free Press*, 3 May 1913; David Ackerman, 153rd Pennsylvania, to Jacob H. Ackerman, 11 May 1863 (Ackerman Letters, 153rd Pennsylvania, P5–3, Cumberland County Historical Society, Carlisle, Pa.); C. V. Strickland, "What a Drummer Boy Saw at Chancellorsville," *National Tribune*, 14 May 1908; Theodore Howell to wife, 10 May 1863 (MPF 502, Lehigh County Historical Society); Colonel Charles Glanz, 153rd Pennsylvania to Governor Andrew G. Curtin, 2 June 1863 (RG-19, 153rd Pennsylvania folder, PASA). Glanz's language here is obviously self-glorifying, but it still conveys the fact that the 153rd stood and fought before retreating.

20. Otto Heusinger, *Amerikanische Kriegsbilder*, 117; William Burghart to A. C. Hamlin, 2 November 1891, bMS Am 1084 (temp. box 22, file N–O), Houghton Library, Harvard University; Luis Keck to "Dearest wife and child," translation and transcript in archives, FSNMP, original letter in memoirs of James C. McCown, in possession of David R. Wiltse, Arlington Heights, Illinois; William J. Halpin, "A German Regiment in the Civil War: The 45th New York State Volunteer Infantry, '5th German Rifles,'" *Mili-*

tary Images 21 (March–April 2000): 20. Hamlin states that about 300 of the 41st and 45th New York managed to cross to the north side of the turnpike and briefly join the stand of the 153rd Pennsylvania and 58th New York, before joining them in running to the rear (Hamlin, 65).

21. Culp, *The 25th Ohio Vet. Vol. Infantry*, 65–66; Hartwell Osborn, "On the Right at Chancellorsville," Illinois MOLLUS, *Military Essay and Recollections*, vol. 4 (Chicago: Cozzens and Beaton Company, 1907), 188; Charles T. Furlow journal, 2 May entry, p. 35, copy in archives, FSNMP, original in Yale University Archives; Luther B. Mesnard Reminiscence, 6 May 1901, Civil War Misc. Collection, USAMHI; John Lewis to wife, 14 May 1863, Lewis Leigh Collection (Books, Folder 39), USAMHI; Jacob Smith, *Camps and Campaigns of the 107th Regiment Ohio Volunteer Infantry*, 74.

22. Hamlin, 56–57, 60, 69; Gustav Schleiter, "The Eleventh Corps: Who Was Responsible for its Disaster at Chancellorsville?" *National Tribune*, 30 July 1885; Carl A. Keyser, *Leatherbreeches: Hero of Chancellorsville* (Rye Beach, N.H.: Amherst Press, 1989), 40–41; Carl Schurz, "Reminiscences of a Long Life: The Eleventh Corps at Chancellorsville," 167–69. Schurz believed the repositioning of these three regiments was the most he could accomplish considering what he called "Howard's singular obstinacy." Howard assented to Schurz's independent preparations only reluctantly.

23. Schurz, "Reminiscences of a Long Life," 168.

24. Jacob and John Ullmann and Mehring quoted in Hermann Nachtigall to A. C. Hamlin, 16 February 1893, bMS Am 1084 (temp. box 22, file N–O), Houghton Library, Harvard University; Hermann Nachtigall, "History of the 75th Regiment, Pa. Vols.," (1886, translation North Riverside, Ill.: n.p., 1987, by Heinz D. Schwinge and Karl E. Sundstrom), 20–21; Hamlin, *The Battle of Chancellorsville*, 42–43; Bates, *History of the Pennsylvania Volunteers*, 4: 919.

25. OR, I, vol. 25, 654–55; Sears, *Chancellorsville*, 276.

26. Martin Seel to Georg Seel, 10 May 1863, copy and translation in archives of FSNMP, original owned by Bob Seel, Tucson, Arizona; *Pittsburgher Freiheitsfreund*, 18 May 1863; Schurz, "Reminiscences of a Long Life," 169; OR, I, vol. 25, 665.

27. Dr. Carl Uterhard to "my dear Marie and Mama," 17 May 1863, reprinted in Helbich and Kamphoefner, eds., *Deutsche im Amerikanischen Bürgerkrieg*, 219; Charles F. Lewis diary transcription, 2 May 1864, Civil War Misc. Collection, 3rd Series, USAMHI; Sears, *Chancellorsville*, 276–77; OR, I, vol. 25, 668; Hamlin, 71–73; Darwin D. Cody to parents, 9 May 1863, copy in archives of FSNMP. Dilger's battery was not the only Eleventh Corps battery active at this time; the corps' reserve batteries also opened up on the advancing Confederates from positions behind Dilger. They retreated, however, before his battery did.

28. Frantisek Stejskal memoir originally published in Josef Cermak, *Dejiny Obcanske Valky* (Chicago: August Geringer, 1889), 219–21, copy and translation in archives, FSNMP; Friedrich P. Kappelman to "Dear Parents," 10 May 1863, transcription and translation in Civil War Times Misc. Collection, USAMHI; *Pittsburgher Freiheitsfreund*, 22 May 1863; Report of Lt. Col. Edward S. Salomon, 82nd Illinois, to Brig. General Alexander Schimmelfennig, found in Carl Schurz Papers, Container 4, LOC. Salomon was not present at Chancellorsville, recovering from an illness in Chicago, yet felt it his duty to submit the official report to Schimmelfennig. This account was written "according to the statements I solicited from the officers of the regiment." How the report ended up in the Carl Schurz Papers is unknown, but it is almost exactly the same one reprinted in the Official Records, Part 1, 663–64.

29. Hamlin, 69; Doerflinger quoted in James S. Pula, *The Sigel Regiment*, 120–21.

30. Adam Muenzenberger to wife, 7 May 1863 and Frank Smrcek diary entry, May 1863, both translated and available at http://www.agro.agri.umn.edu/~lemedg/wis26/; Pula, *The Sigel Regiment*, 126–29; Wickesberg quoted in Pula, 125.

31. Hamlin, 70; Pula, 126; William H. Clark, 157th New York, to sister, 8 May 1863, copy in archives, FSNMP; A. B. Searles quoted in "On Picket at Chancellorsville"; Benjamin B. Carr memoir, "Sketch of the Battle of Chancellorsville," p. 5, copy in archives FSNMP, original in Misc. Records, Civil War Collection, North Carolina State Archives; Martin Seel to brother, 10 May 1863; Hecker quoted in *Pittsburgher Freiheitsfreund*, 22 May 1863.

32. Furgurson and Sears disagree about the approximate timing of Howard's incident. Sears places it after the Wilderness Church line crumbled and Furgurson inserts it after the disintegration of Devens's division but before Schurz's men assembled at the church. I am inclined to agree with Sears on this account. See Sears, *Chancellorsville*, 277, and Furgurson, *Chancellorsville*, 181. Howard quoted in Furgurson, 181; J. H. Peabody, 61st Ohio, quoted in Furgurson, 182; Hartwell Osborn, 55th Ohio, "On the Right at Chancellorsville," *Military Essays and Recollections* (Chicago: MOLLUS Illinois, 1907), 4: 188.

33. Hamlin, *The Battle of Chancellorsville*, 74–75; Furgurson, 186, OR, I, vol. 25, 645.

34. Hamlin, 75.

35. Ibid.; Mark H. Dunkelman, "Hardtack and Sauerkraut Stew," 81; Donald C. Pfanz, "Negligence on the Right," 10.

36. OR, I, vol. 25, 657.

37. Ibid., Hamlin, 76; William Clegg to "Dear cousin," 8 May 1863, copy in archives, FSNMP, original in Clegg Papers, The Filson Club, Louisville, Ky.; Jacob Smith, *Camps and Campaigns of the 107th Regiment Ohio Volunteer Infantry, From August, 1862, to July, 1865* (n.p., n.p., 1910), 74; John Haingartner Civil War Memoir, Historical Society of Pennsylvania.

38. OR, I, vol. 25, 645–46.

39. OR, I, vol. 25, 665; Adolph Bregler to "Dear Parents," 10 May 1863, Bregler Pension File, 27th Pennsylvania, App. 172.294, certif. 128.498, NARA; James Emmons letter quoted in Mark H. Dunkelman and Michael J. Winey, *The Hardtack Regiment: An Illustrated History of the 154th Regiment, New York State Infantry Volunteers* (Teaneck, N.J.: Fairleigh Dickinson University Press, 1981), 61; Charles Cresson Pension File, 27th Pennsylvania, App. 846278, certif. 629.838; Bates, *History of the Pennsylvania Volunteers*, I: 389–90, and IV: 865; Hamlin 76. The casualties in the 73rd Pennsylvania were especially grievous. Its colonel, lieutenant colonel, major, and most of its captains were wounded, one mortally. It suffered 103 casualties total.

40. Both Ernest B. Furgurson and Stephen W. Sears allot one paragraph each to the stand of Buschbeck's brigade. As one veteran of the brigade put it in 1908, most histories "hurry past to tell about the great charge of a division of the Third Corps into the woods in front of Jackson's advance," but neglect the "very gallant defense" of Buschbeck's men. See C. W. McKay, 154th NY, "Buschbeck's Brigade," *National Tribune*, 8 October 1908; Hamlin, 74; Dunkelman and Winey, 57–59.

41. This number excludes Barlow's brigade, which was still en route from the south.

42. Hamlin, 77; Pfanz, "Negligence on the Right," 11–12.

43. Fritsch, 173–74; Bates, IV: 865; Philadelphia *Freie Presse*, 8 May, 1863. Fritsch's reaction to the term "Dutchmen" is interesting, indicating a foreigner's lack of understanding with what had become almost a standard term used by Anglo Americans to describe any ethnically German group.

44. Charles E. Davis, *Three Years in the Army: The Story of the Thirteenth Massachusetts Volunteers from July 16, 1861, to August 1, 1864* (Boston: Estes and Laurist, 1894), 203; Hamlin 127, 131; Pfanz, "Negligence on the Right," 12.

45. By using the term "Pennsylvania German" here I am referring to all German-speaking regiments that hailed from Pennsylvania, not simply those composed of Pennsylvania Dutch troops. For a detailed explanation of the difference between "German

Americans" and "Pennsylvania Dutch" (frequently called "Pennsylvania Germans"), see Valuska and Keller, *Damn Dutch*, chapter one.

46. OR, I, vol. 25, 660; "Report of killed wounded and missing of the 75th Reg't. PV," RG-19, Box 45, folder 13, PASA; 73rd and 75th Pennsylvania Morning Report Books, April–May, 1863, RG-94, NARA; Philadelphia *Daily Evening Bulletin*, 8 May 1863; Philadelphia *Freie Presse*, 17 and 18 May 1863; *National Tribune*, 12 January 1893; Samuel H. Hurst, *Journal-History of the Seventy-third Ohio Volunteer Infantry* (Chillicothe, Ohio: n.p., 1866), 57; Sears, *Chancellorsville*, 280.

47. Philadelphia *Freie Presse*, 18 May 1863; *National Tribune*, 12 January, 1893, Sears, 487–88.

48. Adin B. Underwood, *The Three Years' Service of the Thirty-third Mass. Infantry Regiment, 1862–1865* (Boston: A. Williams and Co., Publishers, 1881), 98; Cortland County Historical Society, *A Regiment Remembered: The 157th New York Volunteers, From the Diary of Captain William Saxton* (Cortland County, N.Y.: The Society, 1996), 57.

49. OR, I, vol. 25, 660; *National Tribune*, 12 January 1893; James S. Pula, *The Sigel Regiment: A History of the Twenty-sixth Wisconsin Volunteer Infantry, 1862–1865* (Campbell, Calif.: Savas Publishing Co., 1998), 136. Of the 359 combined casualties of the 26th Wisconsin and 82nd Illinois, 275 were dead and wounded.

50. *National Tribune*, 12 January 1893; Sears, 280, 487.

51. Hamlin, 79; Adolph Bregler to "Dear Parents," 10 May 1863, Adolph Bregler pension file, NARA; Wilhelm Roth to "Dear Brother," 11 May 1863, Civil War Times Miscellaneous Collection, USAMHI. Bregler lamented that he could not stay with his wounded brother, as "the rebels were pressing hard behind us." He "had to stay with the regiment" after leaving Karl in "a little house where a hospital was set up." Predicting Karl had survived the wound but was now a prisoner, Bregler tried to assuage his parents' fears by claiming the "rebels treat their prisoners well." Bregler mentioned nothing about the wounding of Stonewall Jackson, the most-remembered event about Chancellorsville in popular memory. Only a few German American soldiers noted anything about the wounding and subsequent death of the famous Confederate chieftain.

4. "Retreating and Cowardly Poltroons": The Anglo American Reaction

1. Abram P. Smith, *History of the Seventy-Sixth Regiment New York Volunteers* (Cortland, N.Y.: Truair, Smith and Miles, printers, 1867), 218; Patrick R. Guiney to "My Dear Jennie," 7 May 1863, reprinted in Christian G. Samito, ed. *Commanding Boston's Irish Ninth: The Civil War Letters of Colonel Patrick R. Guiney, Ninth Massachusetts Volunteer Infantry* (New York: Fordham University Press, 1998), 187–88; Oscar D. Ladley to "Dear Mother and Sisters," 8 May 1863, reprinted in Carl M. Becker and Ritchie Thomas, eds., *Hearth and Knapsack: The Ladley Letters, 1857–1880* (Athens, Ohio: Ohio University Press, 1988), 121–22; Carl Schurz to Franz Sigel, 25 June 1863, quoted in Engle, *Yankee Dutchman*, 162; William C. Bryant to Lincoln, 11 May 1863, reprinted in Roy Basler, ed., *The Collected Works of Abraham Lincoln*, 9 vols. (New Brunswick, N.J.: Rutgers University Press, 1953), 6: 216.

2. Carol Reardon, "The Valiant Rearguard: Hancock's Division at Chancellorsville," in Gary W. Gallagher, ed., *Chancellorsville: The Battle and its Aftermath* (Chapel Hill: The University of North Carolina Press, 1996), 171; James Biddle to wife, 9 May 1863, James Biddle Civil War Letters, HSP; Colonel Robert McAllister, 11th NJ, to Ellen McAllister, May 1863, in James I. Robertson, ed., *The Civil War Letters of General Robert McAllister* (New Brunswick, NJ: Rutgers University Press, 1965), 301; Abram P. Smith, *History of the Seventy-Sixth Regiment New York Volunteers*, 218; "Laird" to "My dear boy, 10 May 1863, George S. Lester papers, Louisiana State University, Dept. of Archives and Manuscripts; Darwin Cody to parents, 9 May 1863, FSNMP; Francis McCarthy letter, 8

May 1863, printed in New York *Irish American*, 30 May 1863, quoted in John Charles Bodger, Jr., "The Immigrant Press and the Union Army" (Ph.D. diss., Columbia University, April 1951), 252; Sears, 433; DeTrobriand quoted in Ella Lonn, *Foreigners in the Union Army and Navy*, 594.

3. For a good analysis of Civil War soldiers' loyalty to each other and their regiments, see Gerald Linderman, *Embattled Courage*.

4. Mark H. Dunkelman, "Hardtack and Sauerkraut Stew: Ethnic Tensions in the 154th New York Volunteers, Eleventh Corps, during the Civil War," *Yearbook of German American Studies* 36 (2001): 72, 75–76.

5. Van Aernum, Smith, Robbins, and Matthewson quoted in Dunkelman, 82–84; Isaac N. Porter to "Friend Murray," 13 May 1863, USAMHI, uncatalogued.

6. E. L. Edes to mother, 4 May 1863, E. L. Edes Papers (P374, Reel 6), Massachusetts Historical Society; W. H. H. Hinds to A. C. Hamlin, 3 August 1893, bMS Am 1084, Houghton Library, Harvard University; George W. Conklin, *Under the Crescent and Star: The 134th New York Volunteer Infantry in the Civil War* (Port Reading, NJ: Axworthy Publishing, 1999), 88–89.

7. John Lewis to wife, 14 May 1863, Lewis Leigh Collection, USAMHI; Wilson French to wife, 10 and 11 May 1863, copies of both letters in archives, FSNMP, originals in possession of Donald V. Richardson, Stratford, Connecticut; Andrew L. Harris to "friend Lough," 7 June 1863, copy in archives, FSNMP, original in Andrew Linton Harris papers, Ohio State Historical Society; William Wheeler to mother, 14 May 1863, transcript available at http://www.realtime.net/~jjc.

8. Williams to "Dear daughter," 18 May 1863, reprinted in Milo M. Quaife, ed., *From the Cannon's Mouth: The Civil War Letters of General Alpheus S. Williams* (Detroit: Wayne State University Press, 1959), 190–91. For Hamlin's questioning of the identity of the mob of men who broke into the Chancellor House clearing, see Hamlin, 99.

9. Thomas H. Elliott to James J. Gillette, 23 May 1863, James J. Gillette Collection, Box 1, LOC.

10. Hamlin, 93, 149–50; Bigelow, 310.

11. David Mouat, unpublished manuscript, "Three Years with Co. G. in the 29th Pennsylvania Volunteers," HSP; James Miller to William Miller, 12 May 1863, William S. Schoff Collection, Clements Library, University of Michigan; Rice Bull quoted in K. Jack Bauer, ed., *Soldiering: The Civil War Diary of Rice C. Bull, 123rd New York Volunteer Infantry* (San Rafael, Calif.: Presidio Press, 1978), 51.

12. Cody quoted in Sears, *Chancellorsville*, 286; Hamlin, 99; Bigelow, 309. Sears also mentions that Colonel Joseph Dickinson of Hooker's staff shot at soldiers, as did Colonel Elliott Cook of the 28th New York, who killed "four or five" with "a navy revolver," according to one of his men.

13. Daniel O. Macomber to "friend Eben," 15 May 1863, Lewis Leigh Collection, Book 6, folder 14, USAMHI; Warren H. Cudworth, *History of the First Regiment (Massachusetts Infantry)* (Boston: Walker, Fuller, and Company, 1866), 360–61; Henry N. Blake, *Three Years in the Army of the Potomac* (Boston: Lee and Shepard, 1865), 178–79.

14. Benjamin F. Robb to "Dear sir," 1 June 1863, Civil War Times Misc. Collection, USAMHI; Dennis Tuttle to wife, 13 May 1863, Dennis Tuttle Papers, Library of Congress; William Peacock to "Dear Sarah," 6 May 1863, Peacock Papers, USAMHI; John L. Smith to mother, 8 May 1863, copy in archives, FSNMP; Grotius R. Giddings to father, 20 May 1863, Joshua R. Giddings Papers, Ohio Historical Society.

15. *New York Times*, 5 May 1863. After Chancellorsville, the northern public identified Schurz with all things German, as they had with Sigel, and any defamation aimed against him was also aimed against his German troops. Engle states that "Schurz commanded a division of Germans who were forced to retreat during the battle . . . and the label 'Flying Dutchman' which had previously been applied to Sigel's military blunders, now

applied to Schurz's exploits." See Engle, *Yankee Dutchman*, xiii, 157, 160–61, and Pula, *For Liberty and Justice*, 119.

16. *New York Times*, 5 May 1863.

17. *New York Herald*, 5, 6, 7 May 1863.

18. *New-York Daily Tribune*, 6 May 1863.

19. Washington *Daily National Intelligencer*, 6 and 7 May 1863; New York *Evening Post*, 5 May 1863; Philadelphia *Public Ledger*, 6 May 1863; Philadelphia *Inquirer*, 6, 7, and 9 May 1863; *Weekly Pittsburgh Gazette*, 6 May 1863; Hartford *Evening Press* 13 May 1863; Chicago *Tribune*, 6 and 7 May 1863; *Pittsburgh Post*, 6 and 8 May, 1863; *Frank Leslie's Illustrated Newspaper*, 23 May 1863. Interestingly, the German Reading, Pennsylvania *Adler* followed a close translation of the *New York Times* 5 May account, noticeably omitting the words "coward" and "poltroon." Reading and Berks County, however, had very few soldiers enlisted in Eleventh Corps regiments.

20. Chicago *Tribune*, 7 May 1863.

21. Philadelphia *Inquirer*, 7 May 1863.

22. Cleveland *Plain Dealer*, 8 May 1863.

23. *Pittsburgh Post*, 12 May 1863; Chicago *Tribune*, 9 May 1863.

24. Bryant to Lincoln, 11 May 1863, and Lincoln to Bryant, 14 May 1863, both reprinted in Basler, ed., *The Collected Works of Abraham Lincoln*, vol. 6, 1953.

25. *New York Herald*, 6 and 12 May 1863; *New York Times*, 12 May 1863.

26. Charles E. Davis, *Three Years in the Army: The Story of the Thirteenth Massachusetts Volunteers*, 203; Kaufmann, *The Germans in the American Civil War*, 198–99; Sears, 432–33.

5. "All We Ask Is Justice": The Germans Respond

1. OR, I, vol. 25, 630–31.

2. 45th New York Infantry Letter, Order, and Index Book, RG-94, NARA. Whether or not the ban on beer was intended as a punishment is unknown, but based on the timing and Howard's evangelizing personality, this is a possibility.

3. Howard's ban on lager beer editorialized and the Wisconsin soldier's letter reprinted in the Philadelphia *Freie Presse*, 11 May 1863 and the *Pittsburger Demokrat*, 8 May 1863; Theodore Howell to "Dearest Wife," 10 May 1863 (Lehigh County Historical Society); Reuben J. Stotz, 153rd Pennsylvania, to "Dear Sister," 2 June 1863, reprinted in Rev. W. R. Kiefer, *History of the 153d Regiment Volunteer Infantry* (Easton, Pa.: The Chemical Publishing Co., 1909), 245–46. Alcoholic beverages were officially forbidden to enlisted men in the Federal army, but officers were afforded some flexibility regarding wine and brandies. Depending on the corps, division, or brigade commander, the drinking of whiskey, beer, or other intoxicating beverages, although unlawful, could be winked at. This frequently occurred in the Eleventh Corps due to the Germans' ethnic predilection for beer consumption.

4. Muenzenberger quoted in Pula, *The Sigel Regiment*, 135; Frederick Winkler letter, 7 May 1863, in Frederick C. Winkler, *Letters of Frederick C. Winkler, 1862–1865*, ed. and trans. by William K. Winkler, 1963 (privately published), 50–51; 119th New York Infantry Regimental Letter and Order Book, 58th New York Infantry Regimental Order Book, 82nd Illinois Infantry Consolidated Morning Report, Letter, and Order Book, all in RG-94, NARA; Register of Letters Received Relating to Leaves of Absence, Resignations, and Furloughs, 11th A.C. 1863, RG-393, pt. 2, entries 5317 and 5322, NARA.

5. Carl Schurz to "Dear Jacobs," 11 June 1863, container 4, Carl Schurz Papers, LOC; 119th New York Infantry Regimental Letter and Order Book, RG-94, NARA.

6. Pittsburgh *Freiheitsfreund und Courier*, 17 June 1863; Rudolph Mueller to Friedrich Hecker, 18 May 1863, available at http://www.geocities.com/Athens/Parthenon/7419/mueller.html; *Philadelphia Demokrat*, 19 May 1863.

7. Howard to Schurz, 8 May 1863, Schurz Papers, Container 4, LOC.

8. Schurz to Howard, 12 May 1863, ibid.

9. Ibid.

10. Schurz to Hooker, 17 May 1863, ibid.

11. Schurz to Edwin Stanton, 18 May 1863, ibid.

12. E. Townsend, Asst. Adjt. General, to Schurz, 21 May 1863; Schurz to Howard, 21 May 1863, both letters found in Schurz Papers, Container 4, LOC.

13. Engle, *Yankee Dutchman*, 161–62; Schurz to Howard, 26 May 1863, Schurz Papers, Container 4, LOC.

14. Schurz to Sigel, 26 June 1863, reprinted in Engle, 162–63; Schurz to Howard, 26 May 1863, Schurz Papers; OR, I, vol. 25, 660.

15. Ibid. Stephen Sears quotes several officers who frowned upon Hooker's assumption to command of the Army of the Potomac because of questionable personal qualities. One wrote that he was "entirely unscrupulous," another claimed to have "little confidence in honesty of purpose." Charles Francis Adams went so far as to rebuke Hooker's integrity, stating his "private character is well known to be—I need not say what." Many of his contemporaries argued that Hooker was elevated to command through intrigue, and thus it seems entirely possible that Hooker was looking out for his own political interests in his dealings with Howard and Schurz. See Sears, *Chancellorsville*, 57–58.

16. See the *New York Herald*, 11 May 1863 and the *New-Yorker Staatszeitung*, 12 May 1863 for examples of Howard letters exonerating Schurz; Hecker's public letter reprinted in Pittsburgh *Freiheitsfreund und Courier*, 22 May 1863; Hecker to Schurz, 21 May 1863, Schurz Papers; Hans Trefousse, *Carl Schurz: A Biography* (New York: Fordham University Press, 1998), 135. Schurz remained extremely sensitive to any allegations of cowardice, both regarding himself and his troops, for the rest of the war. He even threatened fellow division commander, Adolph von Steinwehr, with a court martial because von Steinwehr delivered a farewell address to the departing 29th New York which insinuated that von Steinwehr's first brigade (of which the 29th was a part) was the only Eleventh Corps brigade to hold firm "while all around were in wild flight." Schurz thought this impugned the valor of the regiments in his division. An angry exchange of letters between the two generals resulted. See Schurz to von Steinwehr, 16 June 1863 and von Steinwehr to Schurz, 16 June 1863, both in Schurz Papers, Container 4, LOC.

17. Philadelphia *Freie Presse*, 15 May 1863; Pittsburgh *Freiheitsfreund und Courier*, 22 May, 1863; Alfred C. Raphelson, "Alexander Schimmelpfennig: A German-American Campaigner in the Civil War," *Pennsylvania Magazine of History and Biography* 87, no. 2 (April 1963): 168–70.

18. Fritsch, 183–84.

19. OR, I, vol. 25, 662–63.

20. Pittsburgh *Freiheitsfreund und Courier*, 15 May 1863. For good examples of other newspapers reporting the casualties alongside the first reports from the Anglo American press, see the *Philadelphia Demokrat*, 8 May 1863, and the losses of the 27th Pennsylvania, or the Cincinnati *Wöchentlicher Volksfreund*, 20 May 1863, and the losses of the 107th Ohio. The great majority of German papers, although steadfast in their defense of the Eleventh Corps' Germans, did not unilaterally disclaim the valor of the Anglo American regiments, either.

21. Philadelphia *Freie Presse*, 15, 18, and 29 May 1863; Highland, Illinois *Highland Bote*, 15 May 1863. Also see the *Louisville Anzeiger*, 12 May 1863 and the Pittsburgh *Freiheitsfreund und Courier*, 8 May 1863 for the translated story from the *Milwaukee News*. The *Milwaukee Seebote* originally printed the translation of the story.

22. *Philadelphia Demokrat*, 12 May 1863; Cincinnati *Wöchentlicher Volksfreund*, 20 May 1863; Belleville, Illinois *Belleviller-Zeitung*, 14 and 21 May 1863.

23. *New-Yorker Staatszeitung*, 15 May 1863. Schirmer may have overestimated both the damage his artillery inflicted upon the enemy and his own losses. Most Confederate reports and accounts give the federal artillery on 2 May some credit, but do not claim it caused substantial casualties. The Official Records, moreover, report that the Eleventh Corps artillery suffered just 40 casualties total (OR, I, vol. 25, 182–83). The actual numbers of dead and wounded artillerymen probably falls in between Schirmer's number and the OR's.

24. *New-Yorker Staatszeitung*, 13 and 15 May 1863; *Philadelphia Demokrat*, 14 May 1863. Some of the editors, lacking firsthand accounts or the factual information necessary to provide accurate editorials, committed gross errors in their haste to defend the German regiments. On 7 May the Chicago *Illinois Staats-Zeitung*, arguably the most powerful of the Midwestern German papers, in response to the English-language press's assertion that McLean's brigade of Devens's division fought well, claimed that "the division of Devens is none other than the grizzled, veteran, and primarily German division of General Stahel." This was not true, nor was the claim that Buschbeck's brigade belonged to Devens's division: "one of his brigades, that of Colonel Buschbeck, is very German, and the other, of McLean, consists of three German and only two American regiments." The last statement was completely false. Even more comically, the editor insisted that Schurz's "brigade contains a large number of non-German elements," citing the 119th New York as one of them. The 12 May *Louisville Anzeiger* also tried to make McLean's brigade German: "Devens' Division consists of the brigades of McLean and Colonel Gilsa; the former is composed of German, the latter of American regiments." However, "the Germans did not run away without firing a shot; on the contrary, Schurz held an entire hour without receiving reinforcements—here fell the brave Schimmelfennig."

25. Philadelphia *Freie Presse*, 7 May 1863. See Engle, *Yankee Dutchman*, 230–33, for a critique of Sigel's performance as a general in the Civil War.

26. Higland, Illinois *Highland Bote*, 8 May 1863; Pittsburgh *Freiheitsfreund und Courier*, 9 and 30 May 1863; New York *Criminalzeitung und Bellestrisches Journal*, 15 and 22 May 1863. Also see the Boston *Pionier*, 20 May 1863. The anti-Halleck rhetoric in the *Freiheitsfreund* was reprinted from an editorial taken from the prominent *Illinois-Staats-zeitung* of a few days earlier. Another editorial in the *Highland Bote* on 29 May also originated with the *Staatszeitung* and offered hope that Sigel would be reinstated.

27. Friedrich P. Kappelman to parents, 10 May 1863, translation and transcription in Civil War Misc. Collection, USAMHI; letter from Lieutenant Knöbel printed in *Pittsburgher Voksblatt*, 9 May 1863; Louis Schleiter, 74th Pennsylvania, to "Dear editor of the Freiheitsfreund," 10 May 1863, printed in Pittsburgh *Freiheitsfreund und Courier*, 15 May 1863.

28. Adam Muenzenberger to wife, 7 May 1863, available at http://www.agro.agri.-umn.edu/~lemedg/wis26/26pgam64.htm; Ernst Damkoehler to Mathilde Damkoehler, 10 May 1863, quoted in Pula, *The Sigel Regiment*, 141.

29. Friedrich A. Brautigam diary entry, 6 May 1863, transcript and translation in Civil War Misc. Collection, USAMHI; *New-Yorker Staatszeitung*, 7 and 8 May 1863. The Democratic *Staatszeitung*, considering itself the spokesman of the eastern Germans, continually bickered with the strongly Republican "radical" German press of Missouri, blaming it and its backers for all the evils brought out by the war. On 9 and 15 May, the *Staatszeitung* followed the old pattern, strongly insinuating that the "radicals of St. Louis" had helped bring about the nativistic backlash against Germans everywhere because of their constant heckling of Halleck and the Lincoln administration.

30. Philadelphia *Freie Presse*, 18 May 1863; Friedrich Kapp, *Aus und über Amerika: Thatsachen und Erlebnisse*, vol. 1 (Berlin: Verlag von Julius Springer, 1876), 292; Pittsburgh *Freiheitsfreund und Courier*, 15 May 1863; *Milwaukee Herold*, 23 May 1863.

31. Culp article in *National Tribune*, 11 December 1884; Hartwell Osborn, *Trials and Triumphs*, 69; Samuel H. Hurst, *Journal-History of the Seventy-Third Ohio*, 56. Devens may have been drunk during the afternoon of 2 May, an allegation supported by Hurst's delicate statement about his "condition."

32. *Pittsburger Demokrat*, 16 May 1863; Jacob Smith, *Camps and Campaigns*, 73; Karl Wickesberg, 26th Wisconsin, to family, 21 May 1863, quoted in Pula, *The Sigel Regiment*, 142.

33. Hecker to Schurz, 21 May 1863, Schurz Papers, LOC.

34. Chicago *Illinois-Staatszeitung*, 7 May 1863; Cincinnati *Wöchentlicher Volkfreund* 13 May 1863.

35. *Pittsburger Demokrat*, 8, 9, and 10 May 1863; Chicago *Illinois-Staatszeitung* 7, 8, 9 May 1863.

36. Cleveland *Wächter am Erie*, 30 May 1863; Pittsburgher *Freiheitsfreund und Courier*, 9 May 1863; Allentown *Friedensbote*, 13 May 1863; Philadelphia *Freie Presse*, 12 May, 1863. The U.S. Ford was one of the primary fords the Union army used to cross the Rappahannock River, and one of its critical routes of retreat.

37. Philadelphia *Daily Evening Bulletin*, 14 May 1863; *Pittsburger Volksblatt*, 13 May 1863. The family of Second Lieutenant Oscar Ladley of the 75th Ohio of McLean's brigade wrote frequently to him after the battle of Chancellorsville, assuring him that the blame of the northern public rested squarely on the Germans' shoulders, not on his Anglo American brigade or the commanding generals. His mother wrote on May 13 that "the papers did not blame any but the Germans. . . . But they spoke in high terms of McLeans Brigade." His sister reiterated this point on 24 May, declaring "the papers blame the Dutch but praise the Ohio boys." See Carl M. Becker and Ritchie Thomas, eds., *Hearth and Knapsack*, 124, 133.

38. Philadelphia *Freie Presse*, 29 May 1863.

39. Ibid. The editor specifically stated that the "morale of the troops is quite low."

40. Heusinger, *Amerikanische Kriegsbilder*, 119; Highland, Illinois *Highland Bote*, 22 May, 1863.

41. Ibid, 4 June 1863. The remarks of the Ohio officers were reprinted at the top of the page, in German. Also see the Pittsburgh *Freiheitsfreund und Courier* on 6 and 7 June 1863 for similar sentiments about the Ohio troops' petition and proposed transfer of the German regiments. Unfortunately, I was unable to locate an English-language copy of the Ohio officers' petition, but evidence of it exists in the National Archives. A letter to the Assistant Adjutant General of the Eleventh Corps from the new colonel commanding the second brigade, first division, on 19 May 1863 reads: "I have the honor to forward herewith a paper bearing the signatures of certain officers of the 25th, 55th, and 75th Ohio Regiments. Also a communication with accompanying resolutions from the 107th Ohio. I do this, in conformity with the wish expressed in the resolutions and in compliance with the request of the officers whose names are attached to the paper above named. I desire, however, to say that the paper was drawn before my connection with this Brigade and that it was circulated without my knowledge. It has my unqualified disapproval" (see "Letters Sent, May 1863–May 1864, Dept. of Florida, Entry 5364, RG-393, pt. 2, NARA).

42. Philadelphia *Freie Presse*, 23 June 1863; Boston *Pionier*, 8 July 1863; Belleviller *Volksblatt*, 8 July 1863; Jörg Nagler, *Frémont contra Lincoln: Die deutsch-amerikanische Opposition in der republikanischen Partei während des amerikanischen Bürgerkrieges* (New York: Peter Lang, 1984), 122–23, 127. The Pittsburgh *Freiheitsfreund und Courier* of 24 and 25 June 1863 also carried coverage of the Washington meeting but did not reprint its proceedings verbatim. The "Washington Conference" as it became known in the German American communities, soon came under fire by Democratic Germans as being

too radical and too dominated by Republicans. The radical Missouri Germans, for their part, claimed it was not radical enough.

43. "The Battle of Chancellorsville and the Eleventh Army Corps" (New York: G. B. Teubner, printer, 1863), 7, 8–12, 16.

44. Ibid., 19–20. The full texts of each major speech were published and distributed in both German and English pamphlets. Following the texts of the speeches was an "appendix" containing the letters of Schurz and Schimmelfennig previously mentioned, letters from other officers of the Eleventh Corps, reprints of the slanders in the American press, and the set of resolutions unanimously passed by those at the rally.

45. Ibid., 22–27.

46. Philadelphia Demokrat, 13 June 1863.

47. New York Times, 3 and 4 June 1863, reprinted in the Philadelphia Freie Presse, 12 June 1863; Philadelphia Freie Presse, 6 June 1863; Philadelphia Demokrat, 4 June 1863; New-Yorker Staatszeitung, 3 June 1863; New York Criminalzeitung und Bellestrisches Jounal, 5 June 1863.

6. Nativism and German Ethnicity after Chancellorsville

1. See chapter 7 of David L. Valuska and Christian B. Keller, Damn Dutch: Pennsylvania Germans at Gettysburg (Mechanicsburg, Pa.: Stackpole Books, 2004), for a detailed analysis of the Eleventh Corps at Gettysburg, especially the Pennsylvania German regiments, and the reactions of the Anglo American and German-language press to that battle.

2. Ibid.

3. Anonymous hospital visitor's letter reprinted in Highland, Illinois Highland Bote, 7 August 1863; Peter Boffinger to "Dear Theodor," 1 December 1863, reprinted in Helbich and Kamphoefner, eds., Deutsche im Amerikanische Bürgerkrieg, 206; Pula, The Sigel Regiment, 182.

4. Carl Schurz to "Dear sister in law," 10 September 1863, reprinted in "Zwei Briefe von Carl Schurz," The American-German Review (June–August 1947): 14–15; Martin Seel to brother, 24 September 1863, translation and transcription at Archives, FSNMP, original in possession of Bob Seel, Tucson, Arizona.

5. Wilhelm Vocke to "editorship of the 'Nashville Union,'" 10 June 1863, reprinted in Wilhelm Vocke obituary, Deutsch-Amerikanische Geschichtsblätter 7, no. 3 (July 1907): 118–21.

6. Gottfried Rentschler to the editor of the Tägliche Louisville Anzeiger, 10 March 1864, published 15 March 1864. Reprinted in Joseph R. Reinhart, ed. and trans., Two Germans in the Civil War: The Diary of John Daeuble and the Letters of Gottfried Rentschler, 6th Kentucky Volunteer Infantry (Knoxville: University of Tennessee Press, 2004), 67–68. Rentschler's observations about the low opinion of Germans in the minds of Americans was reiterated in the normally uncontroversial Cincinnati Protestantischen Zeitblätter, which declared on 15 August 1864, "How shameful, how base, yes, how inhuman has the treatment of German immigrants by the natives become!" The future of the country was bleak indeed "If the [Americans] convince future German immigrants that the Germans here in America are viewed only as a type of Spartan helot or Chinese Coolie to be exploited and oppressed by the natives!"

7. Carl Schurz to "the editors of the Louisville Journal," 6 November 1863, typescript in Carl Schurz Collection (Box 181, General Correspondence 1863), LOC; New York Tribune, 19 November 1863; Hans L. Trefousse, Carl Schurz, 141–42.

8. [Illegible name] to Carl Schurz, 19 November 1863, Carl Schurz Papers, Container 4, LOC; Philadelphia Freie Presse, 26 November 1863; Pittsburgh Freiheitsfreund und Courier, 20 November 1863; Philadelphia Demokrat, 19 November 1863.

9. *Philadelphia Demokrat*, 10 and 19 November 1863; Wilhelm Kaufmann, *The Germans in the American Civil War*, 377–78.

10. Trefousse, *Carl Schurz*, 141; Rochester *Beobachter*, 16 February 1864. Buschbeck's brigade of von Steinwehr's division of the Eleventh Corps performed well again at Tunnel Hill during the battle for Missionary Ridge, but Schurz's division missed most of the action because of its rearward position. In the forefront of the charge on the rebel works at Tunnel Hill, the 27th and 73rd Pennsylvania "displayed a courage almost amounting to rashness," according to General William T. Sherman. The 73rd ran out of ammunition, however, and most of the men were captured in that battle, while the 27th suffered heavy casualties: 132 out of 240 engaged. See Samuel P. Bates, *History of the Pennsylvania Volunteers, 1861–1865*, 5 vols. (1869–1871; reprint 1993, Broadfoot Publishing Company), 2: 392–93; Bates, 4: 867–68, 920–21.

11. Carl Schurz, *Reminiscences of Carl Schurz*, vol. 3 (New York: McClure, 1907–8), 85–94; Trefousse, 143–44; Rochester *Beobachter*, 16 February 1864; Pittsburgh *Freiheitsfreund und Courier*, 27 February 1864; Pula, *For Liberty and Justice*, 150–56; Charles A. Dana to Carl Schurz, 24 March 1863, Schurz Papers, Container 4, LOC. Schurz was not down for the count. In the 1864 presidential election he campaigned extensively for Lincoln while still retaining his army rank, and later returned to field command near the very end of the war.

12. Rochester *Beobachter*, 29 April 1864.

13. Lt. Colonel Alexander von Mitzel, 74th Pennsylvania, to "Provost Marshal at City Point, Va," 19 September 1864 (74th PA Unbound Regimental Papers Filed with Muster Rolls, RG-94, Box 4378, NARA); Lt. Colonel J. Chamberlin, Pennsylvania Military Agency, Nashville, to Col. Samuel B. Thomas, a.d.C., 20 March 1865 (RG-19, Box 45, Folder 13, PASA); Lt. Colonel Charles Reen to General A. L. Russell, Adjt. General, Pennsylvania, 18 February 1865 (RG-19, Box 62, Folder 14, PASA). The 74th, 75th and 98th Pennsylvania had each been officially reorganized as veteran regiments after being mustered out in 1864. There was only lukewarm enthusiasm, apparently, among the men to re-enlist. About one-third of the men of the 74th and 75th Pennsylvania refused to re-enlist, and almost one-half of the 98th was discharged. Was this caused by dissatisfaction with nativistic prejudice? See above citations for documents related to mustering-out and re-enlistment. The members of the 27th PA were strongly against re-enlisting: 325 men mustered out May 31, 1864 (August Riedt to Brig. General William Whipple, 21 May 1864, RG-94, 27th Pennsylvania Unbound Regimental Papers filed with Muster Rolls, Box 4259, NARA). The 27th mustered out en masse partly because the men were not permitted to muster out officially on 5 May due to the exigencies of the coming campaign against Atlanta. The frustration among the ranks caused by this action was extreme and many men believed themselves wronged by the government. See Bates, *History*, 2: 393.

14. Former Colonel Adolph von Hartung, 74th Pennsylvania, to Andrew Curtin, 28 July 1864 (RG-19, Box 44, Folder 16, PASA); Capt. Gottfried Bauer, 98th PA, to Colonel Samuel B. Thomas, a.d.C, 6 February 1865 (RG-19, Box 62, Folder 14, PASA); Colonel John Ballier, 98th Pennsylvania, to Andrew Curtin, 19 August 1863 (ibid.). Both von Hartung and Ballier were medically discharged in 1863 due to wounds received in battle: Ballier at Salem Heights and von Hartung at Gettysburg.

15. "Roster of Commissioned Officers of the 74th Regiment Penna. Volunteers, for the Month of March, 1864" (74th Pennsylvania Unbound Regimental Papers Filed with Muster Rolls, RG-94, Box 4378, NARA).

16. "Roster of Commissioned Officers of the 75th Regiment Penna. Vet. Vol. Inf. for the Month ending March 31, 1865" (RG-19, Folder 13, Box 45, PASA).

17. See Burton, *Melting Pot Soldiers*, pp. 111 and 227 for these quotes. It is important to note that Burton drew much of his material from Ella Lonn's book, which also clearly argues for the Americanization thesis.

18. Otto Heusinger, in his memoirs of service with the German 41st New York, substantiates the idea that German officers routinely prevented the promotion of non-Germans in the ethnic regiments and thus preserved their ethnic character. In October 1863 the 41st received 600 new recruits to fill up the regiment. Two-thirds of them were Irish, French, or Americans, and the rest German. "It happened that the officer corps was composed only of German members; nonetheless several attempts were made to shove in American officers. The majority of the non-commissioned officers were also German, so that the regiment therefore remained classified as a German one." Otto Heusinger, *Amerikanische Kriegsbilder*, 162. Heusinger's contention is reinforced by a letter sent home by Private Albert H. Richards of the 41st, who complained to his father on 29 November 1864, "I am in a Dutch regiment, all dutch but a few officers and men." See Albert H. Richards Pension File, App. 268.384, Certif. 205.943, NARA.

19. Charles Power to Hon. Eli Slifer, 25 May 1865 (RG-19, Box 44, Folder 14, PASA).

20. 1st Sergeant Ezra W. Merrill, 75th PA, to "His Excellency Hon. A. G. Curtin," 8 October 1862 (RG-19, Box 44, Folder 14, PASA); Irving W. Combs, Co. K, 74th PA, to A. G. Curtin, 30 August 1864 (RG-19, Box 44, Folder 13, PASA).

21. Results of Election held at the Headquarters of the 74th PA, Beverly, West Virginia, 8 April 1865, contained in RG-19, Box 44, Folder 14, PASA.

22. Capt. G. Hoburg, 74th PA, to Brevet Maj. General McMillan, 8 April 1865 (RG-94, Carded Records, Volunteer Orgs: Civil War Personal Papers, Pennsylvania, 74th Regiment, Boxes 157–158, NARA).

23. Hoburg to Curtin, 21 April 1865; A. C. White to A. G. Curtin, 13 April 1865 (both letters in RG-19, Box 44, Folder 14, PASA).

24. List of officers of the 74th Pennsylvania, including promotions, honorable discharges, and dismissals up to June 1865. No date or location for this roster was given, but every officer was listed, along with his rank, company, date of original commission, date of muster, birthplace, current residence, and special notations. There was a separate section for promotions and dismissals, with Pealer, Wilson, McLain and others prominently featured (RG-19, Box 44, Folder 13, PASA).

25. Samuel Pealer, John Wilson, Gavin McLain, James McGregor, and S. Hendricks to Andrew G. Curtin, 30 June 1865 (RG-19, Box 44, Folder 13, PASA). These men must have traveled to Harrisburg to personally meet with Curtin as their letter's heading lists "Harrisburg, Pa." Whether or not they actually spoke with the governor is unknown.

26. "Company F, 74th PA" to "Mr. Andrew G. Curtin, Guv of pa," 20 July 1865 (RG-19, Box 44, Folder 13, PASA). Unlike most company-wide petitions discovered, the men did not sign their individual names, but instead signed only "Co. F."

27. Ibid.; "Descriptive List of Deserters from the 74th Regiment of Pennsylvania Volunteer Infantry," compiled from the records of Provost Marshal General's Bureau, James B. Fry commanding, Washington, D.C., 26 June 1866. This comprehensive list, along with similar lists for all the Pennsylvania regiments, was found in a Gettysburg antique shop in a bound leather volume marked "Deserters." Such volumes were issued to each county after the war, to determine voter eligibility. Interestingly, the same source revealed deserter information on other ethnically German regiments that may reflect prejudicial treatment: Of 72 deserters from the 73rd Pennsylvania from July 1862 to the end of the war, 36 were non-German. Similarly, from June 1863 to April 1864 only 70 out of 107 deserters from the fractious 27th Pennsylvania were clearly non-German. In both regiments, birthplace was clearly indicated. No doubt Hoburg wanted the Colonelcy of the 74th for more than simply ethnic reasons; the difference in pay and prestige between a captain and a colonel, not to mention the increased pension he would receive, were certainly additional motives.

28. Jörg Nagler, *Frémont contra Lincoln*, 150, 356; Chicago *Illinois Staatszeitung*, 22 October 1863; Carl Wittke, *Against the Current: A Life of Carl Heinzen* (Chicago, 1944), 191.

29. Nagler, 150–54; Philadelphia *Freie Presse*, 24, 26, 28 October 1863; Carl Wittke, *Refugees of Revolution; The German Forty-Eighters in America* (Philadelphia: University of Pennsylvania Press, 1952), 245–46; Chicago *Illinois-Staatszeitung*, 23 October 1863.

30. Franz Sigel to "the President of the German Convention in Cleveland, Dr. Greiner," 19 October 1863, reprinted in Pittsburgh *Freiheitsfreund und Courier*, 30 October 1863; [Illegible, but probably E. F. Schmidt] to Carl Schurz, 8 November 1863, Container 4, Carl Schurz Papers, LOC.

31. Wittke, *Refugees*, 246; Nagler, *Frémont contra Lincoln*, 154–55; [Illegible] to Carl Schurz, 8 November 1863; Philadelphia *Freie Presse*, 9 December 1863; Rochester *Beobachter*, 17 March 1864.

32. Nagler, 154; *Philadelphia Demokrat*, 13 June 1863; Taussig quoted in Otto C. Schneider, "Abraham Lincoln und das Deutschtum," *Deutsch-Amerikanische Geschichtsblätter* (April 1907): 73–74; Henry Boernstein, *Memoirs of a Nobody: The Missouri Years of an Austrian Radical, 1849–1866*, trans. and ed. Steven Rowan (St. Louis: Missouri Historical Society Press, 1997), 372–73; Wittke, *Refugees*, 246.

33. St. Louis *Neuen Zeit* article reprinted in Pittsburgh *Freiheitsfreund und Courier*, 6 February 1864; Cincinnati *Volksblatt*, 11 March 1864; Stephen D. Engle, *Yankee Dutchman*, 168–69; Strother quoted in Cecil D. Eby, ed., *A Virginia Yankee in the Civil War: The Diaries of David Hunter Strother* (Chapel Hill: University of North Carolina Press, 1961), 213.

34. Engle, *Yankee Dutchman*, 187–92, 198; Columbus *Westbote*, 26 May 1864; *Pittsburgher Volksblatt* editorial reprinted in Columbus *Westbote*, 26 May 1864.

35. Rochester *Beobachter*, 24 March 1864; Francis Lieber, "Lincoln or McClellan: Appeal to the Germans in America" (New York: Loyal Publication Society, 1864), 2, 4.

36. *New-Yorker Staatszeitung*, 31 August 1864, 1 September 1864; James S. Lapham, "The German Americans of New York City, 1860–1890" (Ph.D. diss., St. Johns University, 1977), 212–13; Pittsburgh *Abendzeitung*, 19, 21, 31 October 1864.

37. Caspar Butz, "Unser Urteil über Lincoln," *Deutsch-Amerikanische Monatshefte* 1 (February 1864): 128; Wittke, *The German-Language Press in America* (Lexington: University of Kentucky Press, 1957), 153–55; Nagler, *Frémont contra Lincoln*, 223, 228, 241–44. Some Germans were disgusted with all three presidential candidates. Captain Rudolph Mueller of the 82nd Illinois wrote to Friedrich Hecker on 9 July 1864, "It is difficult to find one's way in this political chaos and find the man who is capable of bringing back to the nation its sinking credit. . . . One cannot go for Fremont; for Lincoln, this sleepy head, in any case only with reluctance. What's left? Is one supposed to wait for the rejuvenation of the corroded Democracy? The best thing would be to plant one's own cabbage and roots far away from the disgusting ways of the world, in the most distant part of the jungle to live only for one's self." Letter translated and transcribed in Eric Benjaminson, "A Regiment of Immigrants," 169.

7. Chancellorsville and the Civil War in German American Memory

1. *Der Deutsche Pionier* 15, no. 8 (November 1883): 330–31.

2. Stephen Engle, *Yankee Dutchman*, 212–28; David W. Blight, *Race and Reunion: The Civil War in American Memory* (Cambridge, Mass.: Belknap Press of Harvard University Press, 2001); Stuart McConnell, *Glorious Contentment: The Grand Army of the Republic, 1865–1900* (Chapel Hill: University of North Carolina Press, 1992), 55, 69, 209, 272; Margaret Creighton, *The Colors of Courage: Gettysburg's Forgotten History* (Cambridge, Mass.: Basic Books, 2005), chapter 8; Martin Oefele, *German-Speaking Officers in the U.S. Colored Troops, 1863–1867* (Gainesville, Florida: University Press of Florida,

2004), 229–33. Another fascinating work at the intersection of the subjects of Civil War memory and German Americans in the war is Peter Sevenson, *Battlefield: Farming a Civil War Battleground* (New York: Ballantine Books, 1992), which does not analyze German American memory of the war at all, but is a charming story of how one man, who bought a large portion of the Cross Keys battlefield, struggled to remember and honor those who died there.

3. Helbich and Kamphoefner, *Deutsche im Amerikanischen Bürgerkrieg*, 82–85; Engle, *Yankee Dutchman*, 230.

4. For some excellent examples of early literature focusing on exclusively German American issues in the war, see, for instance, a poem celebrating the return of the German 24th Illinois: "Die Heimkehr: Dem 24. Illinois (Hecker) Regiment Gewidmet," *Deutsch-Amerikanische Monatshefte* 2 (August 1864): 169–70, or one honoring the German dead buried in Monroe, Michigan, entitled, "Unsere Todten," in the January issue of the same publication. For examples of good biographical sketches of German military leaders, see the installments "General Adolph von Steinwehr," "General August Willich," and "General Hugo Wangelin," in *Der Deutsche Pionier* 9, no. 1 (April 1877): 17–28; 10, no. 2 (May 1878): 69–71; 10, no. 3 (June 1878): 114–17; 10, no. 4 (July 1878): 144–47; and 15, no. 10 (January 1884): 408–10. Some good examples of anecdotes about German soldiers may also be found scattered throughout the issues of the *Pionier*, but see especially "Ein paar Soldaten-Geschichten," in vol. 18, no. 1 (1886), 12–13 and "Merkwürdiges Wiedersehen von zwei deutschen Veteranen," in vol 18, no. 2 (1887) 111–12. Obituaries of prominent officers often carried with them short histories of German American arms during the war, such as that of Lieutenant Colonel Heinrch von Trebra of the 32nd Indiana, which appeared in the January 1910 issue of the *Deutsch-Amerikanische Geschichtsblätter*, 31–33. Even a history of the Chicago Turnverein in 1905 was dominated by a history of the organization's involvement in the Civil War. See *Deutsch-Amerikanische Geschichtsblätter* (July 1905): 42–46.

5. Rudolph Lexow, "Zur Erinnerung," *Deutsch-Amerikanische Monatshefte* 3 (January 1866): 2–26.

6. Ernst Reinhold Schmidt, *Der Amerikanische Bürgerkrieg: Geschichte des Volks der Vereinigten Staaten vor, während und nach der Rebellion*, II (Philadelphia and Leipzig: Verlag von Schäfer und Koradi, 1867): 155, 226–27, 251–52.

7. E. Schlaeger, *Die sociale und politische Stellung der Deutchen in den Vereinigten Staaten* (Berlin: Puttkamer and Mühlbrecht, 1874): 25; Martin Luecke, *Der Bürgerkrieg der Vereinigten Staaten, 1861–65* (St. Louis: Druck und Verlag von Louis Lange, 1892), 177.

8. Wilhelm Kaufmann, *The Germans in the American Civil War* (1911; reprint and translation, Carlisle, Pa.: John Kallman Publishers, 1999): 2, 198–200, 210–11. Kaufmann's book was heralded all throughout the German American press even before its publication. Several sections of it were originally published in serial form in over eighty German-language newspapers before the author compiled them and created the final product (Kaufmann, reprint, v).

9. Schurz, *Reminiscences*, 2:407–43; 3:51, 85–95; Schurz, "Reminiscences of a Long Life," *McClures Magazine* (June 1917): 161–76; Mary Elizabeth McMorrow, "The Nineteenth-Century German Political Immigrant and the Construction of American Culture and Thought" (Ph.D. diss, New School for Social Research, 1982), 119–22; Trefousse, *Schurz*, 135.

10. T. A. Meysenberg, "Reminiscences of Chancellorsville," *War Papers and Personal Reminiscences* (St. Louis: MOLLUS Missouri, 1892), 1:306; Hamlin, *Chancellorsville*, 159. It is interesting to note what Meysenberg left out of his paper, namely, any criticism of General Howard, whom he dutifully served during the war, and, according to several

believable accounts, may have protected by "pocketing" Hooker's famous "9:30 order." See chapter 2.

11. Hubert Dilger to Augustus Hamlin, 12 July 1892 and 3 April 1893, both in bMS Am 1084 (temp. box 22, file N-O), Houghton Library, Harvard University; Karl Doerflinger, "Familiar History of the Twenty-sixth Regiment Wisconsin Volunteer Infantry: I. Personal Reminiscences of the Battle of Chancellorsville; particularly on Hawkins' Field," 18 March 1911, original at State Historical Society of Wisconsin, copy at archives, FSNMP.

12. "General Adolph von Steinwehr, *Die Deutsche Pionier* 9, no. 1 (April 1877): 17–28.

13. "Carl Schurz: Sein Leben und Wirken," *Deutsch-Amerikanische Geschichtsblätter* 3 (July 1906): 6–9.

14. William Vocke, "Our German Soldiers," *Military Essays and Recollections* (Chicago: MOLLUS Illinois, 1899), 3:350–57.

15. Stuart McConnell, *Glorious Contentment*, 55, 272; Hermann Nachtigall to Augustus C. Hamlin, 28 January 1893, Augustus Hamlin Papers, bMS Am 1084 (temp. box 22, file N-O), Houghton Library, Harvard University. Post 8 in Philadelphia was also primarily composed of German-born veterans.

16. Address of Lieutenant T. Albert Steiger in "Dedication of Monument: 75th Regiment Infantry, Orchard Knob, November 14, 1897," Chickamauga and Chattanooga Battlefield Commission, *Pennsylvania at Chickamauga and Chattanooga: Ceremonies at the Dedications of the Monuments* (Harrisburg: William S. Ray, 1900), 167–85.

17. Ibid.

18. "Dedication of Monument, 41st Regiment Infantry, 'De Kalb Regiment,' July 3, 1893: Historical Sketch"; "Dedication of Monument, 45th Regiment Infantry, October 10, 1888: Oration of Comrade Christian Boehm"; "Dedication of Monument, 58th Regiment Infantry, July 2, 1888: Historical Sketch" all in William F. Fox, ed., *New York at Gettysburg: The NY Monuments Commission Final Report on the Battlefield of Gettysburg* (Albany: J. B. Lyon Company, 1900), 306, 377, 429. "Dedication of Monument, 68th Regiment Infantry: Historical Sketch," in *New York Monuments Commission for the Battlefields of Gettysburg and Chattanooga: Final Report on the Battlefield of Gettysburg* (Albany: J. B. Lyon Company, 1902), 2: 568.

19. Address of Captain Paul F. Rohrbacker in "Dedication of Monument, 74th Regiment Infantry, July 2, 1888," in Gettysburg Battlefield Commission, *Pennsylvania at Gettysburg: Ceremonies at the Dedication of the Monuments Erected by the Commonwealth* (Harrisburg: William S. Ray, 1914), 1:427–30.

20. Ibid.

21. Some of the early leaders of the cultural pluralist school are Michael Novak, *The Rise of the Unmeltable Ethnics* (New York: Macmillan, 1973); Thomas Sowell, *Ethnic America: A History* (New York: Basic Books, 1981); Joseph A. Ryan, ed., *White Ethnic Life in Working Class America* (Englewood Cliffs, N.J., 1973); and Nathan Glazer and Daniel P. Moynihan, *Beyond the Melting Pot: The Negroes, Puerto Ricans, Jews, Italians, and Irish of New York City*, 2nd ed. (Cambridge, MA: MIT Press, 1970). Werner Sollors, ed., *The Invention of Ethnicity* (New York: Oxford University Press, 1989); Kathleen Neils Conzen, "German Americans and the Invention of Ethnicity," in Frank Trommler and Joseph McVeigh, eds., *America and the Germans: An Assessment of a Three-Hundred Year History*, vol. 1: Immigration, Language, Ethnicity (Philadelphia: University of Pennsylvania Press, 1985); David L. Salvaterra, "Becoming American: Assimilation, Pluralism, and Ethnic Identity," in Timothy Walsh, ed., *Immigrant America: European Ethnicity in the United States* (New York: Garland Publishing, Inc., 1994); and more recently, Matthew Frye Jacobson, *Whiteness of a Different Color: European Immigrants and the Alchemy of Race* (Cambridge, Mass.: Harvard University Press, 1998), have added a great deal to the earlier scholars' studies of immigrant groups' pluralistic behavior, especially for the last few decades of the nineteenth century, which is my focus in this chapter. I have been

especially influenced by Conzen's work. Russell A. Kazal's *Becoming Old Stock: The Paradox of German American Identity* (Princeton: Princeton University Press, 2004) is an excellent study of how Philadelphia's German Americans ultimately assimilated, modeled on the cultural pluralist school, but chronologically begins only in 1900.

22. Friedrich Kapp, "Rede, gehalten am 19. Juli 1865 in Jones Wood, in New York, zum Schluss des neunten deutschen Sängerfestes," reprinted in *Deutsch-Amerikanische Monatshefte* (August 1865): 182–88; "Der Nativismus in den Staatsschulen," in J. B. Stallo, *Reden, Abhandlungen und Briefe von J. B. Stallo* (New York: E. Steiger and Co., 1893), 193–96.

23. Friedrich Lexow, "Die Deutschen in Amerika," *Deutsch-Amerikanisch Monatshefte* 3 (January 1866): 149–54, and March 1866, 255–61. Lexow welcomed those who disagreed with him, as evidenced by two lengthy articles written by Charles L. Bernays, former editor of the powerful *Anzeiger des Westens*. Bernays was an "anti-Germanizer" as much as he was an assimilationist, taking great issue with the pluralist attitudes of Lexow. See "Ein Beitrag zur Geschichte," and "Betrachtungen" in *Deutsch-Amerikanische Monatshefte* 4 (February 1867): 91–108 and May 1867, 386–99.

24. "Deutsch-Amerikaner, aber keine amerikanisirte Deustche," *Deutsch-Amerikanische Monatshefte* 4 (April 1867): 348–56.

25. Article from *Philadelphia Demokrat* reprinted in *Der Deutsche Pionier* 14, no. 6 (September 1882): 216; article from *Pittsburgher Volksblatt* reprinted in *Der Deutsche Pionier* 3, no. 5 (July 1871): 149–50. Also see reprints of similar articles from the *Illinois-Staatszeitung*, the Allentown *Weltbote*, and the St. Louis *Anzeiger des Westens* in the *Pionier* 6, no. 8 (October 1874): 265–67; 7, no. 6 (August 1875): 221–22, and 13, no. 5 (August 1881): 201–2. The *Weltbote* article also mentioned that the Franco-Prussian war had an "electric" effect upon the emigrated Germans, and that now "the Germans of the old and new world are united like never before through the magical bond of blood relationships, language, ideas and feelings, customs, and desires . . . they are now a harmonic whole."

26. L. W. Habercom, *Unser Adoptiv-Vaterland: eine Geschichte der Vereinigten Staaten mit Berücksichtigung des deutsch-amerikanischen Elementes* (Milwaukee: the Milwaukee "Herold," 1889), 337–88.

27. "Denkmal der Deutsch-Amerikaner in Dayton, Ohio," *Deutsch-Amerikanische Geschichtsblätter* (January 1911): 8–15.

Bibliography

Abbreviations

FSNMP   Fredericksburg-Spotsylvania National Military Park Archives
HSP   Historical Society of Pennsylvania
NARA   National Archives and Records Administration
OR   *The War of the Rebellion: A Compilation of the Official Records of the Union and Confederate Armies*
PASA   Pennsylvania State Archives
USAMHI   United States Army Military History Institute

Archival Materials

Bowdoin College Library Special Collections
    O. O. Howard Letters

Clements Library, University of Michigan
    William S. Schoff Collection

Cumberland County Historical Society, Carlisle, Pa.
    David Ackerman Letters

Fredericksburg-Spotsylvania National Military Park Archive
    Benjamin B. Carr Memoir
    William Clegg Letters
    William H. Clark Letters
    Darwin D. Cody Letters
    Karl Doerflinger Reminiscence
    Charles T. Furlow Journal
    Wilson French Letters
    James C. McCown Memoirs
    Martin Seel Collection
    John L. Smith Letters

Historical Society of Pennsylvania, Philadelphia
    James Biddle Civil War Letters

John Haingartner Civil War Memoirs
Jacob C. Kappler Collection
David Mouat Manuscript

Houghton Library, Harvard University
    A. C. Hamlin Letter Collection

Lancaster County Historical Society, Lancaster, Pa.
    MG-18, Civil War Collection

Lehigh County Historical Society, Allentown, Pa.
    Theodore Howell Letters

Library Company of Philadelphia, Philadelphia
    Rare American Collection

Library of Congress Manuscripts Division, Washington, D.C.
    Diary of Friedrich Otto Baron von Fritsch
    James J. Gillette Collection
    Frank Jacobs Diary, 1862
    MMC Sebastian Mueller Letterbooks
    Carl Schurz Papers
    Dennis Tuttle Papers

Louisiana State University Dept. of Archives and Manuscripts, Baton Rouge,
La.
    George S. Lester Papers

Massachusetts Historical Society, Boston, MA
    E. L. Edes Papers

National Archives and Records Administration, Washington, D.C.
    RG-15, Pension Office Files
    RG-94, Records of the Office of the Adjutant General
        82nd Illinois Infantry Consolidated Morning Report, Letter, and Order
            Book
        45th New York Infantry Letter, Order, and Index Book
        54th New York Infantry Regimental Letter and Order Book
        58th New York Infantry Regimental Order Book
        119th New York Infantry Regimental Letter and Order Book
        27th Pennsylvania Order, Letter, and Endorsement Book
        27th Pennsylvania Regimental Descriptive Book
        27th Pennsylvania Unbound Regimental Papers filed with Muster Rolls

  73rd Pennsylvania Carded Records, Volunteer Orgs.: Civil War Personal Papers
  73rd Pennsylvania Order, Letter, and Endorsement Book
  73rd Pennsylvania Regimental Descriptive Book
  74th Pennsylvania Carded Records, Volunteer Orgs.: Civil War Personal Papers
  74th Pennsylvania Order, Letter, and Endorsement Book
  74th Pennsylvania Regimental Descriptive Book
  74th Pennsylvania Unbound Regimental Papers filed with Muster Rolls
  75th Pennsylvania Order, Letter, and Endorsement Book
  75th Pennsylvania Regimental Descriptive Book
  75th Pennsylvania Unbound Regimental Papers filed with Muster Rolls
  97th Pennsylvania Order, Letter, and Endorsement Book
  98th Pennsylvania Order, Letter, and Endorsement Book
  98th Pennsylvania Regimental Descriptive Book
RG-393, pt. 2, Records of U.S. Army Corps
  Letters Sent Dec. 1861-Nov. 1863, 11AC
  Letters Received, January 1863–1864, 11th A.C.
  Register of Letters Received Relating to Leaves of Absence, Resignations, and Furloughs, 11th A.C. 1863
  Letters Sent, May 1863-May 1864, Dept. of Florida

Ohio State Historical Society, Columbus, Ohio
  Joshua R. Giddings Papers
  Andrew Linton Harris Papers

Pennsylvania State Archives, Harrisburg, Pa.
  RG-19, Records of the Adjutant General of the State of Pennsylvania
    27th Pennsylvania Unbound Regimental Papers filed with Muster Rolls
    73rd Pennsylvania Unbound Regimental Papers filed with Muster Rolls
    74th Pennsylvania Unbound Regimental Papers filed with Muster Rolls
    75th Pennsylvania Unbound Regimental Papers filed with Muster Rolls
    98th Pennsylvania Unbound Regimental Papers filed with Muster Rolls
    153rd Pennsylvania Unbound Regimental Papers filed with Muster Rolls

United States Army Military History Institute, Carlisle Barracks, Pa.
  Civil War Times Illustrated Collection
  Civil War Times Misc. Collection
    Eugene Blackford Memoir
    Friedrich A. Brautigam Diary
    Friedrich P. Kappelman Letters

Charles F. Lewis Diary
Luther B. Mesnard Reminiscence
Benjamin F. Robb Letters
Wilhelm Roth Collection
Leonhard Schlumpf Diary, 1862
Franz Henry Schwenzer Letters, 1861–1862
Harrisburg Civil War Roundtable Collection
Lewis Leigh Collection
    John Lewis Letters
    Daniel O. Macomber Letters
Peacock Papers
Isaac N. Porter letter, uncatalogued
Michael Winey Collection

Virginia Historical Society, Richmond, Va.
Friedrich Wilhelm von Schilling Collection

Privately Owned Materials

"Descriptive List of Deserters from the 74th Regiment of Pennsylvania Volunteer Infantry." Compiled from the records of Provost Marshal General's Bureau, James B. Fry commanding, Washington, D.C., 26 June 1866. Found in Gettysburg antique shop.

Newspapers

Allentown Friedens-Bote
Allentown *Unabhängige Republikaner*
Allentown *Weltbote*
Baltimore American
Belleviller Zeitung
Belleviller *Volksblatt*
Boston Journal
Boston *Pionier*
Chicago *Illinois-Staatszeitung*
Chicago *Tribune*
Cincinnati *Daily Gazette*
Cincinnati *Protestantischen Zeitblätter*
Cincinnati *Täglicher Volksfreund*
Cincinnati *Woechentlicher Volksfreund*

Cleveland *Plain Dealer*
Cleveland *Wächter am Erie*
Columbus *Westbote*
Easton *Daily Free Press*
Egg Harbor Pilot
Frank Leslie's Illustrated Newspaper
German-Reformed Messenger
Gettysburg Compiler
Harper's Weekly
Hartford *Evening Press*
Harrisburg Daily Telegraph
Highland Bote
Milwaukee Herold
Milwaukee Seebote
The Moravian
National Tribune
New York Herald
New York *Evening Post*
New York Times
New-York Daily Tribune
New-Yorker Criminalzeitung und Belletristisches Journal
New-Yorker Staatszeitung
The Pennsylvania Fifth
Philadelphia Demokrat
Philadelphia *Daily Evening Bulletin*
Philadelphia *Inquirer*
Philadelphia *Evening Bulletin*
Philadelphia *Freie Presse*
Philadelphia *Lutheran and Missionary*
Philadelphia *Morning Pennsylvanian*
Philadelphia *Public Ledger*
Pittsburgh *Abendzeitung*
Pittsburger Demokrat
Pittsburgh *Freiheits Freund und Pittsburger Courier*
Pittsburgh Post
Pittsburgher Volksblatt
Reading Adler
Reading *Banner von Berks*
Rochester *Beobachter*
Skippackville Neutralist und Allgemeine Neuigkeits-Bote

St. Louis *Anzeiger des Westens*
Tägliche Louisville Anzeiger
Washington *Daily National Intelligencer*
Weekly Pittsburgh Gazette

Primary Sources on the World Wide Web

Rudolph Mueller letters, *http://www.geocities.com/Athens/Parthenon/7419/mueller* .*html*

Adam Muenzenberger letters, http://www.russscott.com/~rscott/26thwis/26 pgam63.htm

Frank Smrcek diary entry, http://www.russscott.com/~rscott/26thwis/frsmrcek .htm

Books

Alba, Richard D. *Ethnic Identity: The Transformation of White America.* New Haven: Yale University Press, 1990.

Anbinder, Tyler. *Nativism and Slavery: The Northern Know Nothings and the Politics of the 1850s.* New York: Oxford University Press, 1992.

Arndt, Carl J. R. and Mary E. Olson. *German/American Newspapers and Periodicals.* Heidelburg, Germany: Quelle and Meyer, 1961.

Bancroft, Frederic, ed. *Speeches, Correspondence and Political Papers of Carl Schurz.* New York: G. P. Putnam's Sons, 1913.

Barclay, David E. and Elisabeth Glaser-Schmidt, eds. *Transatlantic Images and Perceptions: Germany and America Since 1776.* Cambridge: Cambridge University Press in association with the German Historical Institute, Washington, D.C., 1997.

Barth, Fredrik, ed. *Ethnic Groups and Boundaries: The Social Organization of Cultural Differences.* Boston, Mass.: Little, Brown, and Co., 1969.

Basler, Roy, ed. *The Collected Works of Abraham Lincoln.* 9 vols. New Brunswick: Rutgers University Press, 1953:6.

Bates, Samuel P. *The Battle of Chancellorsville.* Meadville, Pa.: Edward T. Bates, 1882.

———. *History of Pennsylvania Volunteers, 1861–5.* Harrisburg, Pa.: B. Singerly, State Printer, 1869–1871; Wilmington, N.C.: Broadfoot Publishing Company, 1993.

"The Battle of Chancellorsville and the Eleventh Army Corps." New York: G. B. Teubner, 1863.

Bauer, K. Jack, ed. *Soldiering: The Civil War Diary of Rice C. Bull, 123d New York Volunteer Infantry.* San Rafael, Calif.: Presidio Press, 1978.

Becker, Carl M. and Richie Thomas, eds. *Hearth and Knapsack: The Ladley Letters, 1857–1880.* Athens, Ohio: Ohio University Press, 1988.

Berkey, Jonathan. "The Foundations of Transformation? The Experiences of Hooker's Command During Chattanooga Campaign." M.A. thesis, Pennsylvania State University, 1994.

Bigelow, John. *The Campaign of Chancellorsville: A Strategic and Tactical Study.* New Haven: Yale University Press, 1910.

Billington, Ray Allen. *The Protestant Crusade, 1800–1860: A Study of the Origins of American Nativism.* New York: Macmillan, 1938; reprint, Gloucester, Mass.: Peter Smith, 1963.

Blake, Henry N. *Three Years in the Army of the Potomac.* Boston: Lee and Shepard, 1865.

Blight, David W. *Race and Reunion: The Civil War in American Memory.* Cambridge, Mass.: Belknap Press of Harvard University Press, 2001.

Bodger, John Charles, Jr. "The Immigrant Press and the Union Army." Ph.D. diss., Columbia University, 1951.

Boernstein, Henry. *Memoirs of a Nobody: The Missouri Years of an Austrian Radical, 1849–1866.* Trans. and ed. Steven Rowan. St. Louis: Missouri Historical Society Press, 1997.

Bright, Eric W. "Nothing to Fear from the Influence of Foreigners:" The Patriotism of Richmond German-Americans during the Civil War." M.A. thesis, Virginia Polytechnic and State University, 1999.

Burton, William L. *Melting Pot Soldiers: The Union's Ethnic Regiments.* 2nd ed. New York: Fordham University Press, 1998.

Cermak, Josef. *Dejiny Obcanske Valky.* Chicago: August Geringer, 1889.

Chickamauga and Chattanooga Battlefield Commission. *Pennsvlvania at Chickamauga and Chattanooga: Ceremonies at the Dedications of the Monuments.* Harrisburg, Pa.: William S. Ray, 1900.

Conklin, George W. *Under the Crescent and Star: The 134th New York Volunteer Infantry in the Civil War.* Port Reading, N.J.: Axworthy Publishing, 1999.

Conzen, Kathleen N. *Immigrant Milwaukee, 1836–1860: Accommodation and Community in a Frontier City.* Cambridge, Mass.: Harvard University Press, 1976.

Cook, Benjamin F. *History of the Twelfth Mass. Vols. (Webster Reg't.).* Boston: Twelfth Regiment Association, 1882.

Cortland County Historical Society. *A Regiment Remembered: The 157th New York Volunteers, From the Diary of Captain William Saxton.* Cortland County, N.Y.: The Society, 1996.

Creighton, Margaret. *The Colors of Courage: Gettysburg's Forgotten History.* Cambridge, Mass.: Basic Books, 2005.

Cudworth, Warren H. *History of the First Regiment (Massachusetts Infantry).* Boston: Walker, Fuller, and Company, 1866.

Culp, Edward C. *The 25th Ohio Veteran Vol, Infantry in the War for the Union.* Topeka, Kans.: G. W. Crane and Co., 1885.

Davis, Charles E. *Three Years in the Army: The Story of the Thirteenth Massachusetts Volunteers from July 16, 1861 to August 1, 1864. . . .* Boston: Estes and Larist, 1894.

Dodge, Theodore A. *The Campaign of Chancellorsville.* 2nd ed. Boston: Ticknor and Fields, 1881.

Doubleday, Abner. *Chancellorsville and Gettysburg.* New York: Scribners, 1882; reprint, New York: De Capo Press, 1994. Introduction by Gary W. Gallagher.

Dunkelman, Mark H. and Michael J. Winey. *The Hardtack Regiment: An Illustrated History of the 154th Regiment, New York State Infantry Volunteers.* Teaneck, N.J.: Fairleigh Dickinson University Press, 1981.

Eby, Cecil D., ed. *A Virginia Yankee in the Civil War: The Diaries of David Hunter Strother.* Chapel Hill: University of North Carolina Press, 1961.

Engle, Stephen D. *Yankee Dutchman: The Life of Franz Sigel.* Baton Rouge: Louisiana State University Press, 1993.

Faires, Nora H. "Ethnicity in Evolution: The German Community in Pittsburgh and Allegheny City, Pennsylvania, 1845–1885." Ph.D. diss., University of Pittsburgh, 1981.

Faust, Albert B. *The German Element in the United States.* New York: Steuben Society, 1927.

Foner, Eric. *Free Soil, Free Labor, Free Men: The Ideology of the Republican Party Before the Civil War.* New York: Oxford University Press, 1970.

Formisano, Ronald P. *The Birth of Mass Political Parties: Michigan, 1827–1861.* Princeton: Princeton University Press, 1971.

Fox, William F., ed. *New York at Gettysburg*: The NY Monuments Commission Final Report on the Battlefield of Gettysburg. Albany: J. B. Lyon Company, 1900.

Furgurson, Ernest B. *Chancellorsville: The Souls of the Brave.* New York: Alfred A. Knopf, 1993.

Gallagher, Gary W., ed. *Chancellorsville: The Battle and Its Aftermath.* Chapel Hill: University of North Carolina Press, 1996.

Gettysburg Battlefield Commission. *Pennsylvania at Gettysburg: Ceremonies at the Dedication of the Monuments Erected by the Commonwealth.* Vol. 1. Harrisburg, Pa.: William S. Ray, 1914.

Glazer, Nathan and Daniel P. Moynihan. *Beyond the Melting Pot*. 2nd ed. Cambridge, Mass.: MIT Press, 1970.

————, eds., *Ethnicity: Theory and Experience*. Cambridge, Mass.: Harvard University Press, 1975.

Gordon, Milton M. *Assimilation in American Life*. New York: Oxford University Press, 1964.

Gould, Benjamin A. *Investigations in the Statistics of American Soldiers*. New York: Riverside Press, 1869.

Grebner, Constantin. *We Were the Ninth: A History of the Ninth Regiment, Ohio Volunteer Infantry, April 17, 1861, to June 7, 1864*. Trans. and ed. Frederic Trautmann. Kent, Ohio: Kent State University Press, 1987.

Greeley, Horace. *The American Conflict: A History of the Great Rebellion in the United States of America, 1860–1865*. G. and C. W. Sherwood, 1866.

Gregory, Winfred, ed. *American Newspapers, 1821–1936: A Union List of Files Available in the United States and Canada*. New York: H. W. Wilson Co., 1937.

Habercom, L. W. *Unser Adoptiv-Vaterland: eine Geschichte der Vereinigten Staaten mit Berücksichtigung des deutsch-amerikanischen Elementes*. Milwaukee: the Milwaukee "Herold," 1889.

Hamerow, Thedore. *Restoration, Revolution, Reaction: Economics and Politics in Germany, 1815–1871*. Princeton: Princeton University Press, 1957.

Hamlin, Augustus Choate. *The Battle of Chancellorsville*. Bangor, Maine.: privately published, 1896.

Handlin, Oscar. *Boston's Immigrants: A Study in Acculturation*. Rev. and enlarged ed. New York: Atheneum, 1974.

————. *The Uprooted*. New York: Grosset and Dunlap, 1951.

Hawgood, John A. *The Tragedy of German-America*. New York: G. P. Putnam's Sons, 1940.

Helbich, Wolfgang and Walter D. Kamphoefner. *Deutsche im Amerikanischen Bürgerkrieg: Briefe von Front und Farm, 1861–1865*. Paderborn, Germany: Schöningh Verlag, 2002.

Hennessy, John J. *Return to Bull Run: The Campaign and Battle of Second Manassas*. New York: Simon and Schuster, 1993.

Hess, Earl J. *A German in the Yankee Fatherland: The Civil War Letters of Henry A. Kircher*. Kent, Ohio: Kent State University Press, 1983.

————. *Liberty, Virtue and Progress: Northerners and Their War for the Union*. 2nd ed. New York: Fordham University Press, 1997.

Heusinger, Otto. *Amerikanische Kriegsbilder: Aufzeichnungen aus den Jahren 1861–1865*. 1869; reprint Wyk auf Foehr, Germany: Verlag für Amerikanistik, 1998.

Higham, John. *Strangers in the Land: Patterns in American Nativism*. New Brunswick: Rutgers University Press, 1955; reprint, New York: Atheneum, 1963.

Hitz, Louise Winkler, ed. *Letters of Frederick C. Winkler, 1862–1865*. N.p.: William K. Winkler, 1963.

Hobsbawm, Eric and Terence Ranger, eds. *The Invention of Tradition*. New York: Cambridge University Press, 1983.

Holt, Michael. *Forging a Majority: The Formation of the Republican Party in Pittsburgh, 1848–1860*. New Haven: Yale University Press, 1969.

Howard, Oliver Otis. *The Autobiography of Oliver Otis Howard, Major General, United States Army*. Vol. 1. New York: Baker and Taylor, 1917.

Hurst, Samuel H. *Journal-History of the Seventy-Third Ohio Volunteer Infantry*. Chillicothe, Ohio, 1866.

Johnson, Robert Underwood and Clarence Clough Buel. *Battles and Leaders of the Civil War*. New York: The Century Company, 1887; reprint, New York: Thomas Yoseloff, 1956.

Jacobson, Matthew F. *Whiteness of a Different Color: European Immigrants and the Alchemy of Race*. Cambridge, Mass.: Harvard University Press, 1998.

"Jahres-Bericht der Deutschen Gesellschaft der Stadt New York, am 31. December 1861." New York: Druck von M. W. Siebert, 1862.

Joyce, William L. *Editors and Ethnicity: A History of the Irish-American Press, 1848–1883*. The Irish Americans Series. New York: Arno Press, 1976.

Kapp, Friedrich. *Aus und über Amerika: Thatsachen und Erlebnisse*. Vol. 1. Berlin: Verlag von Julius Springer, 1876.

Kaufmann, Wilhelm. *The Germans in the American Civil War*. Trans. Steven Rowan. Carlisle, Pa.: J. Kallman Publishers, 1999.

Kawaguchi, Lesley Ann. "The Making of Philadelphia's German-America: Ethnic Group and Community Development, 1830–1883." Ph.D. diss., University of California, Los Angeles, 1983.

Kazal, Russell A. *Becoming Old Stock: The Paradox of German-American Identity*. Princeton: Princeton University Press, 2004.

Keil, Hartmut, ed. *German Workers' Culture in the United States, 1850–1920*. Washington, D.C.: Smithsonian Institution Press, 1988.

Keyser, Carl A. *Leatherbreeches: Hero of Chancellorsville*. Rye Beach, N.H.: Amherst Press, 1989.

Kiefer, Rev. W. R. *History of the One-Hundred and Fifty-third Regiment PA Vol. Infantry*. Easton, Pa.: Chemical Publishing Co., 1909.

Kleppner, Paul J. *The Cross of Culture: A Social Analysis of Midwestern Politics, 1850–1900*. New York: The Free Press, 1970.

Knobel, Dale T. *"America for the Americans:" The Nativist Movement in the United States*. New York: Twayne Publishers, 1996.

———. *Paddy and the Republic: Ethnicity and Nationality in Antebellum America*. Middletown, Conn.: Wesleyan University Press, 1986.

Koerner, Gustav. *Das Deutsche Element in den Vereinigten Staaten von Nordamerika, 1818–1848*. Cincinnati, Ohio: A. E. Wilde and Co., 1880.

Krick, Robert K. *Conquering the Valley: Stonewall Jackson at Port Republic*. New York: William Morrow and Company, 1996.

Lapham, James S. "The German-Americans of New York City, 1860–1890." Ph.D. diss., St. Johns University, 1977.

Levine, Bruce. *The Spirit of 1848: German Immigrants, Labor Conflict, and the Coming of the Civil War*. Chicago: University of Illinois Press, 1992.

Lieber, Francis. "Lincoln or McClellan: Appeal to the Germans in America." New York: Loyal Publication Society, 1864.

Linderman, Gerald F. *Embattled Courage: The Experience of Combat in the American Civil War*. New York: Free Press, 1987.

Lonn, Ella. *Foreigners in the Union Army and Navy*. Baton Rouge: Louisiana State University Press, 1951.

Luebke, Frederick C., ed. *Ethnic Voters and the Election of Lincoln*. Lincoln, Nebr.: University of Nebraska Press, 1971.

———. *Germans in the New World: Essays in the History of Immigration*. Chicago: University of Illinois Press, 1990.

Luecke, Martin. *Der Bürgerkrieg der Vereinigten Staaten, 1861–65*. St. Louis: Druck und Verlag von Louis Lange, 1892.

Mahin, Dean B. *The Blessed Place of Freedom: Europeans in Civil War America*. Washington, D.C.: Brasseys, 2002.

Martin, David G. *Carl Bornemann's Regiment: The Forty-First New York Infantry (DeKalb Regt.) in the Civil War*. Hightstown, N.J.: Longstreet House, 1987.

McConnell, Stuart. *Glorious Contentment: The Grand Army of the Republic, 1865–1900*. Chapel Hill: University of North Carolina Press, 1992.

McMorrow, Mary Elizabeth. "The Nineteenth-Century German Political Immigrant and the Construction of American Culture and Thought." Ph.D. diss., New School for Social Research, 1982.

McPherson, James M. *Battle Cry of Freedom*. New York: Oxford University Press, 1988.

———. *For Cause and Comrades: Why Men Fought in the Civil War*. New York: Oxford University Press, 1997.

———. *What They Fought For, 1861–1865*. New York: Anchor Books, 1994.

Meysenberg, T. A. "Reminiscences of Chancellorsville." *War Papers and Personal Reminiscences.* Vol. 1. St. Louis: MOLLUS Missouri, 1892.

Miller, Albert G. *History of the German Hospital of Philadelphia and its Ex-Resident Physicians.* Philadelphia: J. B. Lippincott Company, 1906.

Miller, Randall M., ed. *Germans in America: Retrospect and Prospect. Tricentennial Lectures Delivered at the German Society of Pennsylvania in 1983.* Philadelphia: The German Society of Pennsylvania, 1984.

——. *States of Progress: Germans and Blacks in America over 300 Years.* Philadelphia: The German Society of Pennsylvania, 1989.

Mitchell, Reid. *Civil War Soldiers: Their Expectations and Their Experiences.* New York: Viking Press, 1988.

——. *The Vacant Chair: The Northern Soldier Leaves Home.* New York: Oxford University Press, 1993.

——. *War Soldiers: Their Expectations and Their Experiences.* New York: Viking Penguin, 1988.

Mueller, Jacob. *Erinnerungen eines Achtundvierzigers: Skizzen aus der Sturm- und Drang Periode der Fünfziger Jahre.* Cleveland: Rud. Schmidt Printing Co., 1896.

Nachtigall, Hermann. *History of the 75th Regiment, PA. Vols.* North Riverside, Ill.: W. P. Printers, 1987. Trans. of *Geschichte des 75sten Regiments, Pa. Vols.* by Heinz D. Schwinge and Karl E. Sundstrom.

Nagler, Jörg. *Frémont contra Lincoln: Die deutsch-amerikanische Opposition in der Republikanischen Partei während des amerikanischen Bürgerkrieges.* New York: Peter Lang, 1984.

Nadel, Stanley. *Little Germany: Ethnicity, Religion, and Class in New York City, 1845–80.* Chicago: University of Illinois Press, 1990.

New York Monuments Commission for the Battlefields of Gettysburg and Chattanooga: Final Report on the Battlefield of Gettysburg. Vol. 2. Albany: J. B. Lyon Company Printers, 1902.

Nickolson, John Page, ed. *Pennsylvania at Gettysburg: Ceremonies at the Dedication of the Monuments Erected by the Commonwealth of PA. . . . .* Vol. 1. Harrisburg, Pa.: William Stanley Ray, State Printer, 1904.

Novak, Michael. *The Rise of the Unmeltable Ethnics.* New York: Macmillan, 1973.

O'Connor, Richard. *The German-Americans: An Informal History.* Boston: Little Brown and Company, 1968.

Oefele, Martin W. *German-Speaking Officers in the U.S. Colored Troops, 1863–1867.* Gainesville, Fla.: University of Florida Press, 2004.

Osborn, Hartwell. "On the Right at Chancellorsville." *Illinois MOLLUS, Military Essay and Recollections,* vol. 4. Chicago: Cozzens and Beaton Company, 1907.

Osborn, Hartwell. *Trials and Triumps: The Record of the Fifty-fifth Ohio Volunteer Infantry.* Chicago: A. C. McClurg and Co., 1904.

Paludan, Phillip Shaw. *A People's Contest: The Union and Civil War, 1861–1865.* 2nd ed. Lawrence, Kans.: University Press of Kansas, 1996.

Pula, James S. *For Liberty and Justice: The Life and Times of Wladimir Krzyzanowski.* Chicago: The Polish-American Congress Charitable Foundation, 1978.

―――. *The Sigel Regiment: A History of the 26th Wisconsin Volunteer Infantry, 1862–1865.* Campbell, Calif.: Savas Publishing Company, 1998.

Quaife, Milo M., ed. *From the Cannon's Mouth: The Civil War Letters of General Alpheus S. Williams.* Detroit: Wayne State University Press, 1959.

Reinhart, Joseph R., ed. and trans. *Two Germans in the Civil War: The Diary of John Daeuble and the Letters of Gottfried Rentschler, 6th Kentucky Volunteer Infantry.* Knoxville: University of Tennessee Press, 2004.

Rice, Owen. *Afield With the Eleventh Army Corps at Chancellorsville.* Cincinnati: H. C. Sherrick and Co., 1885.

Rippley, La Vern J. *The German-Americans.* Lanham, Md.: University Press of America, 1984.

Robertson, James I., ed. *The Civil War Letters of General Robert McAllister.* New Brunswick: Rutgers University Press, 1965.

―――. *Soldiers Blue and Gray.* Columbia, S.C.: University of South Carolina Press, 1988.

Rosengarten, Joseph. *The German Soldier in the Wars of the United States.* Philadelphia: J. B. Lippincott, 1886.

Rowan, Steven, ed. and trans. *Germans for a Free Missouri: Translations from the St. Louis Radical Press, 1857–1862.* Intro. James Neal Primm. Columbia, Mo.: University of Missouri Press, 1983.

Ryan, Joseph A., ed. *White Ethnic Life in Working Class America.* Englewood Cliffs, N.J.: Prentice-Hall, 1973.

Samito, Christian G., ed. *Commanding Boston's Irish Ninth: The Civil War Letters of Colonel Patrick R. Guiney, Ninth Massachusetts Volunteer Infantry.* New York: Fordham University Press,.1998.

Saxton, William. *A Regiment Remembered: The 157th New York Volunteers: From the Diary of Capt. William Saxton.* Cortland, N.Y.: Cortland County Historical Society, 1996.

Scharf, J. Thomas and Thompson Westcott. *History of Philadelphia, 1609–1884.* Philadelphia: L. H. Everts and Co., 1884.

Schlaeger, E. *Die sociale und politische Stellung der Deutchen in den Vereinigten Staaten.* Berlin: Puttkamer and Mühlbrecht, 1874.

Schmidt, Ernst Reinhold. *Der Amerikanische Bürgerkrieg: Geschichte des Volks der Vereinigten Staaten vor, während und nach der Rebellion.* Vol. 2. Philadelphia and Leipzig: Verlag von Schaefer und Koradi, 1867.

Schurz, Carl. *Reminiscences of Carl Schurz.* Vol. 2. New York: McClure, 1907–8.

———. *The Reminiscences of Carl Schurz.* Garden City, N.Y.: Doubleday and Company, 1917.

Sears, Stephen W. *Chancellorsville.* New York: Houghton Mifflin Company, 1996.

Seidensticker, Oswald. *Erster Teil der Geschichte der Deutschen Gesellschaft von Pennsylvanien.* Philadelphia: Neudruck von Graf & Breuninger, 1917.

———. *Geschichte des Männerchors in Philadelphia, 1835–1885.* Philadelphia: Verlag des Männerchors, 1885.

Sevenson, Peter. *Battlefield: Farming a Civil War Battleground.* New York: Ballantine Books, 1992.

Shore, Elliott, Ken Fones-Wolf and James P. Dankey, eds. *The German-American Radical Press: The Shaping of a Left Political Culture, 1850–1940.* Chicago: University of Illinois Press, 1992.

Sibley, Joel. *A Respectable Minority: The Democratic Party in the Civil War Era, 1860–1868.* New York: W. W. Norton, 1977.

Simmers, William and Paul Bachschmid. *The Volunteer's Manual: Or Ten Months with the 153d Penn'a Volunteers.* Easton, Pa.: D. H. Neiman, Printer, 1863.

Small, Abner R. *The Sixteenth Maine in the War of the Rebellion, 1861–1865.* Portland, Maine: B. Thurston and Co., 1886.

Smith, Abram P. *History of the Seventy-Sixth Regiment New York Volunteers.* Cortland, N.Y.: Truair, Smith, and Miles, Printers, 1867.

Smith, Jacob. *Camps and Campaigns of the 107th regiment Ohio Volunteer Infantry from August, 1862 to July, 1865.* N.p, 1910.

Sollers, Werner, ed. *The Invention of Ethnicity.* New York: Oxford University Press, 1989.

Sowell, Thomas. *Ethnic America: A History.* New York: Basic Books, 1981.

Spaeth, Mrs. Adolph, ed. *Life of Adolph Spaeth, D.D., LL.D.* Philadelphia: General Council Publication House, 1916.

Sperber, Jonathan. *Rhineland Radicals: The Democratic Movement and the Revolution of 1848–1849.* Princeton: Princeton University Press, 1991.

Stackpole, Edward J. *Chancellorsville: Lee's Greatest Battle.* Harrisburg, Pa.: Stackpole Co., 1958.

Stallo, J. B. *Reden, Abhandlungen und Briefe von J. B. Stallo.* New York: E. Steiger and Co., 1893.

Struve, Gustave. *Diesseits und Jenseits des Oceans: Jahrbuch zur Vermittelung der Beziehungen zwischen Amerika und Deutschland.* Coburg, Germany: F. Streit's Verlagsbuchhandlung, 1864.

Swinton, William. *Campaigns of the Army of the Potomac.* 1867; reprint, New York, Smithmark Publishers, 1995.

Tap, Bruce. *Over Lincoln's Shoulder: The Committee on the Conduct of the War.* Lawrence, Kans.: University Press of Kansas, 1998.

Trefousse, Hans L. *Carl Schurz: A Biography.* 1982; reprint, New York: Fordham University Press, 1998.

———. *Germany and America: Essays on Problems of International Relations and Immigration.* New York: Brooklyn College Press, 1980.

Trommler, Frank and Joseph McVeigh, eds. *America and the Germans: An Assessment of a Three-Hundred Year History.* Vol. I, *Immigration, Language, Ethnicity.* Philadelphia: University of Pennsylvania Press, 1985.

Underwood, Adin B. *The Three Years' Service of the Thirty-Third Mass. Infantry Regiment 1862–1865.* Boston: A. Williams and Co., 1881.

United States. *Report of the Joint Committee on the Conduct of the War.* Vol. 4. Reprint: Broadfoot Publishing Company, 1999.

United States. War Department. *The War of the Rebellion: A Compilation of the Official Records of the Union and Confederate Armies.* Washington, D.C.: Govt. Print. Office, 1880–1901.

Valuska, David L. and Christian B. Keller. *Damn Dutch: Pennsylvania Germans at Gettysburg.* Mechanicsburg, Pa: Stackpole Books, 2004.

Vautier, John D. *History of the Eighty-Eighth Pennsylvania Volunteers in the War for the Union, 1861–1865.* Philadelphia: J. B. Lippincott, 1864.

Vocke, William. "Our German Soldiers." In *Military Essays and Recollections; Papers Read Before the Commandery of the State of Illinois, Military Order of the Loyal Legion of the United States.* Vol. 3. Chicago, 1891.

Walsh, Timothy, ed. *Immigrant America: European Ethnicity in the United States.* New York: Garland Publishing, Inc., 1994.

Wiley, Bell Irvin. *The Life of Billy Yank: the Common Soldier of the Union.* New York: The Bobbs-Merrill Company, 1951.

Winkler, Frederick C. *Letters of Frederick C. Winkler, 1862–1865.* Ed. and trans. William K. Winkler. N.p, 1963.

Wittke, Carl. *Against the Current: A Life of Carl Heinzen.* Chicago, 1944.

———. *The German-Language Press in America.* Lexington, Ky.: University of Kentucky Press, 1957.

———. *Refugees of Revolution: The German Forty-eighters in America.* Philadelphia: University of Pennsylvania Press, 1952.

Yans-McLaughlin, Virginia, ed. *Immigration Reconsidered: History, Sociology, and Politics.* New York: Oxford University Press, 1990.

Zucker, Adolf E. *The Forty-Eighters: Political Refugees of the German Revolution of 1848.* New York: Columbia University Press, 1950.

Journal Articles

Benjaminson, Eric. "A Regiment of Immigrants: The 82nd Illinois Volunteer Infantry and the Letters of Captain Rudolph Mueller." *Journal of the Illinois State Historical Society* 94, no. 2 (2001): 137–80.

Bergquist, James M. "German Communities in American Cities: An Interpretation of the Nineteenth-Century Experience." *Journal of American Ethnic History* 4, no. 1 (Fall 1984): 9–30.

Bernays, Charles L. "Ein Beitrag zur Geschichte," *Deutsch-Amerikanische Monatshefte* 4 (February 1867): 91–108.

Butz, Caspar. "Unser Urteil über Lincoln." *Deutsch-Amerikanische Monatshefte* 1 (February 1864): 128.

"Carl Schurz: Sein Leben und Wirken." *Deutsch-Amerikanische Geschichtsblätter* 3 (July 1906): 6–9.

Conzen, Kathleen Neils. "The Paradox of German-American Assimilation." *Yearbook of German-American Studies* 16 (1981): 153–60.

Conzen, Kathleen and others. "The Invention of Ethnicity: A Perspective from the U.S.A." *Journal of American Ethnic History* 12, no. 1 (Fall 1992): 3–32.

Delpech, David. "La longue marche de la division Blenker." *Le Courier de la Guerre d'Amerique* 52 (4th quarter 1999): 18–26.

"Denkmal der Deutsch-Amerikaner in Dayton, Ohio." *Deutsch-Amerikanische Geschichtsblätter,* January 1911, 8–15.

"Deutsch-Amerikaner, aber keine amerikanisirte Deustche." *Deutsch-Amerikanische Monatshefte* 4 (April 1867): 348–56.

"Die Heimkehr: Dem 24. Illinois (Hecker) Regiment Gewidmet." *Deutsch-Amerikanische Monatshefte* 2 (August 1864): 169–70.

Dunkelman, Mark H. "Hardtack and Sauerkraut Stew: Ethnic Tensions in the 154th New York Volunteers, Eleventh Corps, during the Civil War." *Yearbook of German-American Studies* 36 (2001): 69–90.

Echterncamp, Jörg. "Emerging Ethnicity: The German Experience in Antebellum Baltimore." *Maryland Historical Magazine* 86, no. 1 (Spring 1991): 1–22.

Engle, Stephen. "Franz Sigel at Pea Ridge." *The Arkansas Historical Quarterly* 50 (Autumn 1991): 249–70.

———. "A Raised Consciousness: Franz Sigel and German Ethnic Identity in the Civil War." *Yearbook of German-American Studies* 34 (1999): 1–17.

Ettinger, Amos A. "An Allentonian in Florida During the Civil War: the Diary and Letters of Alfred C. Pretz, 1861–1865." *Proceedings of the Lehigh County Historical Society* 12 (December 1939): 50–80.

"General Adolph von Steinwehr." *Der Deutsche Pionier* 9, no. 1 (April 1877): 17–28.

Halpin, William J. "A German Regiment in the Civil War: The 45th New York State Volunteer Infantry, '5th German Rifles.'" *Military Images* 21 (March–April 2000).

Hardt, Hanno R. E. "A German-American Editor Supports the Union, 1860–62." *The Journalism Quarterly* 42, no. 3: 457–60.

Hess, Earl J. "The Obscurity of August Mersy: A German-American in the Civil War." *Illinois Historical Journal* 79 (Summer 1986): 127–38.

———. "Sigel's Resignation: A Study in German-Americanism and the Civil War." *Civil War History* 26, no. 1 (1980): 5–17.

Higham, John. "Integrating America: The Problem of Assimilation in the Nineteenth-Century." *Journal of American Ethnic History* 1, no. 1 (1981): 7–25.

Kamphoefner, Walter D. "German-Americans and Civil War Politics: A Reconsideration of the Ethnocultural Thesis." *Civil War History* 37:3 (1991): 232–46.

Kapp, Friedrich. "Rede, gehalten am 19. Juli 1865 in Jones Wood, in New York, zum Schluss des neunten deutschen Sängerfestes." *Deutsch-Amerikanische Monatshefte* (August 1865): 182–88.

Kawaguchi, Lesley Ann. "Diverging Political Affiliations and Ethnic Perspectives: Philadelphia Germans and Antebellum Politics." *Journal of American Ethnic History* 13, no. 2 (Winter 1994): 3–29.

Keller, Christian B. "Pennsylvania and Virginia Germans in the Civil War: A Brief History and Comparative Analysis." *Virginia Magazine of History and Biography* 190, no. 1 (July 2001): 37–86.

———. "The Reaction of Eastern Pennsylvania's German Press to the Secession Crisis: Compromise or Conflict?" *Yearbook of German-American Studies* 34 (Winter 1999): 35–61.

Lee, Alfred E. "The Battle of Cross Keys." *Magazine of American History* 15 (1885): 488.

Lexow, Friedrich. "Die Deutschen in Amerika." *Deutsch-Amerikanisch Monatshefte* 3 (January 1866): 149–54, and March 1866, 255–61.

———. "Zur Erinnerung." *Deutsch-Amerikanische Monatshefte* 3 (January 1866): 2–26.

Pfanz, Donald. "Negligence on the Right: The Eleventh Corps at Chancellorsville, May 2, 1863," available at http://www.morningsidebooks.com/notes/eleventh.htm.

Raphelson, Alfred C. "Alexander Schimmelfennig: A German-American Campaigner in the Civil War." *Pennsylvania Magazine of History and Biography* 87, no. 2 (April 1963): 156–81.

Schneider, Otto C. "Abraham Lincoln und das Deutschtum." *Deutsch-Amerikanische Geschichtsblätter*, April 1907.

Schurz, Carl. "Reminiscences of a Long Life: The Eleventh Corps at Chancellorsville," *McClure's Magazine,* June 1907, 175.

"Wilhlem Vocke obituary." *Deutsch-Amerikanische Geschichtsblätter* 7, no. 3 (July 1907): 118–21.

Zunz, Olivier. "American History and the Changing Meaning of Assimilation." *Journal of American Ethnic History* 4 (1985): 53–72.

"Zwei Briefe von Carl Schurz." *The American-German Review* (June–August 1947): 14–15.

Index

The North's Civil War Series

Paul A. Cimbala, series editor

20. Paul A. Cimbala and Randall M. Miller, eds., *An Uncommon Time: The Civil War and the Northern Home Front.*

21. John Y. Simon and Harold Holzer, eds., *The Lincoln Forum: Rediscovering Abraham Lincoln.*

22. Thomas F. Curran, *Soldiers of Peace: Civil War Pacifism and the Postwar Radical Peace Movement.*

23. Kyle S. Sinisi, *Sacred Debts: State Civil War Claims and American Federalism, 1861–1880.*

24. Russell L. Johnson, *Warriors into Workers: The Civil War and the Formation of Urban-Industrial Society in a Northern City.*

25. Peter J. Parish, *The North and the Nation in the Era of the Civil War.* Edited by Adam L. P. Smith and Susan-Mary Grant.

26. Patricia Richard, *Busy Hands: Images of the Family in the Northern Civil War Effort.*

27. Michael S. Green, *Freedom, Union, and Power: The Mind of the Republican Party During the Civil War.*

28. Christian G. Samito, ed., *Fear Was Not In Him: The Civil War Letters of Major General Francis S. Barlow, U.S.A.*

29. John S. Collier and Bonnie B. Collier, eds., *Yours for the Union: The Civil War Letters of John W. Chase, First Massachusetts Light Artillery.*

30. Grace Palladino, *Another Civil War: Labor, Capital, and the State in the Anthracite Regions of Pennsylvania, 1840–1868.*